LEAVING

LEAVING

A NARRATIVE OF ASSISTED SUICIDE

Anthony Stavrianakis

UNIVERSITY OF CALIFORNIA PRESS

University of California Press
Oakland, California

© 2019 by Anthony Stavrianakis

Library of Congress Cataloging-in-Publication Data

Names: Stavrianakis, Anthony, author.
Title: Leaving : a narrative of assisted suicide / Anthony
    Stavrianakis.
Description: Oakland, California : University of California
    Press, [2020] | Includes bibliographical references and
    index.
Identifiers: LCCN 2019040146 (print) | LCCN 2019040147
    (ebook) | ISBN 9780520344464 (cloth) |
    ISBN 9780520344471 (paperback) |
    ISBN 9780520975545 (epub)
Subjects: LCSH: Assisted suicide—Switzerland—21st century. |
    Suicide victims—Case studies.
Classification: LCC R726 .S674 2020 (print) |
    LCC R726 (ebook) | DDC 179.7—dc23
LC record available at https://lccn.loc.gov/2019040146
LC ebook record available at https://lccn.loc.gov/2019040147

29 28 27 26 25 24 23 22 21 20
10 9 8 7 6 5 4 3 2 1

For Linda and Emmanuel, my parents

CONTENTS

A NOTE OF GRATITUDE

I began research for this book at the end of 2013, after having left UC Berkeley, where I had finished my PhD dissertation under the guidance, care, and friendship of Paul Rabinow on the topic of collaboration between the natural and human sciences. I left for France with my wife, fellow anthropologist Laurence Tessier. We were both in the transition phase between PhD theses and conducting new lines of inquiry, as well as becoming new parents: our son Marcel was born at the beginning of that year. The inquiry unfolded mainly over the course of the years 2014, 2015, and 2016. I conceived of it as a test case of the mode of inquiry I had learned and forged with Paul, as we continued our collaborative work, asking the question of how to develop a form of anthropological inquiry after the breakdowns and waning of modernisms in the human sciences.

I had the good fortune to meet Swiss anthropologist Marc-Antoine Berthod as I began this work. The dialogue with Marc turned into a long-standing collaboration, and I continued to develop the project in conversation with him through multiple phases and stages. As the project developed, Marc and I submitted a proposal to the Swiss National Science Foundation, as a way for me to be hired as a post-doc; initially unsuccessful, it worked the second year we submitted it (at the end of 2015), by which time I had entered the Centre national de la recherche scientifique, in France, as a tenured researcher. The second time we applied was in collaboration with Dolores Angela Castelli Dransart, a sociologist with long-standing experience working on the theme of suicide and grief. The collaborative project began at the end of 2017, and with the funds from the project we were able to hire a post-doctoral researcher, Alexandre Pillonel, providing a strong collaborative team basis to take further, and in different directions, inquiry into voluntary assisted dying in Switzerland. This book is the product of five years of conversations with, and support from, Laurence, Marc, and Paul.

I am indebted to Nicolas Dodier, whose generosity and guidance was crucial in orientating me to the academic environment in Paris and whose consistently exacting questions were an intellectual boon. I have been very fortunate over six years in Paris to have had the chance to work with and learn from many colleagues at the Laboratoire interdisciplinaire d'études sur les réflexivités (LIER), the Centre de recherche médecine, sciences, santé, santé mentale, société (CERMES3), and the Laboratoire d'ethnologie et de sociologie comparative (LESC), as well as friends from Berkeley. I would like to thank especially Janine Barbot, Isabelle Baszanger, Simone Bateman, Marine Jeanne Boisson, Baptiste Buob, Jason Carpenter, Emily Chua, Gregory Delaplace, Lyle Fearnley, Roy Fisher, Graham Hill, Bruno Karsenti, Trine Korsby, Vololona Rabeharisoa, Catherine Rémy, Gildas Salmon, and Pierre Thévenin.

I owe a debt, moreover, to Robert Desjarlais and Todd Meyers, whose generous readings of the manuscript were an instantiation of that hope, occasionally admitted to, of wanting to be read as intended. It was truly a gift.

Finally, I wish to acknowledge the generosity of all those individuals and families who shared their experience of assisted suicide with me. In particular, I would like to thank Erika Preisig from *lifecircle*; Jerome Sobel, Daphné Berner, and Suzanne Pletti from Exit; and Christine, Fabienne, Sylviane, Clément, Pascal, Clara, Florian, and Françoise for their collaboration.

Introduction

In Switzerland, as in the vast majority of countries in the world, euthanasia—the active ending of a person's life by a medical professional—is not, and has never been, legal. In 1982, however, two organizations were founded that would come to develop practices to help people with the task of managing how they die. These two organizations—one Francophone (based in Geneva and Lausanne), the other Germanophone (based in Zurich)—which both took the name "Exit," were joined in the mid-1990s by a handful of other associations. The practices that these organizations developed included both advice on how to draft advanced planning documents for end-of-life care and, crucially, practices of assisting people with voluntarily ending their lives by their own hand. The associations existed, and still exist today, outside of formal medical institutions, with the vast majority of assisted suicides taking place at home.

The latter characteristic renders the case of Switzerland distinct from several states in the US, as well as Belgium, Luxembourg, and the Netherlands—countries that have legal frameworks for managing medical assistance with the active practice of ending life. The specificity of the Swiss legal situation concerning assisted suicide pertains to Article 115 of the 1937 Swiss Penal Code, which considers assisting in suicide a crime if, and only if, the motive is "selfish." As such, Switzerland has the particularity of having developed a political and ethical form for assisted dying that exists, unlike those other countries in which either euthanasia or assisted suicide is legal, in a zone adjacent to institutionalized medicine—a zone that is tolerated, although at times scrutinized, by legal, political, and medical institutions.

The problem space of the practice of requesting and being assisted with voluntary death is constituted through multiple vectors: personal reflection, bodily experience, medical diagnoses and prognoses, fears, and care, among others: the complex position of the person(s) who is (are) willing to assist with voluntary death, which in the typical case includes a medical doctor willing to use her or his capacity and right of prescription to authorize a lethal dose of barbiturate, to be administered by the individual herself or himself. The practice is therefore facilitated through the nonegoistic concern of one person, for the manner of dying of another person, using recourse, typically, although not always, to a doctor's medical authority, in order to provide a person with humane means to end her or his own life. A further vector is the variable positions of different people who, for different reasons, observe such requests, as well as their manner of observing, which will include the forms and aims of such observation.

The core *question* I posed during this inquiry was two-pronged: how does a person come to the judgment that they have had enough, and then, in relation to and with the assistance of others, how do they come to the judgment that dying voluntarily is the appropriate course of action to take given the situation in which they find themselves, of having had enough?

The *problem* that I take up in this book is connected to, but also distinct from, that question, to wit: how can an inquirer, in this case an anthropologist, who wishes to inquire into this practice, grasp such a judgment of having enough: enough, that is to say, of an experience of ill health, enough of an experience of care (or its lack), and enough of a life.

More than a century ago, Max Weber wrote with characteristic elegance that "Abraham or any other peasant in olden times died 'old and fulfilled by life'[1] because he was part of an organic life cycle, because in the evening of his days his life had given him whatever it had to offer and because there were no riddles that he still wanted to solve. Hence he could have 'enough' [*genug*] of life. A civilized man, however, who is inserted into a never-ending process by which civilization is enriched with ideas, knowledge, and problems may become 'tired of life,' but not fulfilled by it."[2] Weber's topic is modern to the hilt: a modern form of life is one "inserted into a never-ending process," a moral orientation to progress, to amelioration. In a certain sense this book takes up precisely the contemporary problem of the conditions under which, today, the human sciences might grasp lives that, in their own ways, have had enough of life and, on that basis, make the judgment to leave it.

A CONTEMPORARY CASUISTRY

From its inception I conceived of this inquiry into assisted suicide as a test case of an "anthropology of the contemporary."[3] The anthropology of the contemporary, forged by Paul Rabinow over more than a decade (since 2007), has sought to conceptualize the parameters of anthropological inquiry into the "present" in terms of a movement-space, *Bewegungsraum*—a term taken from the work of German intellectual historian Hans Blumenberg. For Blumenberg the term indexes a space of existence between two poles of what he calls the "ontological distance," poles that he labels "oppositionality" (*Gegenständigkeit*), and "extrapositionality" (*Inständigkeit*).[4] The former is the pole of the self-assurance and self-understanding of a subject grounded in method, exemplified by Husserl and Descartes, through which both knowledge of the world and action in the world are justified. The latter, exemplified by Heidegger's analysis of *Dasein*, is the pole "in which human existence spurns the assurances offered to it by reason, religion, and tradition to face up to its own contingency."[5] Translator and commentator Robert Savage highlights the fact that "Blumenberg marks his own position by vindicating the 'fallen' or 'inessential' realm of history against those who would transcend it in either direction."[6] A pragmatic anthropology of the contemporary likewise endeavors to refuse both the modern epistemological self-assurance of method as the means by which a subject can come to know both itself and the world, within limits, and at the same time refuse the modernist valorization of contingency for its own sake. The *contemporary* is a term that endeavors to identify ratios in inquiry composed of an experiential vector of the observation of practice and historical vectors that gauge the transformation of the forms through which practices are enacted, with their epistemological, affective, ethical, and aesthetic characteristics or dimensions. As Rabinow stated, in a formulation that has served as a meditative device in the decade of work on the "contemporary" that has followed: "Just as one can take up the 'modern' as an ethos and not a period, one can take it up as a moving ratio. In that perspective, tradition and modernity are not opposed but paired: 'tradition is a moving image of the past, opposed not to modernity but to alienation.' The contemporary is a moving ratio of modernity, moving through the recent past and near future in a (nonlinear) space that gauges modernity as an ethos already becoming historical."[7] The historical space in which my own inquiry moves begins in a present, a present in which both I, as subject conducting the inquiry, and those people with whom I sought to engage, together making up a situated "object" of inquiry, are in motion.

There are at least three temporal vectors that make up the space of motion of the inquiry: one is the temporal vector of the social environment in which this practice takes place, dying in Switzerland. As will be narrated in part I, what is important to understand is how end-of-life options are managed by medical professionals. How are these options given a particular form when an individual poses to herself or himself the question of "what to do" when faced with a situation of living that is restricted by illness? Over time, Swiss medical practitioners have strived not to come to a resolution about norms for medical care of suffering patients, in relation to the legitimacy (or illegitimacy) of allowing patients themselves to determine when to end their lives. The second vector of the movement space is the experiential one of the sequence of people whose stories I followed and narrate, thus tracking the motion of their own reflection and movement toward death, and my endeavor to find a position from which to track that motion. The third temporal vector stages an encounter among the epistemological, the affective, and the ethical character of the inquiry: how can this anthropological endeavor to understand a practice of assisted suicide be situated within the historical movement and transformation of the human sciences: what are the lessons learned, and the limitations of the available human sciences for inquiry into the practice of assisted suicide today?

The challenge can be stated as one of adopting a posture and relation to a moving present, both in terms of fieldwork and in terms of the disciplines of the human sciences, a present one endeavors both to be part of and to observe, and yet relative to which one is often slightly too early or too late, slightly too close or slightly too far. The movement space of the present produces a back-and-forth motion between the near future and the recent past: the near future of those participating in the space of the inquiry and the recent past of the endeavor of the human sciences to grasp the objects and problems at stake in the inquiry, an object that can be summed up as the search to give a form to the voluntary ending of life. The challenge I take up in this book is to forge a mode of inquiry through which to grasp the motion of the practice of inquiry within the movement space of the inquiry.[8]

To put it more concretely: if Weber stated that "man," under conditions of modernity and the metrics of progress, knowledge, prosperity, and amelioration, can be tired of life, but cannot have had enough of life, it is only in the fallen realm of history that an observer might gauge what difference today makes with respect to Weber's diagnosis of modern man. It is this difference, the gap, and the ratio between the present, and the modern, that can be considered a problem space of the contemporary. Unlike Blumenberg, however, the space of history as the zone in which such investigation takes place must be transformed and adapted for pragmatic anthropological inquiry.

What might such a transformation look like?

For quite some time Rabinow, myself, and others who participated in what was the Anthropology of the Contemporary Research Collaboratory (2005–18) were curious about what an anthropological "case"[9] of inquiry into the contemporary would consist in, if an inquirer were to refuse the classic understanding of the "case study" as forged by, among others, Max Gluckman. For Gluckman, "the most fruitful use of cases consists in taking a series of specific incidents affecting the same persons or groups, through a long period of time, and showing ... [the] change of social relations among these persons and groups, *within the framework of their social system and culture*."[10] In his major conceptual intervention, *Anthropos Today: Reflections on Modern Equipment*, which spurred the epistemological and ethical stakes of the anthropology of the contemporary that he would later pursue, Rabinow opened a line of thought on how casuistry is a plausible approach to cases in anthropology to the degree that it is a form of case-based reasoning, which is to say it consists in a logic of inquiry that moves from case to case, without either hypostatizing the single case as an end in and of itself or making the case an example of an encompassing object that gives the case significance—"social system," for example, in Gluckman's terms.

Casuistry, understood as case-based reasoning, is perhaps best known in its guise within Jesuit moral theology.[11] It would be "excessive" as a mode of inquiry for anthropology, if the theological model were taken for anthropology, to fix guiding principles that could tell the inquirer how to move from case to case. Similarly, "casuistry is deficient when the case becomes an end in itself. Singularity becomes the goal and not the parameter through which enrichment of other cases can be taken up and related."[12] The challenge of an anthropological casuistry in this book is to track the motion from case to case. The term *case*, in my use here, refers to a narrative form given to my effort to occupy a position within a movement space of inquiry and to give a form to, and to the degree possible to seize, through understanding or sensibility (or both, or neither, as the case may be), the request for an assisted suicide by an individual in relation to others.

What makes it a specifically "anthropological" casuistry is precisely the effort to track my shifting position through the unfolding of the inquiry and to track not only how people came to the judgments that they came to, in relation to the question of whether and how they would leave life, but also to see how reflection on those judgments and observation of the practice of the movement of leaving depends on the position that I was able to occupy in relation to the person making the request. As such, what is specific to the "casuistry" is the order and sequence of cases, the movement space in which they can be sequenced, and the problem space (of the human sciences) in which they can be put to the test of further reflection.

What is specifically "contemporary" about the project and the book I present here, contemporary in Rabinow's sense of ratios of a present in relation to wider historicizing historical vectors of the norms and forms of modernity,[13] is the effort to invent a "point of view" within the movement space of inquiry, one that both works over an experience in the present and reconnects such experience to the recent past of the modern human sciences. It is, then, an effort to take stock of a certain kind of breakdown in both modern and modernist norms of anthropological writing (the excessive poles in Blumenberg's orientation).[14]

To find out what this point of view could consist in, it is necessary to reconsider a maxim taken from Max Weber's methodological writing. Weber wrote in 1904 that "it is not the 'factual' interconnection of 'things,' but rather the conceptual interconnection of problems, which forms the basis for zones of inquiry. A *new* 'science' emerges where *new* problems are pursued by *new* methods and truths are thereby discerned which open up significant standpoints."[15] Today, what had been those new sciences at the dawn of the twentieth century—and in particular for my purposes: psychoanalysis, sociology, and fieldwork-based anthropology—have waned, if not completely worn themselves out. The challenge for a contemporary inquirer in the so-called human sciences is to confront and interconnect experiential knowledge (*Erfahrung*; participant-observation) as a way of going about doing inquiry, with the knowledge domains that were once known as the human sciences.

My aim is not, then, with all due respect to Weber, to establish a *new* science with *new* problems and *new* methods: a modernist challenge *par excellence*.

Rather, my aim is to see what the limits are to our old sciences, what we can still learn from them, and what remediation might involve—which is to say, to paraphrase Weber, a problem of whether or not a remediation of our old sciences "might yet be of some use to the one who puts the question correctly" given that, as he expressed it with characteristic trenchancy, drawing on the "simplest reply" provided by Tolstoy, science (*Wissenschaft*) gives us "no" answers to the only question that counts: "What shall we do and how shall we live?"[16]

Let me be clear: I am not advocating that we jettison the human sciences, for the simple reason that, at least for now, the human sciences are the *logoi*—reasoned discourses—available for thinking about ethos (character). For an anthropological casuistry, such as the one I am endeavoring to engage in here, dedicated to the dual aim of characterizing a human practice, and discerning its didactic significance for the author and reader, whose ultimate aim, I consider, is to provide a source for, but not a determination of, moral reflection, or an ethical pedagogy, the fulcrum between the didactic and characteristic purposes of such reflection is constituted through just such an object of inquiry—namely, "ethos."[17] As such, with these dual aims this book parts ways with a recent, and I hope passing, interest from some of my colleagues in an anthropology "beyond the human" (a modernist revival *par excellence*) and seeks to vindicate the worth of continuing to pose questions about the ethos of human beings under variable conditions.

The price to be paid, following Weber, of a logos of ethos, reasoned discourse about the character of human beings, which has an ethical pedagogical aim, is the condition of pathos, the pathos that such a science cannot tell the author or reader how to live. This point is necessary to underscore with respect to this book, since my claim is twofold: that the reader and I should learn something about the character of those people with whom I have talked and observed, including about our relation to the themes of the inquiry, perhaps most importantly reflection on the uses of the margins of freedom available to individuals, in relation to others, under significant constraints; yet I also insist that the analysis cannot determine a singular judgment on these cases. I can only share with the reader how, through the unfolding inquiry, through the sequence of cases, I came to a series of determinations, of stopping points, each of which parameterized the further unfolding of, and reflection in, the inquiry.

Leaving is thus composed of three parts, which open through the following sequence: (1) an orientation to the "zone" in which this practice is situated, on the borders of institutionalized medical care; (2) a series of cases of participant-observation with practices of assistance with suicide in which people are reflecting on, and pursuing the means to leave, their experience of illness; and (3) a trio of studies that asks how to grasp the ethos or character of those who say "enough," and who want, on that basis, to leave life. The three studies take up three specific technical points (and in that sense they are *études*) in knowledge domains of the modern human sciences that deal with "ethos" or "character"—the psychological, the sociological, and the anthropological. In relation to each knowledge domain, and a specific technical understanding of character—in terms of ego and desire in psychoanalysis, in terms of a sociology of virtue, and in terms of the "arts of existence" (*technē tou biou*) in anthropology—I ask how to take up these forms of knowledge in relation to the determinations of my participant-observation work.

In asking this, I am endeavoring first to find a form for the particular kind of fieldwork in which I engaged, to produce not just a description but a form of observation that produces an active kind of reflection and intervention, pithily summed up in the term *Betrachtung*, the noun form of the verb *betrachten*, whose semantic range includes considering, as well as esteeming. Second, in insisting on the relation of the form of the narrative to the mode of observation/intervention (*Betrachtung*), I am trying to constitute a narrative bearing or attitude with which to clarify the subject positions that I and the people with whom I worked occupied during the time of the inquiry, positions for which we are, each of us, in the end, responsible.[18]

PART ONE

Restricted Action, an Orientation

Near Death

"Prostate cancer. Bone metastases. Diagnosis of bipolar disorder. And hallucinations." Anne took her turn to drive for our last visit of the day, while Sylvie read out a synopsis of the man we were about to see: in his eighties, near death (*vraiment en fin de vie*). She handed me the folder as I sat in the backseat. I skimmed the stapled pages as Anne bounced the cramped car around the outskirts of Geneva, my inner voice interrupted by one of Sylvie's hardnosed observations: "You know, the reality of dying, for most people is shitting your pants and deliriously screaming *maman*," she said, her gaze fixed on the road ahead.

We entered a large detached peri-urban house at the edge of the city. A remainder of the April evening's apricot sunset trickled through fretwork clouds, across the garden, and through the wide sliding doors of the living room, where we sat facing two women: the dying man's paid caregiver, who had also accompanied his wife in her last months, and his daughter-in-law. In the garden his grandchildren stood talking to a friend of his, a woman in her eighties, sitting, dressed in black, looking away through dark glasses. A grand plane tree, ruling the garden, was strangely still. The atmosphere inside was saturated. In the living room the silence around the table was broken only by short exchanges that clarified what had happened since the team saw him last week. One of the children came in from the garden. Walking slowly, she never lifted her gaze from the floor.

"He had slept well but woke up very agitated. When we touch him, he screams," his daughter-in-law said.

"Friday he cried out a lot," said the caregiver. She looked down at her hands.

"When he screams, does it seem like he is having hallucinations?" Sylvie asked.

"I don't know. He's looking for a specific person: a wine-seller. . . . But he's very confused."

Anne and Sylvie mumbled some medical nouns to each other, getting the measure of the situation and the evolution of his pain treatment. They were trying to understand how his medications had been changed by the nursing team that worked in tandem with their home palliative care service. The caregiver interrupted: "He's having trouble swallowing. It is possible that the lorazepam is staying in his mouth. We found a small piece this morning that he hadn't managed to swallow."

"Ok. We should see him," Sylvie said. The four of us went upstairs, thick carpet absorbing our solemn steps. He was in a small room dominated by a large medical bed, the kind that can be moved up and down electronically. It was just before Easter. A live performance of the Matthäus-Passion emanated from a small radio in the corner of the room. A novel of the life of Jesus had been set down on a small table next to the bed. On the other side were medical materials. I stood back, my little notebook and pencil at my side, trying to move as little as possible, absorbing the scene, looking at the quiet, quick, restrained movements taking place in this small space. The man was on his back—his body long and static on the bed, and pale too, his damp thin gray hair slicked back. His face was pulled tight, or perhaps it was only the skin, as though gripped by emotion. A grimace. Fixed. No one mentioned this. Eyes wide and fixed on the ceiling. I wondered when this happened. What had he seen? A sign, perhaps? I feared breaking the concentrated atmosphere of work and said nothing. The man wore a nappy and a loose white T-shirt that said *Champion* on it. Two tubes entered and exited his body: one went into his belly and the other out of his thigh. They were connected to a machine that made a short pulsing sound every thirty seconds.

Psssssssss.   Psssssssss.   Psssssssss.

The radio audience clapped.

Sylvie examined his belly. She lifted up his T-shirt just a little and pressed him. Both Anne and Sylvie stroked his hands with small movements. They were expertly gentle with him. Sylvie examined his legs, running her hands slowly down them. It was always the legs that interested her—her touch searching for water. She moved the leg, lifted it up and to the side in a circular motion. He screamed, without looking away, without moving. She put the leg down and apologized. Softly she said she should have told him that she was about to do that.

The caregiver explained that it has been very difficult to clean his mouth. Anne looked in the nurses' equipment box to find materials. She took a sponge on a stick and dipped it into a solution. She was wearing latex gloves. She wondered aloud whether there were any masks. After having rummaged around in the stacks of medical equipment lined along the walls, she abandoned the search; there were none. Anne shot an uncharmed look at Sylvie. "*Monsieur,* I am going to clean your mouth," she announced. He bit down on the sponge. "It's not easy to clean. We have to explain," she said to no one in particular. "His tongue. It's all dry with scabs and ulcers [*elle est rôtie*]. It's important that the nursing team comes here tonight to change his medication." She either gave up on her task or considered it finished, snapping off the gloves and wrapping them around the swab, popping them into the waste container.

The caregiver stood at the foot of the bed, her hand on her mouth. "We can't do much for him now," she brought herself to say. Anne moved toward her, facing the woman, touching her arm, responding to her drained and deflated attitude.

"But your presence," Anne said, and she held her.

"It's been ten days he hasn't eaten. A few days now he hasn't drunk anything."

"Do you always give him the extra doses of morphine?"

"Any time we are going to change him or move him."

"We will have to stop the morphine and switch to hydromorphone," Sylvie said.

"It's the screams we don't understand."

The man remained on his back, his gaze fixed, his body gripping itself. Sylvie phoned his son, a doctor, to explain the change of medication, a courtesy not typically extended to those outside the profession, and then we left.

––––––––––

The doors of the car closed. There was a tiny pause and then Sylvie and Anne burst into laughter. "Watch out, we'll get a call in half an hour!" Sylvie exclaimed. They were hunched over, laughing into their seatbelts. Anne composed herself and started the engine. "We have to explain," Sylvie eventually said, for the benefit of the observer, as Anne started to pull the car around to leave.

"There was a man, a little while ago, very religious family, similar state to this man. His tongue was similar," Anne said. "I went to clean his mouth, it was *dis—gust—ing*. A large crust fell off as I was cleaning it. I had no gloves or a mask. I thought I was going to vomit. So I cleaned the mouth. And half an hour later he was dead."

"There's more than one manner of euthanasia!" Sylvie said. "We'll let you know tomorrow what happens."

He died in the night.

Parazone

There is room for misunderstanding. I have picked out this first scene in which I had followed this Geneva-based home palliative care team, not because I had wanted to study home palliative care but because I thought that what I had wanted to study, assisted suicide in Switzerland, could only be initially grasped by first gaining some experience of more common ways of dying and more typical ways of caring for those suffering from serious, life-threatening, illness. One possible misunderstanding is that I picked out this first scene as an exemplar of a way in which people die, against which assisted suicide could then be contrasted as a "dignified death," as it is sometimes called. The possible dignity of assisted suicide would then be embossed by the laughter of the medical professionals. Such a contrast, and relief, is not the point.

Rather, significant for me in this first scene is what it shows about how the limits on possible action, in a given situation, are both invested with and afford kinds of affect. In this situation I have been taken with how I think I have seen that the work of managing the situation of the man whose life was ending occurred within a relatively restricted range of possible actions: not leaving him alone, "being there," as Anne put it, is a thing to do in response to the limits of what can be done for him technically—in this case the simple act of switching from morphine to hydromorphone to ensure that his pain is managed, as well as the act of cleaning his mouth.

Moreover, what I think is worth underscoring is that in such a situation of restricted capacity to do something—"we can't do much for him now," as the caregiver said—there was a deflated affect, a listlessness, on the part of the caregiver that seemed to be connected to this cramped situation and to an acknowledgment that they had done enough. Importantly, the caregiver's affect and Anne and Sylvie's affect in relation to her and the man were then at variance with the outburst expressed by the pair later in the car.

The situation of doing something, albeit a small gesture of cleaning his mouth, to endeavor to make the man more comfortable as his vital processes broke down, caused a heightened intensity of affect for the palliative care team, a comic outburst, which brought into proximity a sense of concern about the relation between doing something and the death to come, a connection and concern predicated on a past experience, and the anxiety attached to a judgment concerning whether doing something could actually be too much—or not enough.

Although Anne and Sylvie did not really think that cleaning the mouth of a dying man could hasten his death—it was a joke—nevertheless, the joke indexed prevalent concerns about possible and appropriate action: what are the right things to do in care at the end of life? What are the right things to do when those who are present think that there is little to be done yet, at the same time, nevertheless do things? Concern with this question indexes the affective ambivalence of those who try to enact such practices of care.

What the scene indicates is that in dying, considered broadly as a "shrunken milieu"—German neurologist Kurt Goldstein's (1878–1965) phrase for the effort to give form to the breakdowns and indeterminations of living with illness or disease[1]—those authorized to act are acting in a space of movement between the poles that the American philosopher John Dewey (1859–1952) identified as "pulses of doing, and being withheld from doing," poles that in his view constitute the dynamics of aesthetic experience.[2] Dewey's poles of aesthetic experience, although expressed at the level of abstract generality, help to distinguish three points on a spectrum for the kind of situations that will be my focus, three points between doing and being withheld from doing: (1) an observation of doing in which the situation of action is relatively open—unrestricted motion; (2) a mode of doing *despite* the fact that the practice occurs in a situation of action in which people are "being withheld" in one way or another from doing; and (3) the variant of actually "being withheld" from doing.

The situations of inquiry that I will narrate are predominantly characterized by the second position. I would suggest, schematically, that whereas the caregiver's listlessness indexed a situation of suspended agency, the palliative care team was in a position in which at the same time, they recognized an injunction to do something and yet were well aware of the limits of any possible action. In consonance with the contemporary literary scholar Sianne Ngai, drawing on her staggeringly original theoretical treatment of affect in situations of "thwarted" action,[3] I read Sylvie and Anne's comic outburst as a heightened affective reaction to the question of what can be done in a situation in which a range of motions and actions becomes significantly reduced and how affects, investments, and judgments—the latter term taken in Dewey's specific sense of the attribution of a mode of being to a situation[4]—emerge in such a space of activity.

As I will explain, in relation to a very general sense that dying occurs within situations of restricted action—situations whose character can be grasped in part through affective investment and effects, as well as aesthetic and ethical judgments—I will describe how assisted suicide became, for a number of contingent reasons, one possible response to the question of what to do under conditions in which people suffering from illness come to the judgment, on the basis of the experience they have and the prognoses they receive, that there is little to be done, that they have had enough, and that affectively and intellectually, the little that can be done is to find a better way out than those ways typically provided by institutionalized medicine. To understand the specificity of Switzerland, it is important to understand that aid with voluntary death, as a possible way out from an experience of illness, emerged in *a zone of practice adjacent to institutionalized medicine*, a kind of "parazone" of assisted action, which persists today. The qualifier "assisted" takes on its sense in opposition to that of "thwarted" action—the endeavor to thwart death, which is one of hospital medicine's aims, the thwarting of the endeavor to thwart death, which is our lot as finite beings, as well as the thwarting of the endeavor to hasten it, which in most countries—and, as we will see, in Switzerland, too—is to a large degree the normative orientation of medical practice.

Unlike what Ngai calls "ugly feelings," which are generated in conjunctures of "suspended agency"—or "thwarted action"—in which affective disorientation is connected to a loss of control,[5] I propose considering gestures of care, broadly, in end-of-life situations, as things done in situations of a reduced range of possible activity and in which the very contraction of the range of possible actions heightens concern about, or else a preoccupation with, or simply a consideration of, the legitimacy of the acts done—for example, the concern about whether a given action has contributed to the hastening of a patient's death. The scene with which I opened renders this point in a theatrical manner, but the point holds more widely—for example, the type of situation in which nursing staff consider that they have accelerated the death of a patient, investing that consideration with a range of affects (concern, serenity, self-reproach), even when objectively the doses of medication administered indicate that this is not the case. Of course, my opening narrative is but one situation, one story, and one observation. Its function is not to serve as an *Idealtypus* [idea-type] of a "context" against which other contexts could be distinguished and compared.[6] Rather, I forged it as an image, an orientation for beginning to sketch a space of preoccupation so as to understand the difference introduced by the invention of a practice of assisted suicide relative to the parameters of practice in more typical forms of care at the end of life. As such, let me underscore that the connection I have picked out is deliberately exaggerated from the norm of day-to-day work; on most visits the home palliative care team would make adjustments to medications, check on vital signs, check on psychosocial things that might not be going well, and so forth. The particular duo I followed were gifted at frequently bringing a light, comedic touch to their encounters with patients, which for the most part the patients seemed to appreciate. The rapport was one of mutual appreciation, as well as mutual recognition of the human dimension of the visits, companionship, and accompaniment—a bit of support in difficult times.

Only a small number of patients at any given time would be near death: in my experience it was one out of twenty for each week I followed them (over the course of a month). And as such, the scene of the man near death was uncommon, although not rare, making visible both the more regular background of their own work, in-home palliative care, and the point of contact with a connected yet highly divergent practice of assisted suicide. This point of contact, to repeat, was the heightened concern with the legitimacy of what to do in a situation of restricted action.

To understand more about this background and possible convergence, I asked Anne and Sylvie about how their patients die and where they die: with sixty years of experience between them, as a nurse and doctor in palliative care, I considered my informants well informed. Anne parried my all-too-general question with the simple statement that there are many scenarios: just because someone wants to be cared for at home does not mean they want to die at home; or else, sometimes it is the family that cannot cope and ask for the patient to be transferred, against the patient's wishes. About a third of their patients die at home, they concurred.

I explained to Sylvie and Anne what I was trying do: to study assisted suicide in Switzerland, taking into account the fact that it is one option among others, an option that is statistically uncommon, slightly more than 1 percent of annual deaths.[7] I had thought, I told the pair, that it would be important to start by understanding how medical professionals, particularly in palliative care, who are not necessarily involved with the associations that facilitate assisted suicide, care for patients who are suffering and how, if at all, requests for hastening death are managed. It seemed to me important because one of things that drew me to study assisted suicide in Switzerland, as a possible object of inquiry, was that, from a distance, and prior to any experience, it seemed as though the possibility of assisting a person to end her or his life voluntarily, with the support of medical means, was a practice that existed in a poorly delimited, porous, but largely separate, zone adjacent to medical practice.

ADJACENT TO THE MEDICAL FIELD

Medical institutions in Switzerland—the Swiss Medical Association (*FMH: Foederatio Medicorum Helveticorum*), the Swiss Academy of Medical Sciences (*ASSM: l'Académie suisse des sciences médicales*), and hospitals, both private clinics and cantonal university hospitals (*Centres hospitaliers universitaires*)— have largely maintained the practice of assisted suicide outside of institutionalized zones of medical practice (the medical "field" in a sociological sense).[8] Unlike the majority of states in which it has been legalized—the Netherlands, Belgium, Luxemburg, several states in the US, Colombia—the practice began by way of associations operating in collaboration with a small number of medical professionals but outside of the main medical institutions. In each of these countries we find different institutional configurations, legal frameworks, habits, customs, norms, and so on, producing arrangements between people who are ill and who request assistance with leaving their experience of suffering, their families and friends, and medical professionals.

In Switzerland, since 1982, a series of associations have been established to help people who, suffering from different kinds of illnesses, wish to end their lives. These associations are heterogeneous in terms of whom they help and, to a degree, how they help: some help only Swiss residents; others also help those from abroad. Typically those who help only Swiss residents work as volunteers, and the cost of the assistance with suicide is minimal (usually only annual membership dues), and those who help with non-Swiss residents typically charge a (large) fee to cover the range of costs that are incurred when dealing with people coming from abroad. All the associations, however, share one common feature: they are all financed uniquely by the subscription dues and fees of their members. Thus, those people who ask for assistance must themselves be members of the association, since these associations do not simply offer a provision of a service but rather a veritable engagement as part of an association. Moreover, these associations are, legally speaking, private ones; thus, they receive no public funding. The latter characteristic is key: the practice of assisted suicide in Switzerland was developed by self-financed activist associations, outside of an institutionalized medical field.

The associations' practices are delimited, of course, by the laws of the state and of the particular cantons in which they each operate; as we will see, there are differences among the Swiss cantons. The federal law, which governs the practice at the most general level, is, however, rather minimal. The Penal Code states, "Any person who for selfish motives incites or assists another to commit or attempt to commit suicide is, if that other person thereafter commits or attempts to commit suicide, liable to a custodial sentence not exceeding five years or to a monetary penalty."[9] At a federal level there is no other defining legal condition. Thus, the law provides no positive criteria for an assistance with suicide to be considered legal. The law requires only the absence of selfish motive. The professional status of the person who helps is not specified (i.e., the law does not stipulate a medical professional), nor the means for the fulfillment of the suicide, nor the type of illness or suffering. The practice is thus not necessarily (i.e., in legal terms) linked to medical activity or framed by medical institutions. Yet, for practical reasons, it is in connection with medicine that this activity has been developed.

This Swiss situation can be compared with two others to grasp some pertinent differences: the situation in the Netherlands and the situation in the state of California in the United States. In all three places assisted suicide is legal, and in the Netherlands euthanasia is also legal, which is not the case in California or in Switzerland. The distinction between the two practices is that with euthanasia a medical doctor is allowed to perform the final act of ending life, whereas in assisted suicide the person him- or herself must perform the final gesture.

In the Netherlands the 2002 law, titled "Termination of Life on Request and Assisted Suicide Act," specifies under its "due care" considerations, several aspects of the necessary diligence required to undertake the facilitation of either an assisted suicide or euthanasia:

> (a) the physician must be satisfied that the patient's request is voluntary and well-considered; (b) she must be convinced that the suffering of the patient is lasting and unbearable; (c) she must have informed the patient of the situation in which he finds himself and of his prospects; (d) the physician and the patient are satisfied that there is no reasonable alternative to the situation in which the patient is located; (e) the physician has consulted with at least one other independent physician who has seen the patient and provided written notice of the due diligence requirements in (a) through (d); and (f) the physician has acted with "due care."

Dutch law offers a very broad approach to illnesses that may involve long-term and unbearable suffering, including psychiatric illnesses.[10] The law also provides for situations in which children are able to access an assisted death, when the parents or guardians agree.

The 2016 California End of Life Option Act has several differences, including:

> (i) in order to receive the lethal drug, a patient must be of age; (ii) he must have an end-stage illness; (iii) a physician must determine that the disease cannot be cured and that the disease will be fatal within six months (which excludes, inter alia, psychiatric illness); (iv) the patient must have the ability, physically and mentally, to take the medication at the time they wish to take it; thus excluding euthanasia for a person who can no longer move his body or express his will, but who has previously made a written statement, fulfilling the relevant criteria.

With regard to California and the Netherlands, the "Swiss model" is therefore distinguished by its low degree of institutionalization, both legal and medical, and by a strong involvement of private associations.

Switzerland is thus a site in which to test a simple and powerful observation from Max Weber, nearly a century ago: "whether life is worth living and when?—this question is not asked by medicine."[11] For forty years Switzerland has been a setting in which the tensions internal to this question have been faced with courage and with pathos, tensions produced by the inability for medical practitioners to answer this question with purely medical reasoning. The consequence of this observation for the inquirer is twofold: on the one hand, to attempt to understand how (and where and by whom and when) the question is asked; on the other hand, to observe how a negative answer (to the question of whether a person should carry on living with illness) is worked through and negotiated, including the management of ambivalence.

The question of whether a life is worth sustaining, and at which point and to what end, is, as Weber points out, a question that cannot be answered scientifically: no calculus or norm alone can answer an ethical question. As such, the technical capabilities of progress in medicine have only technical limits: Sharon Kaufman's 2005 work, *And a Time to Die*, an ethnographic account of end-of-life care in California, shows how, in this part of the US, at this particular historical conjuncture, medical practice was (like Weber's early twentieth-century German doctors) unable to ask whether life is worth living and rather was inserted within a medico-scientific infrastructure that aimed to preserve life at all costs.[12] Kaufman shows how in the US, at that moment, pathways of heroic interventions assembled from progress in techniques for intervening in life processes, protocols, and institutional norms produced a milieu for the technical mastery of bodies even into indeterminate zones between life and death. The new law in California, in principle, has intervened in this practice. The case of Switzerland offers an important counterpoint of comparison within the sociological and anthropological literature, a site where affective and ethical challenges of how to pose the question of whether a life is worth living exist in parallel, and occasionally overlap, with the technical protocols of care at the end of life.

In a key work on euthanasia in the Netherlands, rather than focus on how requests were negotiated and ultimately accepted, Frances Norwood's 2009 *The Maintenance of Life: Preventing Social Death through Euthanasia Talk and End-of-Life Care—Lessons from The Netherlands* shows the palliative function of "euthanasia talk," discussions that, she suggests, often obviate recourse to the euthanasia act.[13] The Dutch medical infrastructure that provides the possibility of the act of ending life is thus shown to have also produced a space of discourse about ending life that serves to sustain life through discussion of death. The observation is an important one for the discussion of Switzerland: as the representatives of the assisted suicide associations in the different cantons all insist, half of those who initially request assistance with suicide do not ultimately follow through with it. For the associations this palliative function is important to underscore. Nevertheless, what then remains open as a question is what happens such that a person then actually does decide to give form to their death in this way? How does it occur, especially given the crucial difference with the Netherlands and states in the US, in collaboration with doctors but adjacent to medical infrastructure? Within the poorly delimited zone constitutive of the practice in Switzerland, I began the inquiry in late

2013 asking how doctors and other medical professionals managed requests from people for aid with a voluntary death. The indetermination is in part a consequence of the minimalist legal means that frame the practice.

The public freedom of this practice in Switzerland, which is not regulated by any positive legal framework, is consequent to a legal debate that occurred at the turn of the last century (1894–1918), during the drafting of the Swiss Penal Code.[14] A discussion arose at that time between lawyers and professors of law sitting on the drafting committee regarding whether participation in another person's suicide was a crime and what elements needed to be present to constitute criminal participation in suicide. Suicide was an act that otherwise did not—and still does not—concern criminal law. The committee was oriented in its decision by a then prominent professor, Ernst Hafter, who argued in 1912 that "it is contrary to the sensitivity of human feeling to punish the friend, who provides the means of suicide for one who has been dishonored by the world by a crime, destroyed in his existence, regardless of whether, in the individual case, incitement or aiding is present. It is contrary to righteousness to punish the assistant, who encourages the hopelessly ill person who is determined in his decision to give himself to death, and gives him the means to do so."[15] Only assistance for "selfish reasons" was taken to be punishable. Available records indicate that the committee did not further pursue the question of the meaning of the qualification "hopelessly ill," a phrase whose semantic openness is a core site of indetermination in the practice of assistance with suicide today.

Such a historical antecedent notwithstanding, the efficient cause of the emergence of such a practice was the mobilization in 1982 of two groups of citizens freely associating in order to work together to provide technical and moral supports for those seeking control over the end of life. One group was based in Geneva, the other in Zurich. Both groups took the name "Exit"—Exit Association pour le Droit de Mourir (Exit ADMD) and Exit Deutsche Schweiz. They were inspired by a group already established in the UK: Originally called the Voluntary Euthanasia Legalization Society, setup in 1935, it was known in the late 1970s as Exit and today is called Dignity in Dying UK.[16]

In Switzerland, since 1982, the Exit associations have been joined by others, whose activities vary according to whether they assist only Swiss residents or also non-Swiss residents, and the working languages and location of the associations, which affect who they are primarily oriented to assisting. As far as federal medical bodies are concerned, the work of these associations, and of any doctor with these associations, involves a personal decision and not a profes-sional obligation: as such, as far as these bodies are concerned, assisted suicide is not part of medical practice. The ASSM put it in the following way in 2006:

> The vocation of doctors caring for patients at the end of life consists in relieving and accompanying the patient. It is not part of their duty to offer assistance with suicide, rather, to the contrary, they have the duty to relieve suffering that could be the cause of the desire for suicide. However, the directives recognize that a dying patient (*en fin de vie*) who can no longer bear the situation, can express his desire to die, and persist in the desire. In such a situation, the personal moral decision of a doctor to provide assistance with suicide should be respected.[17]

Georg Bosshard of the Zurich *Institut für Rechtsmedizin* (Forensic Medical Institute), in his work with many colleagues over the last two decades, has persistently reflected on assisted suicide as it pertains to clinical and other institutionalized practices. Bosshard has frequently inquired into whether doctors' involvement with requests for suicide should be within the "routine clinical setting, encompassed by the doctor-patient relationship," or whether medical judgment should be sought and offered in a separate setting, outside of the institutionalized clinical encounter, with what he calls "a neutral medical opinion given prior to assistance."[18] From this work it is clear that the character of relationships between medical practitioners and patients, some-times of substantially lengthy duration, should be taken into account, or a clarification of the nature of short-term relations between medical practitio-ners and the people who request their help in their search for a form of suicide should be provided. Bosshard's work is situated within a large field of bio-ethical studies in Switzerland that have asked, usually through surveys, whether assisted suicide is considered a part of medical practice or whether it is a nonmedical intervention with which it can be judged as legitimate or illegitimate for a physician to cooperate.[19] This question is primed by the fact that statistical studies have shown that in a comparison of different organizations—for example, the two Zurich-based organizations Exit Deutsche Schweiz and Dignitas that figured in a study from 2008— Exit Deutsche Schweiz more frequently aids people with what they call "non-fatal illness."[20] This statistical point echoes my own understanding, developed through processes of field inquiry, that the nature of the illness is not in itself the determining factor of the request for suicide. This claim is put to the test in the case of requests for assistance with suicide stemming from those with diagnosed psychiatric disorders. The question at stake is whether the illness itself causes the desire to die, and it constitutes the apex of the inquiry in the final segment of part 1 of this book ("Judgment on Trial").

PARALLEL DEATHS

Although assisted suicide in Switzerland is a practice distinct from the medical field, both from the point of view of the ASSM and from the point of view of assisted suicide's legal status, it nevertheless tends, in practice, to implicate doctors. Associations that help with suicide need physicians, with their knowledge and their specific rights, such as the right to prescribe barbiturates—the privileged means by these associations to end life. Given these parameters, I thought it would be important to find out how care for the dying is done in practice, at home, by professionals who are not facilitating assisted suicides, to find out both how care for those with serious chronic illness is enacted and how the practice of requesting assistance with suicide is understood. The short narrative with which I began, "Near Death," concretizes one situation of dying, one that was relatively normal, in which the team did what they could to care for the person concerned, acknowledging, through humor, their own limits: limits in which the gesture of cleaning the dying man's mouth, which can generally be important for keeping people comfortable, was associated with an impending death and thus reflecting the link between the medical professionals' own action, under heavily constrained conditions, and the death to come. I characterized this linking as a preoccupation with the relation between legitimate interventions on the body and the timing of death, a preoccupation expressed through the humor of recoding care as actively ending a life ("euthanasia"). The team's own interrogation of what they were doing to help him at the moment of death was echoed, negatively, by the sad resignation of the caregiver saying simply that there was not much to do now, to which the only possible response under the circumstances was to insist on the significance of someone being there—which is not to minimize its importance. The core concern for the palliative care team seemed to turn on what counts as appropriate activity in relation to a person with a serious illness or, even more basically, what can in fact be done when it seems as if there is nothing to do.

I asked Anne the next day whether she had had patients who ultimately decided to end their lives with the help of Exit and whether the palliative care team collaborated with Exit. She said yes, that there had been a case like that, and then quickly gave me a counterexample: "But we had other situations where we felt the people were pressured by Exit to sign up: you remember the lady who kept having visits from Exit?" she said to Sylvie, who nodded. "They came almost every week. Once the person from Exit was even helping install a TV set. I said to them, 'Ooh I see you've got projects together!'" We walked to the car to begin the day's visits. "You mentioned Exit; well the person we're about to see is a member."

"Her husband, too," Sylvie added. "Madame Vasseau . . . she stresses me out."

"It's her husband that stresses me out," Anne replied. "He always attends our consultations and just sits there, not saying anything. I have the impression he is judging all the time." Anne gave me the medical report to read. Pancreatic carcinoma: refused surgery; reduced appetite; obstructive jaundice; pain is managed by three doses of morphine during the night. The report suggests increasing to four times 10 mg over twenty-four hours.

"The last time a doctor examined her was on Monday and reported that her condition is rapidly declining. An ophthalmic consult was proposed in order to investigate flashing lights that she is seeing," Sylvie said. I handed the file back to Anne.

"She probably has cerebral metastases, but we don't know," Anne said.

"Has she talked to you about it during your visits?"

"Just once at the beginning."

"She has the 'Exit look,'" Sylvie said.

"Do I have the Exit look?" Anne asked.

"No, you don't have the capacity for discernment." We laughed, and then Anne's phone rang.

"We're right outside."

"We're six minutes late and he's phoning to see where we are?!"

A beautiful cottage. An elegantly dressed man in his sixties opened the door: neat gray hair, a soft well-kempt beard, blue patterned silk shirt, with glasses hanging from his neck. We went in, and he explained that she has been in bed since the previous day, half-asleep. She had not eaten anything for several days and had not drunk anything for twenty-four hours. "I phoned you just now because she had said yesterday morning that she had phoned, but given her state of confusion now, I wondered suddenly whether she really had phoned." He explained that he has several questions regarding what technical things he can prepare, how to make sure he is properly equipped if she is unable to get out of the bed.

"Do you have the impression that she is in pain?"

"No, I don't think so. She seems quite peaceful. Last night she just wanted me to be with her; as we slept she kept coming closer to me wanting to be held. It was really quite nice. I held her hand." Monsieur Vasseau looked at each of us. His look was not interrogative but rather what I can only think to call "constative," not looking to question, or even to be recognized, but rather to allow us to participate in something that he now knew we should know if we too were to observe and participate in what was to come.

I was deeply moved by the look in the man's eyes, his sadness that was expressed in consonance with the milieu, something I can only qualify weakly, paradoxically perhaps, as a kind of bourgeois pastoral: the pastel, pastoral, tonality of the interior, the calm of the setting at the limits of the city-state, and what seemed to me to be his preparation for the unknown turns that were to come, a turning point that would lead necessarily to an end, but to what end, he didn't know. We went upstairs to see her.

As we entered the room, I saw that there was an old oak bookshelf to the left, a sofa and chairs in front of us illuminated by large windows that looked out onto fields. A large four-poster bed was to the right. Madame Vasseau was a tiny figure in a mass of soft pillows and duvet. Anne and Sylvie approached her to introduce themselves. I kept my distance, close enough to see and to hear, as well as close enough to her husband and their son that I could see what they were doing.

"Hello Madame," Sylvie leaned over, gently.

"Merci," a voice said quietly.

"Oh you're welcome, but we haven't done anything yet!"

"Merci, merci."

"How do you feel?"

"OK." She did not open her eyes but turned a little. Anne and Sylvie attempted to get her to sit up.

"Has she been to the toilet?"

"Perhaps once," her husband said.

"Are you thirsty?"

"Yes."

"Could we have some water please?"

"I have a plastic bottle and a small bucket with a wet towel to make sure her lips are not too dry," her husband said, concerned to make sure that he has been doing the right thing. Her son came back with the bottle, and she was able to swallow a few drops of water.

"Does she have sleeping pills?" Sylvie asked Madame Vasseau's husband.

"Yes."

"Does she take them?"

"No, never."

"Do you mind if I take a look at her medications?"

"Please do. They are in the drawer there, next to her."

"The sleeping-pill box is full. Is it possible that accidentally two patches [of morphine] were put on?"

"I don't know; it's possible." Sylvie and Anne rummaged in the duvet, moving her body looking for a second patch.

"Oooo, it's cold."

"My hands are a little cold. Does that hurt when I touch your belly?"

"A little yes." They continued to look but did not find anything.

"I will be honest. I'm stumped as to what could be causing her to sleep like that," Sylvie said. Madame Vasseau turned over and submerged herself back into the pillows.

"You just want to be left alone to sleep?"

"Ça va, ça va. Merci."

"We are going to discuss now with your husband and your son about what we can do for you."

"Should we go downstairs or stay up here?"

"I think she can hear us, so let's stay up here."

"I took out the advance directives that she filled in, in case you need to see those," her husband said. "What she said is that she doesn't want to be fed artificially but that hydration was ok; that hurts right, being dehydrated? Most of all, she doesn't want to suffer." Sylvie replied that being dehydrated is not per se painful.

"Well, what she doesn't want is unnecessary prolongation of life [acharnement]."

"My suggestion is that we could give her subcutaneous hydration; that way she is not hooked up to an intravenous drip all day. We could do that for twenty-four or forty-eight hours and see if that improves the confusion."

"Her big anxiety was about taking her medications correctly."

"Would it be acceptable, do you think, for you and for her to have a nurse come daily?"

"Yes, it would be."

Their son then said that he was very pleased that we are able to have this discussion among all of us so that they could come to a decision collectively and so that the responsibility for making decisions for his mother did not fall solely on his dad. Sylvie corrected him by saying that what they were in fact in the process of doing was coming to a consensus in order to make the decisions that his mother would have wanted or that were in keeping with what she would want.

"What if she asks for Exit? Would that be a possibility?" her husband asked.

"In her current state she wouldn't be allowed to. But also, there is the question of to what end she would ask for Exit?"

"I'm not sure, but if she regained her capacity and then asked for Exit, I'm not sure what we should do."

"Well, if she is capable and has discernment, she can of course then telephone Exit; we cannot stop her from doing that. It would then be a decision to be made following that course of events. But in her current state it is not a possibility."

"Yes, ok, I see."

"Would you be disappointed if she didn't die with Exit?" Anne asked.

"No no, not all," her husband said. "I just don't want her to suffer." Anne went to make the telephone call to arrange for the nursing team to come daily and to start hydrating her.

FOG

Although Anne and Sylvie frequently narrated their mistrust regarding relations between their patients and Exit, we can see how in relation to their patient they are able to facilitate a conversation about its parallel status: "she can of course then telephone Exit," and the question of the purpose, "to what end" she would call them. This is a principal feature of the adjacent space in which assisted suicide exists: it is not illegal; it exists in a separate channel of practice; and then depending on the specificity of the situation—the person who is ill, the family members who know about the request, and the medical team in charge of care—there will be more or less information shared, more or less of a discussion. Ultimately, if and when a choice is made, then a transfer of responsibility occurs for managing the timing, form, mode, and practice of the ending of life. Again, as the pair underscored, this transfer can occur more or less de facto and with more or less awareness of what is going on for the palliative care team.

Anne and Sylvie, and also other palliative care professionals, stated quite openly that, with respect to the association Exit and the patients in contact with them, generally, "They [Exit] hide things and ask the patient to hide it from us." Anne exemplified the point through an anecdote of going to see a patient and then asking about the next appointment, proposing another visit two weeks later. "And they say, 'Oh yes, well, . . . I'll call you.' And then it turns out they went with Exit. Or else, we had a situation where the Exit doctor phones our nursing team in order to prepare a visit at home, and he asks for an intravenous perfusion to be put in. They ask him why: 'Oh, to hydrate her.' Hydrate her? [*Incredulous*] And it turns out it was for barbiturate perfusion for her to do an assisted suicide!" Such statements will then, depending on the audience and occasion, be tempered with historical claims, coming from both the associations and palliative care-givers, suggesting that relations between palliative care teams and the associations have become much better over the last twenty years. The ultimate aim for some in the associations for medical institutions is to fully integrate assisted suicide and eventually to push for the legalization of euthanasia, as is the case in the Netherlands and Belgium.

Such an image of the relations of those who do palliative care and assisted suicide is, however, often undermined by a sentiment that "there is a lot we don't know about," with respect to the practice of assisted suicide, as one senior palliative care doctor put it to me, and that with respect to the limited information that they have that the practices are "sometimes on the limit of the acceptable." This addition is crucial: not only, as with Anne and Sylvie, is it a matter of hidden projects existing in parallel, but the very character of those projects is put in question, albeit without specifying exactly which type of practices, or specific instances, were being criticized and what limit or limits passed. This kind of imprecise statement, rarely explicit enough to be an accusation, has circulated frequently throughout the four years I inquired into the subject and circulates in tandem with the efforts of the association to render practices public (through different forms of media, TV and newspapers principally), and to develop better relations with medical institutions. I read the besmirching statement less as a statement that aims to undermine the associations' practices per se (although it also has that effect), but more importantly it has the effect of halting a too-easy or -rapid integration of the activity into medical practice proper. The point of the vague statement is not to say that Exit conducts its practice improperly, and thus to make the case for clarification about the "rules," and hence to either ban certain forms of the practice, as happened in Germany, or to legalize the practice, including euthanasia within the hospital, as is the case in the Benelux countries. Rather, the point is to establish an affective and practical zone in which professionals can sit on the fence, being neither for nor against, expressing understanding for why some people want to do it, in relation to statements of compassion and reference to the value of choice. Yet the same professionals will then state that it is a practice that can easily exceed appropriate limits, limits that they are nevertheless not in a position to clarify; hence, the statement turns on a vague evaluation *that must remain vague.*

There is, however, an important addendum to this claim about the parazone in which assisted suicide is practiced in Switzerland and a counterclaim to my proposal that we see the parazone as existing within a fog that is actively maintained. The counterclaim turns on practical efforts to "clarify" the legal framing of assisted suicide.

IN LIEU OF CLARIFICATION

Since 2013, there has been a legal framework in several cantons of Switzerland for the management of assisted suicide requests within medical institutions. In the eyes of some medical professionals, political authorities, and key players from the associations, the change in law in Vaud (2013) and Neuchatel (2014), as well as the recent changes in Geneva (2018) indexed a possible integration of the practice within institutionalized medicine proper, a clarification of "the rules," and the existence of collaborative relations. At the same time, however, the emergence of a specific law in Vaud and Neuchatel, I argue, reaffirms and reinstantiates in many respects the particularity of a Swiss institutional configuration of assisted dying that turns on keeping the norms and the forms of the practice, more broadly, foggy.

In January of 2013 the canton of Vaud voted in favor of a law, applicable at the cantonal level, concerning assistance with suicide within health institutions officially recognized as beneficial to the general public (*établissement sanitaire reconnu d'intérêt public*). A similar law followed in Neuchatel the following year. All health institutions receiving public funds are now unable to refuse the request and practice of an assisted suicide within the institution when the following criteria are in place: the person is capable of discernment;

the request is persistent; the condition concerns an illness or physical state that is serious and incurable; and alternatives linked to palliative care have been discussed. The responsible doctor in the institution, however, has the right to ask for the opinion of another doctor or of an evaluating committee internal to the institution. The responsible doctor must then reply to the request from the person in writing within a "reasonable delay."

Importantly, if the person has access to accommodations external to the institution, and under conditions in which the institution in question does not fulfill the aim of providing housing (such as would be the case in a care home), then the responsible doctor can ask for the assistance with suicide to take place outside of the institution, on the condition that the return of the person to alternative housing is a "reasonable" request. The personnel of the institution may not participate in a professional capacity in the assistance with suicide, thus maintaining one of the key aforementioned aspects of the para-zone: exclusion of the act from professional duty. When the implementation of assisted suicide takes place within the institution, the doctor who is responsible must ensure that the means used is subject to medical dictates (since no means are specified in the law).

The Vaud law is seen by some as an example of the slow, incremental movement toward the institutionalization of the practice of assisted dying within the medical professional milieu and is seen as a constitutive part of a more general movement by Swiss associations that facilitate assisted suicide to get the medical corps and its institutions to integrate the practice. The specificity of the law, and the means for putting it into practice, however, indicate that this is far from obvious: hospitals to a very large degree force people to leave hospital to do assistance with suicide. Those that are unable to go home are for the most part blocked from fulfilling an assisted suicide.

It is true, as of this writing, that the requirement that people with a home to which they can be returned must leave nonresidential medical institutions is a point of contention within the main teaching hospital in Vaud. For the time being, however, hospital medicine still tends largely to exteriorize the practice; there is not usually more than one assisted suicide per year at the main hospital in Vaud. In conversation with a senior figure in psychiatry in the canton, I learned that it was already in 2004 that the issue of forced ejections of individuals who had made requests for assistance with suicide, prior to the existence of a law, had provoked an internal discussion within the main teaching hospital, concerning the possibility of accepting requests and fulfilling the act within the institution. The story concerned a man who was suffering from advanced prostate cancer. He was described as an incredible man, and his character and uniqueness seems to have been important in the capacity of those who cared for him to listen to him and to reform their practice based on what they heard (and subsequently saw). The man told the team that he wanted to end his life by assisted suicide. Owing to hospital regulations, he was forced to do it at home, since the hospital up until then would not allow assistance with suicide on its premises under any circumstances. Because of his physical state and the configuration of his apartment, on the fifth floor of the building, he had to be lifted and moved into the apartment with a furniture lift through the window—"like an object," the psychiatrist explained, with an affect of perturbation, a decade after the fact, concerning the memory of the man's situation. The image is perhaps not lost on the reader that this man had to go through the window, albeit *in* through the window rather than *out* through it, in order to end his life—associating the movement with images and fantasies of violent death. Frequently, those I would talk to about their decision to contact an assisted suicide association would precisely contrast the form of death with "real suicide," which they then instantiate with the image of a person jumping out a window.

This episode prompted a move on the part of a group within the institution to try to change hospital policy, "not for political or moral reasons, but just so that patients have the same rights in the hospital as out of it," the psychiatrist explained. In January of 2006 the hospital decided to "allow" assisted suicide within its walls, "causing ethical and practical dilemmas for the hospital's palliative care consult service," as one of its former palliative care specialists has written.[21] While all the published accounts of the decision focus on ethical and practical reflection that emerged in the wake of the decision, a decision whose status is, to say the least, unclear, more importantly, when it comes to actually knowing anything about how assisted suicide happens when conducted in the hospital, which is to say, to get hospital doctors to talk about a concrete case, no one seems to be familiar with the details. This intrahospital situation seems to have been intensified by the passing of the Vaud law.

Today there is a law that institutes this possible manner of dying within the hospital yet at the same time makes it less likely: under the current situation the same man from 2004 may still have had to go home, through the window, in order to die, depending on a discussion at the hospital as to whether it is reasonable for him to have to be moved in this specific way. Moreover, knowing that a person cannot be moved home is often interpreted by the assisted suicide association in Vaud as part of the power dynamics of the situation of request. As a longtime accompanier with Exit explained to me in general terms, "Every time we have a request for assistance with suicide from within the hospital the services mobilize the psychiatric team in order to say that the person no longer has their decision-making capacities." I asked how they do that.

"The last time, the neuro-oncology team called psychiatry, and a team of five came down. They said that the cerebral tumor had advanced so as to make the woman incapable of expressing herself clearly and thus of making decisions. I knew the woman well and that even before this she had had trouble expressing herself; she was a bit simple. But we can't only help intellectuals. Since she was unable to be moved home, which they knew, she had to stay in the hospital."

The hospital, as a field site, remained basically impenetrable to me (2014–17): I was able to talk with doctors and conduct interviews; but given the rarity of the discussions with patients, and of the practice of the act within the hospital, I decided to focus my fieldwork efforts on the setting of the majority of assisted suicides—private residences, both in the cases of Swiss residents and of foreigners who come to Switzerland in order to die at the rented apartments of the associations that are willing to help foreigners.

Nevertheless, the situation relative to the hospital is important as part of the more general endeavor to characterize how this practice of assisted suicide, whether in relation to the hospital, care homes, or private residences, is situated in a zone adjacent to institutionalized medicine, one over which a layer of practical fog hangs. The point can be exemplified: a cantonal public health official, at a daylong workshop that brought together all relevant stakeholders on the issue of assisted suicide in Switzerland,[22] stated publicly that the law in Vaud was explicitly framed without specific norms or values in mind, meaning that lawmakers explicitly decided not to include specific illnesses, and they hoped that it would be for "society" to respond one way or another. Speaking to an audience that included medical professionals and assisted suicide associations in early 2018, he explained that there would have to be specific instances, examples, jurisprudence, and conflicts, possibly, but that currently, it is impossible to inscribe norms; each case has to be considered separately. He gave an example similar to the one narrated by the Exit accompanier, albeit with the inverse outcome: he explained that he appreciated it when care teams in the hospital reflect on the capacity of discernment of a person, when strictly from a medico-technical point of view they are not capable of discernment; nevertheless, taking into account the ensemble of the person's biography, they might come to the decision that the person is capable. If there were strict norms, he explained, then it would be black and white. He is in favor of laws, as a general principle, but when it comes to this practice, he stated, he is not going to encourage them, preferring to let nature take its course and letting people expose themselves.

Two things are important to draw from this: (1) the character of the judgment and (2) the dimension of risk, which together constitute two further aspects of the parazone's fog, which accompany the first three that have already been outlined: (1) the exclusion of the practice from professional activity; (2) the intentional lack of clarity about rules, and (3) the vague sense of mistrust between the associations and institutional medical professionals. In terms of judgment there is a tension between technical determinations and the nontechnical, which includes aesthetic and ethical considerations. As the cantonal health official expressed, within the jurisdiction of the hospital there is the discretionary power for the doctors concerned to draw on technical or ethico-aesthetic judgment (feeling about the patient, in relation to her or his biography, narrative form). This unpredictable parameter has to be taken into account by those working for these associations.

Regarding the second point, the public health official's position underscores a very general phenomenon: that the normative fog of the parazone operates through a game of exposure. To be considered legitimate, and to avoid the suspicion of engaging in nefarious practices, the associations endeavored to bring their practice into the public domain and endeavored to formalize, as much as possible, the internal norms of practice: a more or less stable protocol for how to manage requests, a division of labor in terms of evaluating the dossiers, and, accompanying the person, a protocol for means of ending life. On the one hand, the associations have, as various members insist, nothing to hide, to the degree that their activity is not illegal. Yet, on the other hand, because of their positioning within this zone adjacent to formalized medical institutions, as well as other political and juridical authorities, given these institutions' reluctance to clarify rules, they put the burden of exposure on those who, for ethical and political reasons, consider it their obligation to aid people suffering in one way or another to leave their experience of life.

An example of this exposure, and perhaps of what the cantonal officer called "society" responding to the development of the practice, appeared in 2014, when Exit ADMD clarified its internal norms about helping people with multiple age-related illnesses (*polypathologies liées à l'âge*). A televised debate was organized in response to this clarification of the association's internal rules about age-related illnesses.[23] It featured two people from the association, the then president Jerome Sobel, a practicing ENT surgeon, and the then vice president Daphné Berner, former cantonal medical officer for Neuchatel, as well as Bertrand Kiefer, a medical doctor, theologian, and ethicist, editor of the *Revue médicale suisse*, as well as a member of the Swiss Advisory Commission on Biomedical Ethics, and a Catholic priest, Nicolas Betticher.

What is noteworthy about the ethicist's opening statement is that rather than refer to the actual legal situation in which this practice exists, he refers to ethical positions of organizations that do not technically have any formal regulatory power over the practice—namely, the Swiss medical association and the national ethics committee:

> *Bertrand Kiefer:* Of course it can be very difficult and very heavy, but with this [change in the internal criteria of the association] we are in a whole other scenario [*cas de figure*] to that which was accepted up until now, which is to say, an assistance with suicide either for people in a terminal phase of an illness or those who have a serious incurable illness. These are the terms which are at the same time those of the national ethics committee, the Swiss medical association and other countries—there are only a handful of other countries who accept it and they all insist that it must be an incurable illness. Now we are going towards something else, much more open, badly defined.

If the reader will permit the intrusion at this point in the discourse, the claim that "now we are going towards something else" is, in point of fact, untrue: de facto, age-related illness had been accepted by the association from the beginning. What changed in 2014 was the formal specification, making sure that all the members *know* that this is the case.

> *Kiefer (cont.):* The question of the end of life is really no longer the one posed to palliative care. It is one posed to society: we are the only ones, in Switzerland, to take this step. So are we Swiss, very advanced in our democracy and in ethics, are we going to be a shining light for other countries? . . . Or, collectively, are we in the process of conditioning ourselves, a social conditioning of thought, without asking the question, why don't these people want to live any longer? That anyhow is the first question.
>
> *TV host:* Is it a step too far to help people without incurable illnesses?
>
> *Daphné Berner:* Wrong, wrong, wrong! (*c'est faux, c'est faux, c'est faux!*) We accompany people who have incurable illnesses: the incapacitating multiple illnesses related to age. I'll give you the case of an old woman who I recently

accompanied [in an assisted suicide], who was ninety-three years old; she was already deaf, she became blind. She adored doing broidery and singing in the choir. She could no longer do either. She already had to grieve for a large part of her existence, and three months prior to calling me, she had become anally incontinent. These things are not curable. No doctor succeeded in healing her.

In terms of rhetorical strategy this is a commonplace tactic by members of Exit: to respond to general statements about values, or principles, with stories about individual lives. Bertrand Kiefer responds with the polar opposite rhetorical strategy.

> *Kiefer:* What place do we [have] in our individualistic society for old people? In our society, that has undermined the value of old age. The solution is not to help people commit suicide but to give their life meaning.
>
> *Jerome Sobel:* These people are adults; they have their life behind them; they have thought about it and argue for values different to your own; they have the right to express themselves; and if we respect them, we must listen to them. The place that we ask for is to be heard.

Lest the discussion be too firmly parameterized by the sociological poles of a methodological and ethical individualism and holism, the framing was disrupted by an intriguing intervention from the Catholic priest, Nicolas Betticher:

> *Nicolas Betticher:* I am shocked tonight, when I read what I have read and hear what I have heard. First of all, no one here has the monopoly on the truth; on the contrary, we all have the monopoly of the duty to search for the truth together (*le monopole du devoir de rechercher la vérité ensemble*), which is a question of society. Life for me is sacred. It is a gift and infinitely dignified. The dignity of life does not depend on the state of health. This is a thesis which it seems to me we must welcome as such. We have in this country two legal bases. The first is the federal charter (constitution), which in its first preamble, says that the law should refer itself to the weakest members of society. I think the most fragile deserve to be accompanied, and not benefit from Exit.

The Swiss Federal charter begins with the following: "In the knowledge that only those who use their freedom remain free, and that the strength of a people is measured by the well-being of its weakest members; we adopt the following Constitution."

> *Betticher (cont.):* The other legal basis is the Penal Code: I remind you that article 115 defines clearly the conditions under which the act you perform is depenalized. But it concerns criminal law, which means that it is in itself

something that is bad (*mauvais*). Since it is in the penal code, the sovereign esteems that it is not ethical.

Crucial for me about this exchange is to understand the rhetorical form that pits a moral principle of individualism against a holism that is equally moralizing, taking its heuristic orientation from the century-old science of the social (a discursive anchor to which I return explicitly in part 3).

In such a moralizing discourse, discussion of assistance with suicide is restricted to an either/or logic in which either individuals are determined by extraindividual forces, and from which they need to be protected, or in rhetorical terms, the individual is reified; its choice and experience is the moral barometer, and there is no room to discuss how it is that a subject comes to determine that it is appropriate to leave the experience of life in such a way, and at a time of the choosing, negotiated together with others. There is no room in this sort of moral debate, and within a process that is supposed to clarify the parameters of the practice, to grasp the paradoxical character of the act. To do so, one would have to listen—and not only to the person concerned or to those authorized to establish talking points. One would have to be open to the sensibility of not knowing already what this practice consists in.

"EVEN THOUGH I WAS THERE"

For those who remain, the vast majority of those whom I have met understood that the decision to die voluntarily could and should be grasped in terms of the desire for autonomy and liberty. Nevertheless, there are also people who recognize that this conceptualization of what happened was not quite right, not quite truthful to their experience, without then occupying a position of external critique that would mobilize the supports of the law (human and divine, as in the discourse of Betticher) and the so-called "societal" (as in the discourse of Kiefer), in which consideration of specific cases is replaced by general moral discourse.

A case in point: I was in contact with the daughter of a woman who ended her life through assisted suicide because of advancing cortico-basal degeneration: a rare neurodegenerative disorder, CBD can lead to severe memory and behavioral problems. The discussions were useful, not only to the degree that I was able to gain information about a specific event but, more important, because of the daughter's manner of describing and reflecting on her experience—not exactly unique but certainly of a rare quality. In the course of our discussions she sent me a text, a written reflection on her mother's death, on her grief, which included a description of her own search to try to understand what happened. Her text was not only a deep reflection on her own experience; it also grasped more broadly a paradox that I had seen but had not been able to name—a paradoxical composition of elements that seemed to provide the thread for the heterogeneous narratives, experiences, episodes, and events that I had heard, seen, and experienced:

> Everyone tells me that she was brave; I reply that I don't know.
> It's totally mad [c'est fou].
> Courageous, maybe, in part, but also completely mad.
> But it was either that [suicide] or madness [. . .]
> As the masterly woman that she had always been, [En maîtresse femme qu'elle a toujours été], she wouldn't tolerate madness [la folie].
> Once she knew what was happening, she drew a red line.
> Die standing.
> This act, rather than madness.
> And I cannot name it.
> Even though I was there.

This observation, meditation, contemplation (Betrachtung) of her experience serves as a device, not an apology but an apologia, for warranting the form that I have endeavored to work with, in order to grasp this act that I too cannot quite name and for which I can provide only a placeholder: leaving.

Judgment on Trial

The first criminal trial concerning assisted suicide in Switzerland was brought against the Zurich psychiatrist Peter Baumann (1935–2011) and unfolded over a five-year period, from 2007 to 2011. It pertained to an event from 2001, when Baumann helped Andreas U., a man in his forties, suffering from psychiatric troubles, to end his own life at his home in Basel. The trial concerned principally the evaluation of the professional legal and moral obligations of a doctor who helps with suicide, in the context of a practice that, as already noted, has been externalized by the medical corps as not pertaining to professional duty but rather concerning a personal moral choice.

I have previously named the activity of a doctor who is dedicated to assisting with suicide in Switzerland as belonging to a weakly institutionalized "parazone," which is adjacent to institutionalized medicine yet draws on elements from practices that are more strongly institutionalized: medical knowledge, juridical rules, and norms of action, such as the fact, for instance, that after an assisted suicide the person who accompanied the individual should telephone the police. The activity of assisted suicide, in a very simple sense, has a capacity, by virtue of its adjacency, to ruffle the institutions to which it is adjacent. And by virtue of this ruffling, those who assist with suicide are exposing themselves to the capacities for action, evaluation, and judgment of these more institutionalized settings.

Prior to narrating the casuistry of participant observation in part 2 of this book, the interest of an in-depth case study of a legal trial pertaining to the relatively uncommon situation of request for help with suicide by a mentally ill person may help us to better grasp the parazone in which this activity takes place; it also underscores one of the parazone's particularities rather than grasping the particularity of the person's request and its unfolding, as will be the endeavor of part 2. Contrary to the Californian and Dutch contexts briefly mentioned, reflection concerning assistance with either euthanasia or suicide for persons suffering from mental illness did not lead to the instauration of a system of explicit and codified rules that govern the activity, as in the Netherlands, nor did it lead to its interdiction, as in the case of California. I will narrate how the trial of Peter Baumann, and its aftermath, served to reestablish, to shore up, the contours of a parazone and its opaque qualities, within which this minor practice is located, adjacent to key institutions such as the media, a police inquiry, a criminal trial, and a court appeal, as well as the political process of a clemency request, without leading to a new explicit framework.[1] The shoring up of the indeterminate institutional contours is a counterpart to the affective and intellectual indetermination of grasping the act.

THE CASE

The Baumann trial, which began in 2007 in Basel, is to my knowledge the first criminal trial concerning the practice of assisted suicide in Switzerland. In this case it was not, first of all, an issue of interpreting Article 115 of the Penal Code, and the danger of a "selfish motive," which makes the person who helps liable to imprisonment. It was rather a case of asking whether Andreas U., a forty-six-year-old man suffering from mental illness, could be considered capable of discernment. Indeed, the Civil Code states explicitly that, from a legal point of view, "a person is capable of judgement within the meaning of the law if he or she does not lack the capacity to act rationally by virtue of being under age or because of a mental disability, mental disorder, intoxication or similar circumstances."[2] It should be noted that Andreas U.'s request for help with suicide was not the first such request that provoked controversy. In the 1990s two other requests from people who had recently left stays in psychiatric clinics had already provoked strong reactions concerning the practices of Exit Deutsche Schweiz. In 1999, when the association decided to help a young woman with a mental illness, the family turned to the cantonal medical officer in Zurich to obtain her forced hospitalization. An investigation was then conducted, and the then president of the association, a medical doctor and professor of medicine who had prescribed the barbiturates for the young

woman, was banned from medical practice for the duration of the investigation. The Zurich cantonal medical officer then stated that the prescription of
a lethal dose of barbiturates to persons without physical illness would result
in the loss of the right to practice medicine for the prescriber within the canton. It is in this context that Exit Deutsche Schweiz adopted a moratorium
on assisted suicide for the mentally ill (*psychisch kranke Menschen*).[3]

The importance of requests of this type has also been analyzed, notably in
a study of the forty-three documented cases of assisted suicide in the Basel
region between 1992 and 1997, of which six cases involved people who had
received treatment in a psychiatric facility.[4] The conclusions of the analysis
testify to the tensions among the medical profession (and more particularly
psychiatry as a specialty), the medico-administrative authorities (institutes of
forensic medicine, cantonal medical officers), and the associations that facilitate suicide. Although the article was published at the time of the adoption
of the moratorium on assistance for people with mental illness by the associations, the authors do not mention it. To the contrary, they express alarm
at Exit's practices with regard to such demands and give a glimpse of what
would become Baumann's doubly problematic position. The final paragraph
of the article states:

> In a latest declaration, the present chairman of EXIT [c. 2001] commends the
> good co-operation with the medical body in general, with the exception of psy-
> chiatrists and psychologists, whose assumption that severely ill people might be
> suffering from depression he still regards as an example of undue paternalism,
> coming from people whose professional shortcomings are easily seen in their poor
> prognoses concerning probation of sexual offenders. Hence, we feel the danger
> cannot be ruled out that assisted suicide carried out by this lay-organisation, which
> clearly disregards the psychosocial implication of suffering, still offers a radical,
> over simplified solution, not only for people suffering from serious medical but
> from difficult social conditions, as well.[5]

One of the authors of the study, a forensic psychiatrist, would be called as an
expert witness by the prosecution in the trial against Baumann.

Following the adoption of its moratorium on psychiatric cases, Exit
Deutsche Schweiz convened an ethics committee including Baumann and the
forensic psychiatrist. In the two years that Baumann sat on this committee,
two core assumptions became clear to him in the reasoning of the majority of
its members: (1) that suicidal thoughts in the absence of physical illness is
sufficient grounds to suspect depression and (2) that depression indexes an

incapacity for judgment.[6] Baumann was not in accord. He founded his own association in 2001, SuizidHilfe (Help with suicide), which aimed to assist people with mental illnesses who wanted help with voluntarily ending their lives. He justified the creation of SuizidHilfe by his anger over the moratorium and said he was outraged that Exit would contravene its own grounds for existence and its aims[7]—namely, to help people with a reasonable serious persistent wish to end their life to do so in a manner that is sure to work and is in accord with their wishes.

In April of 2001 Andreas U. contacted Peter Baumann, who assisted Andreas with suicide at home in Basel. Baumann was alone with Andreas during the suicide and thus decided to film it, to prove to the police that the latter had performed the act himself. Given the inability to use a lethal prescription of barbiturate and the risk of being accused of abusing his professional position, Baumann resigned from the order of Swiss doctors. He and Andreas discussed possible means of suicide, given the injunction against the use of a lethal dose of barbiturate. To clarify what would be appropriate action under the prevailing conditions, he wrote to the Cantonal Pharmacy (*Kantonsapotheke Zürich*) to ask about effective and painless alternative methods, given that, legally speaking, assistance with suicide is not illegal. The pharmaceutical authority did not reply.

The practical solution Baumann came up with, to which Andreas agreed, was to use a closed breathing system, a painter's mask, equipped with soda lime, a chemical that absorbs carbon dioxide. With this device death should have been achieved through suffocation, without Andreas becoming breathless. There were three unsuccessful attempts, a breathless Andreas is said to have pulled off the mask. After the third attempt, Baumann suggested using nitrous oxide, which should be filled in a plastic bag, itself to be secured to the painters mask. Andreas agreed. Baumann left the apartment to go to the local supermarket, where he purchased chargers for whipped cream siphons, which are filled with nitrous oxide. The method was successful. Baumann then called the police and waited with Andreas's body, and he cooperated with their inquiry, as is habitual during any assisted suicide.

PUBLICITY

Baumann only later gained media attention, in November of 2002, when he agreed to appear on a television segment called "Auf Dem Stuhl" (In the chair)—which aired as part of the weekly hard-hitting current-affairs program *Rundschau* (In review), in which host Reto Brennwald asks tough questions of his guests.[8] Baumann was invited to discuss his association, the death of Andreas (although he wasn't named, and specific details were not made public), and the police investigation, which had not been brought to any definitive result. The interview is of interest given its timing, four months before he would be arrested, and gives insight into Baumann's reasoning at that time, his expectations, and his justification, prior to being brought before the law.[9]

Indeed, one could also say that this media exposure perhaps played a role in his subsequent interpolation by the law, although such a claim is entirely speculative and cannot be proved either way. It remains, nevertheless, a plausible parameter in the evolution of the case, as I will later attempt to explain.

> *Reto Brennwald:* Peter Baumann, a very central question is whether you are active in such a situation, or passive. If you were active you would have to face prison. And that is why that is the central question. Now, we hear that you filmed it [the suicide]. Why is that?
>
> *Peter Baumann:* Because I was there alone. Normally, there are always two people there, a relative/close person and the assistant (*Sterbehelfer*). And when I was alone, I brought along my witness "electronically." I did that for the police, to show them what I did.
>
> *RB:* ... and why didn't you bring someone with you, as in a witness?
>
> *PB:* [*Thinks*] ... That was a very personal relationship, between that man and me, and we don't have ... how should I put it ... a formula [*Schema*] or something like that, that it always has to be the same way. I could have brought someone along. That would have been possible, but also strange.
>
> *RB:* OK. So you filmed it, we can see it in all detail, also the justice system can see very precisely whether you possibly, in one way or another, helped or not. Is it actually possible not to help at all, for example, that you don't hold/give a hand, ... or, if something goes wrong, to give a little "push"? ...
>
> [PB reacts excitedly]
>
> *PB:* That "push," well with regard to that, I first have to say: I was misquoted on that. I wrote once that the question would come whether one could possibly be allowed to give the final "push"—in the distant future. So that also this question wouldn't be a taboo anymore. In very specific cases.
>
> *RB:* Well, I was talking about that concrete case [implying but not referencing Andreas U.]. That he is falling asleep slowly and he is holding that plastic bag open over his head. Now when his hand drops in a wrong way, or when the plastic bags falls in a wrong way ...

PB: ... No. The bag over his head, for that he has to be seated, in principle ... So when he falls asleep his hand simply drops down, and with that, with that ... he is just doing it by himself.

RB: How long does it take, how long, for example, does it take in that film?

PB: Well, in that film it was without the plastic bag. There I did it with a [painter's] mask, and he had to strap it around his head and fix it with an elastic band. And so he knew, from now on it counts. So from now on, the next breath means it counts. And from that moment on I don't have to do anything anymore, other than [sitting] next to him, he was lying, [corrects] sitting in his bed. And of course I am sitting next to him, I'm holding his hand, that was very important then. He was pressing it very gently, slowly, rhythmically. I am sure that I would have felt it if he had been afraid.

RB: Herr Baumann, when I hear you talk I feel cold and hot at the same time. When I hear masks, elastics, sleeping pills ... That sounds ... creepy [unheimlich]?

PB: Well, we looked at it together with that man, in advance, whether he is OK with it, if he objects to it, or not. And I don't use an optimal suicide method, but the best there are.

RB: So you mean a "beautiful" one ...

PB: Well, an ideal one. So, for example, dignified is always taken to mean "falling asleep." [But] Dignified means something different to the people I have talked to—safe, nonaggressive towards other people.

RB: Again, to close this part: So you have these films, you are certain that you were not [involved] active[ly]. But you are under investigation. Aren't you a little bit nervous?

PB: Well ... one can be nervous for a little while, and then you have to move on again. Of course, you have ... that's there. In my view, it is also a massive demonstration of power by the state, in front of everyone: Now we interrogate him for seven hours and then we'll search his home, so he will know that with every such action he will have to face that. Then he will stop.

RB: And you are determined to make this also a topic ...

PB: That has to be made a topic!

RB: ... otherwise you probably wouldn't be here? The crucial point is that you're saying it's not enough what Exit and Dignitas are offering so far. It is not enough if only terminally ill, incurable patients can be sent to death. There has to be more. Why for heaven's sake has there to be more?

PB: We don't send [anyone to their deaths]. Those people want it. And they can choose between bad ways—barbiturates, getting saved, with liver damages, brain damages, with the psychiatric ward for eight months and then still suicide; jumping, being a paraplegic, etc.—between bad ways, incredibly bad ones—and I also think society offers those people just all the bad ways. And I find this very unethical.

RB: But you also say that the crucial point is that not only seriously, terminally ill people are concerned; you even say also that people in good health are concerned.

PB: It can be . . . they can decide freely about their own life, that's a human right, a fundamental right. And we cannot define who is entitled to this right. But we have to define who is not entitled to this right. So we are not allowed to say . . . the concept of mental disease; it's completely pointless to use it, useless; it is too undefined. No one knows what that means.

RB: But you say, yes, also healthy people, when you say they are in sound judgment [*urteilsfähig*], I want to make use of that help.

PB: You cannot diagnose healthy people, the healthy . . .

RB: Just because you told me on the telephone in our conversation before this show that also healthy . . .

PB: Yes, in principle everybody. And then you have to look at it and say who is not allowed. And I think this is very simple. That is . . . that shows immediately, an acutely suicidal, acutely psychotic person, someone acutely depressive. First, they definitely wouldn't call me, definitely would not come to me. And afterwards that would be a whole different conversation, and we would be at a completely different point.

RB: The central point, again, is, however, if these people make their decision freely, if they have sound judgment [*urteilsfähig sind*], and Exit, for example, states that especially people with depressions are very often, [corrects] no actually most rarely are of sound judgment.

PB: We will have to have a debate about that. Who will it have to be to demonstrate this sound judgment [*Urteilsfähigkeit*]—after the person's death!

RB: So you're saying you can do it all by yourself; it is very easy. There is no need for a doctor . . .

PB: First of all, he is coming to me.

RB: . . . there is no need for a psychiatrist . . .?

PB: Yes, yes that is true. One can see that this person is undecided. Or that he wavers. Most importantly, he doesn't want it!

RB: Herr Baumann, there are studies showing so clearly that a depression is a phase, after two months, after three months the situation can present itself completely differently. There are people who regret that they even had the wish to commit suicide!

PB: There are those people. I'm not talking about two months, or three months, but I'm talking about eight years or fifteen years. That's what I am calling a chronic depression. And these people know whether they can expect anything from psychiatric therapy. So, keeping apart these two things, these two categories: those for whom it is absolutely no question, and those for whom it is definitely a question.

Several observations can be made about this exchange. First, Baumann agreed to expose himself in the media domain, in order to make assisted suicide a "topic." It can be said that he took a risk at a moment when his practice was under heavy scrutiny from the juridical realm.

Baumann insists above all in the interview on the specific character of his relationship with Andreas U.: theirs was a personal relationship. When Brennwald asks if he thinks a doctor should participate in the process, Baumann insists on the nature of his relationship with Andreas U. and replies, "He comes to me." This answer is both direct and a way of not answering the question. His reply goes to the heart of the problem of action within the parazone: Baumann is a doctor, but this status is not put forward during the interview. When he says, "He comes to me," he implies, I think, that Andreas U. sought out Baumann not per se as a doctor but as a person ready to listen to him and to help him. But even if Baumann insists on his personal relationship with Andreas U., which is not conditioned by medical protocol, nevertheless this rapport, for Baumann, is also based on his medical knowledge and experience.

For Baumann, this does not seem to be a problem in itself: to mobilize medical knowledge for an ethical purpose that is also heavily criticized by medical authorities. Nevertheless, I note that it is this simultaneity of capacities (medical and ethical) and subject positions, psychiatrist and president of the association SuizidHilfe, which will be a problem for the public authorities. According to them, there is an incompatibility between these two positions that concern the skills of the same person, trained as a psychiatrist. If such a mixture is acceptable in the case of a person with a physical illness (for example, to mobilize an oncological knowledge for an ethical purpose to relieve suffering at the end of life, when there is no more hope), in the late 1990s several political authorities decided that this was not legitimate for psychiatric illnesses. Baumann refused to acknowledge this incompatibility.

It must be remembered, however, that Baumann withdrew from the Swiss medical order (FMH) and that he was subject to the prohibition pronounced by the cantonal medical authority regarding the administration of a lethal dose of barbiturate to people not suffering from physical diseases. In the interview Baumann did not explain what had forced him to invent his DIY solution, qualified by Brennwald as "uncanny": a recurrent everyday element, a silver canister for a whipped cream siphon, queuing at the supermarket while Andreas waited at home, to create the means to be able to leave his experience of suffering behind. This kind of aesthetic judgment, of the uncanny creepiness of the situation, will count in the wider reception of the event. The aesthetics of the act will be an important element in the construction of ethical, legal, and political judgments.

Finally, in this exchange, Brennwald mobilized a commonplace regarding "depression," namely that it is a treatable disease, which should be, according to him, a reason for refusal of the request for help with suicide. Baumann, for his part, insists on the need to distinguish between people who suffer from an acute mental illness (psychosis or acute depression) and those who suffer from a chronic illness. In the case of an acute illness these people would not come to him anyway, he suggests. For others it is about knowing what "society" is ready to do or accept. And today, according to Baumann, it offers only "bad ways" to end life voluntarily. Baumann explains that he offers them an alternative, as do doctors engaged in assisting suicide for people with physical illnesses.

At the end of the exchange Baumann raises the question that will be at the heart of the trial: are people suffering from depression capable of discernment? More specifically, he asks, who would be able to evaluate Andreas's judgment after his death?

JUDGMENT

Baumann was arrested in February of 2003 and was released on bail provided he ceased his assisted suicide activity. In the summer of 2007 he was charged by the Basel cantonal prosecutor with intentional homicide. The trial focused on two issues: (1) Was Andreas U. capable of judgment? In other words, was his request for assisted suicide legitimate, and the help provided lawful? (2) What was the nature of Baumann's assessment of Andreas U.'s capacity for discernment? Was it a medical judgment? And if so, was it wrong? What were his responsibilities at stake in the situation?

A series of legal judgments were made about Baumann's assessment of Andreas U.'s ability to decide about his own death. Baumann was found guilty of "negligent homicide" in July of 2007 in the Basel Criminal Court. He lost on appeal in October of 2008. The judgment of the court of appeal reclassified his act as "intentional homicide" and increased the sentence from three to four years in prison. In June of 2009 the federal court upheld the judgment of the appeal court. Baumann was then supposed to serve his prison sentence, at which point his wife appealed for clemency (*Begnadigung*), a move that his lawyer had thought hopeless. In the jurisdiction of Basel, clemency can only be granted by a political decision: a vote of the cantonal parliament. The Grand Council of the Canton of Basel-City agreed to launch a clemency commission (*Begnadigungskommission*) and in February of 2010 voted for pardon (sixty-nine votes in favor, seven against and four abstentions). Baumann died the following year of cancer.

I will address this series of actions in two ways: (1) describe the different stages of reasoning in each legal or political body; (2) analyze the transformation of the judgments rendered from the court of first instance to the court of appeal, and from the court of appeal to the clemency commission.

In his defense plea in the court of first instance (Basel Criminal Court) Baumann's lawyer took the liberty of reminding the court of a basic principle of criminal law procedure: "The object of the penal judgment is the outlined act described in the indictment (intentional homicide). The court is bound to the description of the facts and not to the legal assessment in the accusation."[10] He summarized the implications of this basic point: "the object of the judgment is that in accordance with the alleged actions in the indictment, assistance with suicide for a person who could be found to be incapable of judgment, on legal grounds [if shown to be true] it would amount to either intentional or negligent homicide."[11] The consequential question is whether the facts support such a legal assessment and how knowledge of such facts is determined.

The importance of clarifying the nature of the judgment to be undertaken is then underscored by Baumann's lawyer. He described his own "harsh reaction" on the first day of the trial, when the court president of the trial "alleged that Andreas did not in fact want to die" and raised the question of whether Baumann should be accused of a new legal qualification: murder.[12] Murder, it should be made clear, is a legal qualification distinct from intentional homicide, under Swiss law, which further requires that "the offender acts in a particularly *unscrupulous* manner, in which the motive, the objective or the method of commission is particularly depraved."[13]

The concern here for Baumann's lawyer, in my understanding, is that the aesthetic and moral qualification of the perceived depravity of the act was mobilized by the court president as a means of establishing a reality for the situation: that the suicide went against Andreas's will. My understanding is supported by the fact that the court president, at the end of the trial, felt entitled to restate his moral and aesthetic disdain: the conduct of the suicide— "the use of a painter's mask, the failed attempts, the change of method"—

was, in his words, an "unacceptable bungled bricolage contemptuous of humanity."[14]

I can only surmise that the court president considered (a value judgment) that no person could willfully submit themselves to such a manner of dying without an *unscrupulous* manipulation from a third party. Baumann's lawyer underscored, against the court president, that not even the expert witness for the prosecution put in question the fact that Andreas expressed a wish to die. What is thus in question is only his capacity to judge that would found such an act, as well as of the nature of Baumann's evaluation of that capacity.

We can summarize, therefore, that there were, broadly speaking, five possible qualifications that could be linked to two questions of fact about judgment, Andreas's capacity to judge, and the nature of Baumann's evaluation of Andreas's capacity to judge:

1. No crime

Andreas U. wanted to die, because of his suffering related to mental illness. His decision was based on an ability to think about his illness and he was able to make such a judgment. The act was facilitated by another person, who did not act out of selfish motive.

2. Negligent homicide

Andreas U. wanted to die, but his wish was itself a sign of his inability to judge—a sign that Baumann did not take into account though he should have (without reference here to his status as a doctor and his knowledge in psychiatry).

3. Negligent homicide with respect to professional duty

Andreas U. wanted to die, but his desire was a sign of his inability to judge. Baumann, as a doctor, had a medical responsibility toward Andreas U., and he had a duty to assess his judgment correctly, which he failed to do.

4. Indirect intentional homicide

Andreas U. wanted to die, but his desire was a sign of his inability to judge—a sign that Baumann, given his expertise as a doctor, has necessarily correctly assessed, but which he ignored to pursue: the goal that he had set himself—namely, helping a person with a mental illness to end his life.

5. Murder

Andreas U. did not really want to die. Baumann knew this, and he used his dual position, as a psychiatrist and president of an assisted suicide association, to manipulate him into killing himself.

EVALUATIONS

Baumann's own account of his evaluation was that it was based on a two-hour meeting and sixteen hours of subsequent telephone calls with Andreas over two weeks.[15] Andreas, in Baumann's view, suffered from a severe obsessional compulsive disorder (*Zwangsstörung*), whose prognosis for amelioration was poor, and Andreas did not wish to attempt more therapy, which he had refused after a first year in 1987. Baumann's evaluation was that therefore Andreas's request to end his experience of his illness was sustained and reasonable.

The Basel public prosecutor asked an expert from the Basel Institute for Legal Medicine (*Institut für Rechtsmedizin*) to write a forensic medical report for the prosecution. He was a former colleague of Baumann's on the ethics committee of Exit. The court was aware that they had long been in disagreement on the question of mental illness and assistance with suicide, leading precisely to Baumann establishing his own association. For this reason Baumann's lawyer requested the recusal of the expert, which the court refused.

According to both the written account of the trial provided by Baumann and according to his lawyer, the prosecution forensic report was surprisingly short and was not based on the available medical reports for Andreas.[16] I have not been able to consult for myself the expert testimony for the prosecution because the person in question declined to speak with me. I have thus reconstructed his argument from three sources: Baumann's own analysis of the argument, his lawyer's description of the arguments in his plea in the court of first instance and appeal court plea, and newspaper reports of the trial. Based on these sources, it seems that the expert evaluation was given in the form of a logical demonstration but not an empirical demonstration.

His reasoning seemed to follow the following logic:

a. Baumann's diagnosis of Andreas U.—obsessive neurosis—must be wrong because obsessive neurosis cannot be so severe as to provoke a desire to end one's life.

b. Since Andreas U. had this desire to die, he had to have suffered from a depressive syndrome.

c. Such a depressive syndrome is serious enough that the person cannot be considered a person with the capacity to act.

d. The decision to terminate his life was not reasonable because not all medical procedures had been exhausted in the treatment of depression.

e. Suffering from a pathological perception of reality, Andreas U. thought, owing to the lack of appropriate treatment, that his condition and prognosis was hopeless.

f. Thus, an objective medical evaluation was not carried out by Baumann, whereas it should have been.

g. Baumann had not exhausted all treatment options. The prognosis was not hopeless, so he was negligent, in terms of his medical duty, helping Andreas U. to commit suicide.

The prosecution expert came to the conclusion of a failure of duty. According to Baumann's assessment, it was clear to him that Andreas U.'s condition was a serious form of obsessional neurosis that was unlikely to improve given what he knew from what Andreas U. had told him. In addition, according to Baumann, people with mental illness also have the right to refuse treatment. In his plea Baumann's lawyer argues that the prosecution expert's requirement of proof by attempted additional treatment stems from a normative and nonmedical attitude toward medical-professional obligation that he then attributes to Baumann.

The defense asked a Zurich psychiatrist to produce his own expert analysis. Unlike the Basel expert's report, this report is based on twenty-six documents produced between 1987 and 2001 (the report is twenty-one pages long). The Zurich report explains that the case is exceptional, that it is a serious long-term mental illness, with sparse interventions and few medical reports. Given the limited information, he explains that a diagnosis of obsessive-compulsive disorder is difficult to separate from a primary depressive disorder. The question to which the report responds is whether, on the basis of the available documents, it is possible to determine Andreas U.'s capacity for discernment.

The counterexpert's criterion for answering this question is that only a diagnosis of "severe depression" can nullify judgment. In addition, severe depression is characterized by a fixed mood. The Zurich psychiatrist concludes that Andreas U.'s primary illness was obsessional neurosis, with some depressive episodes, but without severe depression. He argues that the reasoning of Andreas U. was not fanciful and that the prognosis for cure of an obsessive chronic illness is objectively wrong. In addition, based on the video of Andreas's suicide, he notes that Andreas U. was not in a state of panic. According to him, the latter achieved the death that he longed for.

Baumann's lawyer then turns to the second issue, which concerns the nature of Baumann's assistance. He argues that Baumann's judgment to assist Andreas was based on his experience as a psychiatrist but that he operated from the position of an accompanier. Recall that it is precisely such a distinction that the Basel expert refused to make. For him, it was as a psychiatrist, from the position of a psychiatrist, that Baumann was wrong not only regarding the diagnosis but also on the obligation he had toward Andreas U.

Baumann's lawyer made this point in order to attack an informal element of the prosecution's accusation, which has an important consequence for the nature of the qualifications that could be produced: "that [according to the indictment] Baumann problematically mixed his role as a psychiatrist and his role as president of SuizidHilfe."[17] Embedded within this reproach is that qua psychiatrist one must be always ready and willing to try further therapies and that there is an obligation to dissuade from suicide. As we have seen, this was the conclusion of the evaluation of the prosecution expert.

His lawyer further argues that the position of Baumann with respect to Andreas was not therapeutic but that of a person from whom assistance with death is requested. As such, the only responsibilities he had, according to the lawyer, were with respect to the legal and the ethical conduct of the suicide, parameterized by the canton's prior decision to deny the use of optimal means of suicide (i.e., barbiturate overdose) for those with mental illness. Baumann's lawyer made the counterclaim that the prosecution, in arguing for Baumann's duty qua doctor to support further therapies, introduced a nonlegal value judgment that a doctor's assistance with suicide, specifically a psychiatrist's assistance for a person with mental illness, is in and of itself objectionable.

The Basel Criminal Court followed the reasoning of the expert from the Institute for Forensic Medicine, judging Baumann guilty of negligent homicide, not intentional homicide, because Baumann had been erroneously convinced of Andreas's capacity for discernment. By following this reasoning, the court linked Baumann's negligence to a professional fault concerning medical obligation, a point that seems not to have been specified in the first judgment and that would become important when Baumann appealed.

TRANSFORMATIONS OF JUDGMENT

After the judgment of the court of first instance, how do we explain the transformations of judgment—the judgment in 2008 by the court of appeal of intentional homicide and then by the Grand Council of the Canton of Basel-Stadt, which, in 2010, granted clemency to Baumann?

In the court of appeal the prosecutor mobilized the conclusions of the first judgment, and therefore the report of the expert from Basel, to insist that Andreas U. was not capable of judgment.[18] The absence of psychopathology, according to the court, is not enough to prove ex ante that he was capable of judgment.[19] The judgment notes, moreover, that Baumann did not request the medical records of Andreas U., and although he conducted a series of interviews with him, these interviews cannot replace "independent expertise." The court of appeal therefore introduced a criticism of the informal nature of Baumann's assistance of Andreas U. and thus of the overall practice of assisted suicide in the country.

The court decided that the prosecution expert's evaluation was sufficient to demonstrate Andreas's incapacity for judgment along with "the circumstances of the suicide, which leave no doubt."[20] These circumstances are not made explicit, but one must assume the court means the manner in which it took place—"the bungled bricolage contemptuous of humanity," as the court president from the court of first instance qualified it.

The court of appeal did nevertheless consider the need to argue against the counterexpertise mobilized by the defense. The court argues, contrary to the counterexpert, that "it is not possible to prevent an evaluation of Andreas's incapacity for judgment by reference to an observation that the suicide did not take place in a 'state' in which the ability to reflect would have been cancelled"; that is, the court made the basic claim that the qualification of an affective state cannot prevent a plausible argument that the individual is incapable of judgment. In effect, and reduced to its most basic point, the court backed the medical authority and normative reasoning instantiated by the prosecution expert in his evaluation that it was not reasonable for Andreas to end his life.

Baumann should have known, according to the judgment, that since the moratorium, his conversation with Andreas U. would not be enough to legitimize his assistance. Furthermore:

> Given his professional qualification the behavior of the accused can only be understood to the effect that he obviously doesn't think much of the evaluation of discernment, in the specified sense. As he says himself, he would want to fulfill a suicide wish even of people with sure psychiatric diagnoses (obsessional patients) if he empathizes with and understands the wish. By showing that he doesn't care

about an appropriate evaluation of judgment and the objectivity of his assessment of the situation, he has acted ultimately in a premeditated way and is, in accordance with the appeal of the public prosecutor, guilty of intentional homicide in indirect perpetration according to article III of the Swiss Criminal Code.[21]

How to understand such a change? It seems to me that the court of appeal requalified Baumann's position. In the first instance, in judging him guilty of "negligent homicide," the court considered Baumann a person who should have mobilized his abilities (and therefore his position and skill) as a doctor with the ethical orientation that correlates to that position. But the court of appeal considered him to be a doctor who intentionally ignored the correlative ethic: as a doctor, the second court judged, Baumann must have known that Andreas U. was not capable of discernment, and he chose, because of his personal ethic, to ignore the ethical obligation that correlates to his professional duty, which required him to dissuade Andreas from ending his life. This requalification constitutes a strong criticism of Baumann and the efforts of his lawyer to try to distinguish and to multiply the positions, the heterogeneous obligations and the ethical actions, that a doctor can occupy and carry out when faced with a person with a mental illness and who would like to die.

From Baumann's point of view, he was both a psychiatrist and accompanier: he linked his "technical" skills with an alternative ethic. The criminal court criticized his level of technical skills. The court of appeal judged Baumann at the level of his personal ethics that he imposed *in spite of* his technical skills.

What, then, is the significance of the grace that was granted to him eighteen months later? Based on articles published in the press, we know that the vote of the Basel Grand Council took place in February of 2010, eight months after the federal court upheld the judgment of the court of appeal. The result of the vote however was not publicized until April of 2010, when the *Basler Zeitung,* the main local newspaper, made it public. Several hypotheses have been raised by journalists for this delay, in particular the fact that Baumann's name was never used during the parliamentary debate.

When the *Basler Zeitung* asked the president of the commission why Baumann had been pardoned, the main reason given was that the Basel Court of Appeal had in fact later ruled in favor of partial pardon. The court of appeal had thus acknowledged that its judgment had been particularly punitive in the case of an act in a "legal transition zone" (*juristischen Übergangsbereich*). Thus, the president of the commission specified that although Baumann was forgiven, his guilt was maintained: "in order not to send a political message, the Parliament decided to revoke the sentence and not the judgment."[22] Nevertheless, a message was sent: it is not the act of assisting a person with mental disorders that constitutes a transgression but the decision to be the only "judge" of the case: to connect, alone, a personal ethic to professional knowledge and medical ethics. Finally, the outcome of the case was to strengthen the visibility and to a limited degree the formalization of the practice, without, however, making the practice more institutional or resolving the tensions produced by its adjacent position.

PART TWO

Leaving, a Casuistry

Part 2 of this book takes up a sequence of narratives that are organized chronologically, according to the unfolding of my own progressive involvement with the phenomenon of assistance with suicide. Concerning the motion of inquiry that generated this empirical knowledge, I have tried to compose and forge it with sensibility, as well as to search for understanding in relation to both knowledge and sensibility. The conceptual testing of the empirical knowledge produced in part 2 will then take place in part 3, as the narratives of experience confront scientific domains and their correlate theoretical presuppositions and tools. The character of the knowledge contained in part 2 is, I submit, a kind of anthropological casuistry. It is casuistic in the sense that I have endeavored to stay at the level of the "case," without either reifying the singularity of a case or justifying the significance of the case by virtue of a principle of anthropological knowledge grounded in terms such as *order, system, culture, society,* and so on. As such, if I may state it baldly, the principle of knowledge at stake in this inquiry is one of casuistry, formed by the sequence of narratives made possible through inquiry, of movement among the cases, in which progressively I endeavored to find a position from which to better observe and think about the actuality of the practice of assisted suicide: the first three cases endeavor to show variable positions, increasingly internal, from which an account of the practice is possible. The first case, Peter's, is narrated through a double mediation, through forms that are phenomenologically closest to how most observers will first come across narratives and events of assisted suicide: through documentary film, and through the narrative of a third person, in this case, that of Peter's wife, Christine. The stakes of the case are to discern the semiotic and ethical indetermination for an outside observer. The second case, which combines two narratives, that of Fabienne and Sylviane, shows the beginning of the effort to occupy a place in relation to two people who were thinking about a request for assistance with suicide, priming the parameters of access and tempo: with Fabienne I was blocked from occupying the position I thought I wanted to occupy, and with Sylviane, in her haste to give me the position that I thought I wanted, I realized that I was in danger of finding myself in a position that I could not warrant, ethically. The third case, with Clément, was in many respects the apex of the inquiry, in which through a careful and tempered feeling out, I managed to find a place in relation to him and his son, Pascal. The position I occupied allowed me to better explore what had appeared as an initial determination: that the medical-biological substrate to any request is not determinate. The way in which it is not determinate, though, is case specific, and I consider that in the case of Clément I was able to go quite some way in specifying it, to wit, the importance of his experience of the murder of his parents in the Nazi death camps and his experience of flight from, and return to, France. The fourth and final narrative, that of Florian, was a limit-case, a limit experience, which functioned, to a large degree as the denouement to the inquiry, the moment at which, in February of 2017, I knew I had gone as far as I could go, having previously occupied a series of places, of points, from which different kinds of grasping of the practice were possible. I had, with Florian, finally reached a position in which I was *beside the point*, a position that helped me to confront both the indeterminate and discordant nature of the practice itself, as well as my own endeavor to grasp it.

Peter

It must have been in early 2013—I no longer remember exactly when—that I found the film *Terry Pratchett: Choosing to Die* on YouTube.[1] My newborn son had just fallen asleep on my chest. It could have been February. I recall drowning out the sound of the rain with my headphones. What had begun as a nascent thought, a possible new project about assisted suicide in Switzerland, was nourished by the prospect of moving from San Francisco to Paris later in the year. Sitting there at our dinner table, small lungs pressing in and out against mine, I watched the late British comic novelist Terry Pratchett—then suffering with Alzheimer's disease—narrate how he had embarked on making a film about assisted suicide, endeavoring to meet people making the trip to Switzerland to die, so as to pose to himself the question—a fundamentally ethical question—of whether he, too, would do the same.

The film served as an orientation to begin honing what I thought might be a question at stake in the practice of assisted suicide: a question of how the search for a form to give to dying is connected to a search for a manner of dying, within a practice of assisted suicide. I had yet to spend four years (2014–17) attempting to contact people who were in the midst of, or were beginning, their request for assistance with suicide from associations in Switzerland. I had yet to reflect on the encounters I would have with a panoply of people—people wishing to end their lives, their husbands, wives, sons, daughters, presidents and vice presidents of associations for assisted dying, volunteer accompaniers, home palliative care teams and their patients whom we would visit, psychiatrists at teaching hospitals, pharmacists in different cities, police officers, and undertakers. Yet this film, and in particular the story of one person within it, Peter, presented me with both a story of a singular life and an image of the search for a form for dying, an image I would revisit again and again, whose stakes and possible significations would accompany me and would be echoed as I, too, would come to follow others from their requests for assistance with dying to its realization.

I observed in the discourse around, and presentation of, Peter's death that there appeared to be a lack of, or rather a lack in, language for adequately grasping the ethical, aesthetic, and intellectual qualities of this relatively new manner of dying. Or, to put it differently, within the form of the film, and within the genre of this kind of documentary, echoed in some arenas of professional discourse, it wasn't possible to explore such a language and such qualities. What had prompted the nascent idea for such an inquiry was the thought that assisted suicide, statistically speaking a minor phenomenon in terms of how people currently die, might be considered a significant historical intervention in the way human beings end their lives—a reconfiguration of available practices so as to give a new form and manner to dying as an experience.

Suicide and euthanasia are social facts, and each has its own history, of course. Watching the film, I was bolstered in thinking that what seemed specific about the reconfiguration produced by practices of assisted suicide was the invention of a negotiated form for voluntary death, one that is mediated in relation to conventions of medical knowledge and judgment but that endeavors to give a different form—a better, less nefarious form—to the power relations between doctors and those who wish to end their experience of suffering.

The language of choice has been primed in relation to this activity, principally within the medical ethics and bioethics literature, as well as among participants in the practice, both as a positive value and as an ideological illusion.[2] Such a language is insufficient. When watching the film for the first time, I did not have an alternative. In what follows, by constructing a sequence of "cases," I seek to find a way to take up the activity of this form of death, the process of negotiation that it involves, its relation to the seeming obviousness of a language of choice, and the multiple significations and multiple indeterminations around meaning that can be grasped within it and in relation to it.

TO WHOM IT MAY CONCERN

Inside the neat yellow folder marked "medical," among email exchanges with friends, doctors' reports, letters to lawyers, and the letters exchanged with Dignitas—the organization that helped Peter to end his life—I came across a letter:

9 November 2010

To whom it may concern,

    In March 2009, I was diagnosed with Motor Neurone Disease. . . . There is no treatment for this disease and no cure. . . . This is a terminal disease, culminating in restricted breathing, loss of mobility and loss of speech, amongst other undignified and debilitating conditions. As I have no wish or intention to suffer such humiliating and truly unpleasant symptoms I have, not surprisingly, investigated methods of escape from this intolerable situation by way of dignified dying. For reasons I believe are obvious, the dignified dying option is the preferable choice and the least distressing course of action for everyone concerned, and principally, myself. . . .

Peter, a retired hotelier, had contacted Dignitas fifteen months previously. Founded in 1998, Dignitas is a nonprofit members' society that provides counseling about advance directives, suicide attempt prevention, palliative care and end-of-life issues, advocacy in patient-doctor relations within medical settings, and, most famously, a service of assistance with voluntary death, for members, both residents and nonresidents of Switzerland, at an apartment that the association maintains in the canton of Zurich.[3]

    He left for Zurich one month later, with his wife Christine, and without their daughter, in order to die on the premises of Dignitas. Peter lamented having to travel to Switzerland. He was highly critical of British society's failure to address the punitive character of the law on assistance with suicide, which remains an illegal act in the UK despite eighty years of active campaigning. To bring "light and air" to the subject, Peter agreed to participate in a documentary about his assisted suicide, produced by the BBC and broadcast the year after his death.

    It was through the documentary that I first learned of Peter's life and the manner of his death. In October of 2015 I contacted his wife, Christine, to ask if we could talk about her husband's decision. She agreed, specifying that she had refused all efforts by journalists who had contacted her after the screening of the documentary. The fact that Peter wanted to bring what he considered "an absurd situation" before "as many members of our society as possible" is perhaps one reason, among others, why Christine agreed both to talk with me and to allow me to consult Peter's files and personal reflections.

When we met, during two days at her home in December of 2015, on the island of Guernsey, I explained that I was interested in the specificity of Peter's decision to die within a wider program of inquiry around assistance with suicide. It seemed to me that we had a reciprocal understanding of what I was seeking to accomplish: to try to understand how people suffering with different illnesses, and the organizations whose help they solicit, come to an agreement that a voluntary end to life is both appropriate and possible. Moreover, I explained that the endeavor was to grasp the possible significations of such a manner of dying, given the current political and legal obstructions it faced in most countries.

I use the documentary as a principal means to grasp Peter's engagement with the medical process for making a judgment as to whether he could end his life. I focus on two situations of interaction made visible in the documentary, which offer channels to pose questions about the determinations, indeterminations, and open significations of such a mode of dying. Before doing so, let me state that all requests by members of Dignitas are examined by the association before they are handed to a medical doctor, or doctors, none of whom are employees of the organization. A key member of Dignitas underscored for me that this is an important control for them: examination by two independent parties. In fact, with Dignitas's procedure there is, in effect, a three-party-examination: (1) the initial review by Dignitas, (2) the independent medical doctor(s), and (3) the accompaniers who do the actual conducting and preparation of the event of the assisted suicide. The accompaniers are independent to the extent that they can refuse to carry out the accompaniment. In fact, they are obliged to refuse in circumstances where they realize that the prerequisites for a legal assisted suicide are no longer present. For example: if the person loses the capacity of discernment in the hours after the doctor's consultation and the granting of definite consent for the assisted suicide, including the prescription of the pentobarbital.[4]

The key moments I have selected are prefigured and given sense through the life history and descriptions of Peter that Christine shared with me and through the medical documents and negotiations with the association, which Peter meticulously archived. A word is necessary, however, before following

Peter's story, about the development of the documentary and the selection of Peter as a key participant. The film was directed by Charlie Russell, a British documentarist whose first film was about his grandmother, the author Dame Beryl Bainbridge, as she tried to live through the "the curse" of her final year: she was convinced that, as with everyone else in her family, she would die at the age of seventy-one. Russell subsequently made a film about another author living with a prefiguration of death, Sir Terry Pratchett, as he came to terms with a diagnosis of Alzheimer's disease. In the wake of that film Pratchett began to explore assisted suicide in Switzerland as a possible way of dying (he ultimately died at home in 2015). Pratchett and Russell collaborated in order to try to find a few British citizens whose cases had been accepted by Dignitas. The organization wrote to all its British members to ask if they would allow someone who was also ill and considering assisted suicide to follow them. By strange happenstance, Peter, I learned from Christine, had known Pratchett well in his younger days in Somerset, when he and Christine owned and ran the five-star luxury hotel Ston Easton Park.[5] It was chance that reunited them, allowing them to revisit a topic they had, in fact, previously discussed at length. The two men, I was told, used to joke together, with good doses of morbid humor, about how they would end their lives if they found themselves stuck with interminable suffering.

THREE OBSERVATIONS

In redescribing Peter's experiences, his narratives, his gestures even, ones already, if partially, mediated and expressed in the form of a documentary, through his personal records and exchanges, and through the retelling of his life and his death by Christine, my aim is to ask how an observer could grasp a voluntary death, an event for which the signification seems to be obvious, as Peter himself indicates. My aim is to observe, through post facto reconstruction, his decision and his manner of dying. Three of Peter's observations are important to emphasize: (1) that he suffered from an illness for which there is no cure and that would cause him to die in a manner he characterized as unpleasant and humiliating; (2) that for Peter, finding a method of escape was better for everyone and principally for himself; and (3) that recourse to dignified dying was obvious given this situation.

Each of these observations drawn from Peter's letter provides us with a theme for inquiry. First of all, it is important to insist on the fact that it is not mandatory for the associations that facilitate assistance with suicide in Switzerland that an illness is incurable or lethal—what is often called terminal illness, as was the case with Peter. A key question, which is taken up through the series of cases I will present through this casuistry, is what particular illnesses, and what experiences of illness, justify assistance and in the eyes of whom? One of the negative determinations that I seek to show through the sequence of cases is that there is no medico-moral norm, or calculus, that regulates acceptance of requests beyond two boundary conditions: that the person who requests assistance is capable of discernment and that the person can enact the suicide (drinking a lethal solution of barbiturate or opening the tap on an intravenous perfusion) himself or herself. The positive side of this determination is the claim that reference to obviousness is opaque. The act should be qualified by those present as a self-enacted ending of life, of a person of sound mind, and this qualification is either supported or contested by those who take care of the medico-legal consequences: the police, forensic medical examiners, and the public prosecutors who must open an inquiry after each suicide, only closing the case once it has been established that it was an assisted suicide that did not contravene any laws. Thus, on the one hand, different situations, different illnesses, differences among individuals who work with assisted suicide associations, and different cantons, at varying historical moments, demand higher and lower degrees of justification and mobilization of evidence to fulfill these conditions of capability. There are also variable amounts of evidence that are required to demonstrate the precise state of the person's illness and variable judgments about how severe the illness has to have become to justify assistance.

In Peter's situation the collaborating doctor in Switzerland, who first read his dossier, wanted evaluations from more recent neurological reports in order to gain a clearer picture of the degree and rate of neuro-degeneration before giving him a "provisional green light." On the other hand, there is the open question of whether those who are asked to accompany the person who requests assistance with suicide agree to the reasons that they give, as a reasonable and capable person, for wishing to end their experience of suffering. Such requests and acceptance are squarely within the ethical domain of recognition, in a register of love (rather than a register of esteem or rights).[6] Such heterogeneity and open ethical terrain primes attention to two principal themes: how a judgment that a person can and should end his or her life is determined and how it makes sense to those concerned, if it does.

Peter determined that assisted suicide was better for everyone and principally for himself. How was this determination produced? There is a model of decision making in operation centered on the individual and often expressed within a language of choice. Experience indicates that this is a key part of the self-understandings of the people who participate in this practice. Yet this model is incomplete. The decision to die, on the one hand, is understood as a personal *choice*, a term that etymologically comes from a Proto-Indo-European root meaning to taste or test, but the decision to proceed toward one form of death and not another is nevertheless also a judgment: that is to say, a discernment and attribution of a quality or character to a situation that necessarily involves others. I have decided to intentionally retain the use of three terms— *choice, decision,* and *judgment*—to refer to three overlapping aspects of the pragmatics of negotiating and doing an assisted voluntary death: that the act must be able to be referred back to the will of an individual, understood as a choice, in keeping with one of the key legal conditions; that the act of going forward cuts off other possible activities and thus counts as a decision; and, finally, in a pragmatic sense, there is a third aspect of the act of going forward with the endeavor that involves the attribution of a mode of being to a situation that has been rendered determinate, which is how the American philosopher John Dewey understood the practice of judgment.[7]

The extra-individual character of such a determination can be investigated in two ways without nullifying its individuated character. In biographical terms I ask how Peter's decision has extra-individual determinants, leading to a judgment that could be shared. In terms of the situation of assistance with suicide I ask how during the period leading up to the act of ending life the situation requires arrangement and negotiation among participants. Moreover, in the observation of the act of ending life itself, the attribution of meaning to the act must take into account the signification given to it by the person concerned, and yet such meaning is also complemented by others, key among whom are the other participants in the situation but also including observers of the film, readers of the newspaper reports that followed the airing of the film, and readers of this book.

LEAVING THROUGH THE FOG

Let me now clarify and synthesize the arrangements of people and things that should come together, at this historical conjuncture in Switzerland, such that a person may end his or her life with assistance from others. The pragmatic ethical question of whether an individual should help another person to end his or her life is an open one, and as an ethical question, it cannot be arbitrated by right and in advance by the law, thus posing an interest for an anthropological account of ethical practice.

As previously discussed, the legal frame in Switzerland, furthermore, provides no stipulation about the means or venue of such assisted suicide, with the vast majority of deaths occurring in private residences, either in homes of Swiss residents or in residences of associations that agree to help foreigners. This practice is one in which a series of supports are arranged to shape whether and how a person can end his or her own life. It is possible to identify three supports put in place for all associations since the late 1990s:

1. Expertise: The preferred manner of dying is a lethal dose of barbiturate. Associations therefore require the collaboration and judgment of medical doctors. Doctors require medical reports indicating the course of illness and treatments pursued, sometimes including a medical certificate indicating the doctor's appraisal of the situation, as well as the agreement of a doctor in Switzerland to write a prescription.

2. Accompaniment: Assisted suicide facilitated by these associations always involves the participation of at least one accompanier from the association (in the case of Dignitas there are always two present). The accompanier is usually a person distinct from the prescribing doctor, and with Dignitas this is a rule. For the associations that work uniquely with Swiss citizens, such as Exit *Association pour le droit de mourir dans la dignité* (Exit ADMD), the accompanier who guides the assisted suicide may have an ongoing relation with the person who wishes to die, or else a more limited relation, meaning that for some accompaniers, in certain cases, it is their practice to communicate regularly with the person who requests assistance, for example visiting them at home, encouraging the person to continue to live a little longer. Other accompaniers think that such involvement is inappropriate and restrict the practice of accompaniment to the event itself. Thus, the accompaniment might be very short-term, involving only two meetings, or it might unfold over a long period, in which the sick person periodically calls for discussion of assistance with suicide, only to then relinquish the plan, and then subsequently make (yet) another request. Although difficult to generalize and formalize across all associa-

tions and all cases, let us simply say that between the association and the specific accompanier, relevant documents are prepared for the police, and a consent form is presented to the person by the accompanier, who explains it and makes sure it is signed. With respect to the procurement of the lethal dose of barbiturate, again, it is not possible to generalize across all associations. In the case of Dignitas the office staff retrieves the prescription. The accompanier receives the prescription from the Dignitas office and with this retrieves the barbiturate (if someone from the office staff has not already fetched it from a pharmacy). The accompanier also calls the police once the assisted suicide has taken place. Accompaniment expresses a person's concern for the manner in which death is brought about for another.

3. Narrative: Through the exchanges among the person who prescribes, the person who accompanies the persons at the office of the organization, and the person who requests assistance with suicide, there is always elicitation of a narrative about the person's wish to end his or her life. In particular, the person who requests assistance must be suffering in such a way that she or he can narrate the experience as warranting help with suicide. Narratives of the experience of illness relative to a person's request for help to end life are then taken up within the multiple relations that make up the person's life, such as those of kinship and friendship. Assistance with suicide in Switzerland is a practice that the law neither positively frames (it doesn't say how to do it, who can help with it, or the reasons that must underlie the request) nor categorically forbids. Elicitation of a narrative, the work of expertise and of accompaniment, when brought into certain arrangements, can provide the turning point through which a date can be set for the ending of life.

PETER'S CHOICE

Driving from the airport to her home, and responding to her own question as to how we should proceed with our discussion, Christine began to narrate Peter's choice to end his life within his family history: "A few years before Peter got ill, we sat down to do his family tree. And I said to Peter, oh look, no male member of the family lived past seventy-two. His father died at seventy." Peter's symptoms started at sixty-nine. Christine went on to explain the significance of Peter's father's death: he died in a hospital in Sussex, England.

The cause of death was supposedly an infection in his leg, subsequent to gangrene, caused by the car crash that hospitalized him. The car crash, according to Peter's mother, was a result of his father's alcoholism, something his father had always denied: he said he didn't drink. Peter's father used to fall over a lot, though, his teetering and wobbling misinterpreted: he would fall down the stairs, fall over in the kitchen—just as Peter would come to do.

Christine explained to me that she and Peter suspected that, in fact, a perceptive doctor had understood the real cause of the car accident, namely the illness that would eventually appear in Peter. She and Peter came to the conclusion that this doctor had offered Peter's father a way out, based on the circumstances before he died: the night prior to his death, Peter's father had had a special meal delivered, and he summoned family and friends to see him; in the morning he was dead. Without attributing causal power to these prior events, I note simply the descriptive significance for Christine of contextualizing Peter's decision relative to their shared understanding of the nature of his father's death: that voluntarily ending life was considered a possible and reasonable way out, whose significance lies not only in the example it sets but also as a counterpoint to his mother's suffering during her death in hospital. Indeed, the more we talked, and the more I learned of Peter's character, the more that biography and parameters of personal history appeared, if not to explain his choice, at least to provide elements for accurately describing how such a voluntary death became thinkable.

Over the course of 2008, Peter's symptoms began to get worse. "He used to ask, 'Can you hold me up darling; can I hold your arm?' And I would say of course, because, he'd say, 'My right foot is dropping.' But of course, that's the sign of motor neurone disease. And Peter became very studied in his walking, as did my father-in-law. And I think it was to make sure it didn't drop, to try and control all that dropping. We got to the point where Peter was called in to the doctors and to the specialists and was told he had motor neurone disease." In March of 2009, after several months of tests and second opinions, Peter received a diagnosis. Initially, Christine interacted with his doctors, relaying to her husband the likely interventions required, as he did not wish to discuss the disease with them. The doctors treating him were looking ahead to the likely need for PEG [percutaneous endoscopic gastrostomy] and noninvasive ventilation. A doctor's report indicates that Christine should try to establish her husband's view on these possibilities in advance. PEG and ventilation were proposed as medical interventions as the nervous system and muscle tone began to break down. Alongside the possible physical interventions, Peter was also contacted by a local occupational therapist, asking about whether they could help adapt the family home to accommodate his likely needs given the probable course of the illness. The therapist reported in April that Peter did not wish to accept a visit from their team at that time. Moreover, the report noted that "he expressed concern as to what anyone could do to help as he stated that his condition is not going to improve."

In June of 2009, however, Peter had a slight change of heart: he contacted his doctor to ask whether occupational therapy services could make an assessment of what they could do for him. His consultant ordered respiratory function tests to give a baseline figure to assess the need for future interventions regarding ventilation. In July Peter contacted the Medical Research Council (UK) Center for Regenerative Medicine. He thanked them for their most recent report and understood from their reply that although research continues, nothing could be done in terms of slowing or curing the illness.

Christine narrated how it was recommended that Peter read a long article about the illness and possible management strategies: "So, I read it from cover to cover and I thought this is going to be really really hard. And he read it. And at the back of it, it has all sorts of things, and it says record your falls, record this, record that. And he read it and he dropped it in the bin. And I said, 'Why did you do that? Don't you want to fill out these things?' And he said, 'No, that's decided it, I'm not staying to the end.'" Peter contacted Dignitas in August of 2009.

Peter had made his decision. He started to arrange his death in August of 2009, and he died by assisted suicide on 10 December 2010. It is noteworthy, however, how the decision was mediated and formed. On the one hand, he couldn't and didn't do it alone. In the first place it required a negotiation with the association itself for the request to be accepted. In the second place Peter accepted having his death filmed as part of an effort to prompt public and personal reflection on assistance with suicide. Third, observing the film shows how during the actual process of going to Switzerland and in the process of dying, the choice and its signification was being mediated and formed along with those around him and in relation to him, principally his family. Even so, we will see how for Peter, being autonomous, to whatever degree possible, and being seen to be autonomous, was crucial to his self-understanding and his conduct. Christine's efforts to situate Peter's choice to die within his family history and the prior event of his father's death provide an impulse to resist taking at face value Peter's own claim that his choice is obvious. I will instantiate such a stance toward the practice by taking up the specificity of the gesture of dying as a way of showing heterogeneous significations for an observer.

A SCENE OF EVALUATION

The scene that follows is drawn from the documentary in which Peter agreed to appear, and serves as part of the available record of the process through which his decision was mediated. Let me clarify that, of course, I am aware that in basing this analysis of the process of Peter's assisted suicide partly on the film, the object of my analysis has already been staged to the degree that, on the one hand, the film itself is an edited point of view on the process, and, on the other hand, what took place may have taken place differently were the camera not there.

Peter meets the doctor, Dr. Erika, in the hotel room where he and Christine are staying. Erika is a Basel-based family doctor who worked with Dignitas from 2006 to 2012, after having assisted her own father to end his life. She subsequently established her own association, *lifecircle*, whose work we will follow in subsequent narratives.

In the film we see Erika evaluate Peter's condition. She evaluates his physical capacity, such as whether he can get out of the chair by himself. She checks his psychological state. The viewer is unaware of the fact that Peter, by this time in December, is now mostly confined to a wheelchair, a physical support that never features in the film, according to Christine, because he didn't want to be seen to be so handicapped. "Have you ever felt depressed during the time of your illness?" she asks.

"No, I'm not a depressed sort of person." Peter pauses and his gaze drops to the floor. "I've had mixed feelings about it, of course. But I wouldn't call it depression." The examination continues; the doctor checks whether Peter is able to hold a glass and whether he can swallow its contents unassisted.

She watches him do so and remarks, "That's perfect. You will have no problem at all. I would like you to think about it again." The following day, the doctor returns for the second examination, which will establish whether Peter will receive the doctor's consent for the accompanied suicide to take place if he wishes to do so that day. She begins by making a general assessment of the problem of decision. "When I see people with these illnesses, for me it is quite difficult to decide, is it the right time to go? If I say no, you have to go home. You can't die."

"Understood." Peter nods respectfully. "Yes, I understand what you are saying and I . . ."

Erika continues, "You are the only one who can decide which is the right moment. You are sure you want to do this?"

"Oh yes, I've always been quite convinced all the time."

"Have you been listening to yourself, or have you been talking to your wife?"

"Oh no, it's my own conclusions."

Christine intervenes. "If he were listening to me he'd stay at home for Christmas."

Erika mediates. "It's amazing but it's much easier for the one who can go than for the ones who have to stay behind."

"Yes I understand that," Peter confirms.

"I obviously don't want him to go, so I feel that it is going to be tough on me, but I think it is going to be a great relief for you," Christine explains.

Dr. Erika has provided a space in which Christine is integrated into the examination, and Christine takes this invitation and redirects the focus of the conversation from her position and affect toward Peter. The doctor pushes the attention back to Christine, as third party, by focusing on Peter:

"She would like you to wait."

"Yes," Peter replies.

"Yes," Dr. Erika says.

"Yes she would," says Peter.

"I mean, Peter's been my other half for forty years and it's going to be a terrible wrench."

"Yes," Peter affirms.

ASIDE FROM A CLINICAL ENCOUNTER

These sequences are far from classic scenes of clinical encounter: they take place in a hotel; they are the only two meetings Erika and Peter will have. Can we call him a patient and their relation that of the doctor to the patient? In her role as medical doctor Erika has, of course, read the formal request to Dignitas, including Peter's personal letter and medical reports; thus, she clearly knows about his personal and medical situation. We see the indetermination in this relation expressed in the transformation from the first meeting to the second. The first thing we notice is how a medical category of "depression" mediates the possibility of a positive verdict for access to assisted suicide. The question is direct, as are the consequences of responding in the affirmative or the negative. If Peter were to say that he was depressed, this could be grounds for halting the momentum toward an assisted suicide. We have no reason to doubt Peter's response. It is rather the situation that is striking, the manner in which his thoughts about his illness are both solicited and qualified: having mixed feelings about having motor neurone disease is acceptable; being depressed about life with the illness would be a reason, however, to question the request for assistance with suicide.

In this first meeting we thus have a double check of a medical and legal, or technical, nature: is Peter depressed? Can he accomplish the act himself (drinking the lethal solution)? That is, is he both reasonable and an agent? In the second meeting a new element is added, one that is not reducible to medical judgment or the question of rational agency: by whom and how can a judgment be made? Since the first meeting established medical authority, and thus the responsibility of the doctor for providing access to the drug, as well as the assurance that it can be taken by the person, in the second meeting medical authority, and responsibility, is downplayed.

Dr. Erika said plainly that it is difficult to decide whether it is the right time for Peter to die. What she has done, then, in the first meeting, the previous day, is to establish the general possibility of assistance with suicide, reaffirming the medical diagnosis, determining that according to medical judgment Peter could end his life: meaning that there is a reason to do it and that there is not a reason not to let him do it, as well as that he is able to do it, which then opens onto the indetermination about whether he should proceed with his suicide. The sincerity and source of his request are tested against a medical category to qualify its reality. It is then up to Peter to decide whether this day is the right day to die. The reality test of the request to die must be passed back to the requester: clearly, only he can decide. The decision might seem to be obviously individual.

It is worth observing, however, how the examination of Peter's intention to be assisted in ending his life involves Christine, his wife. Erika, the doctor responsible for access to a prescription for a life-ending dose of barbiturate, mediates—in a limited fashion—both Peter's request to exit his illness and Christine's expression of the wish that he stay home for Christmas. We see how Christine is integrated into the examination at the moment in which

Peter's sincerity is examined: "Have you been listening to yourself, or have you been talking to your wife?" Erika asks. The coordinating conjunction *or* could be taken as a formulation crystallizing an abstract conception of personhood and freedom: either he is only listening to himself, in which case he is an autonomous individual, or he is listening to his wife, in which case his autonomy may be put in question by an external constraint—as he said, "Oh no, it's my own conclusions."

The answer Peter gives is the official answer of an autonomous individual. The question solicited this response, and indeed, it is confirmed as true. The question, however, also opens up a space in which his own conclusions, as he put it, can be put in relation to a range of people and things, which was of importance for the doctor: not least the care of Christine, who confirms that he hasn't been listening to her since she would like him to wait until after Christmas. But it is thanks to the love and support of Christine, both emotional and physical, that he could go ahead with his plan. A crystallization of this double register was in play in the relation of friends and neighbors toward Peter after his diagnosis: he absolutely did not want anyone to know he was ill, and Christine promised him she wouldn't tell them. In fact, she did. She told their friends, who then would drop in "unexpectedly" in order to spend time with Peter, given that it was increasingly difficult for him to go out. They would make up plausible reasons for being in the area near Peter and Christine's home and would explain that they had a moment to pop in, if it was convenient. Even his last meal with friends was arranged as a sequence of unexpected visits to which Christine then asked if they would all like to stay for dinner. "Do you think they suspect anything?" he had asked her. "Nothing at all," Christine had replied. The doctor's careful mediation parallels this care for autonomy and wish to include others in the situation: Peter's response and Christine's intervention in relation to Erika's query allow all three people to participate in the question of how Peter's expressed wish has been forged and how a judgment can be made. Such participation among a triad of positions in the making of a judgment, and not only the taking of a decision or making of a choice, is clearly evoked in the series of statements that elicits Christine's participation and elicits acknowledgment that her wish has been heard and her support recognized.

The decision, although ultimately attributed to Peter, is the result of the unfolding of a situation, not given in advance, for coming to the judgment that he can end his life, one that shows those present the range of exterior things with respect to which he is in relation: (1) his position as husband to his wife, (2) his experience of illness, (3) the clinical presentation of illness, (4) its anticipated course, (5) the image he has of what the end of his illness looks like, (6) Christmas, and (7) the loss with which Christine will live if he decides to go through with it.

When Peter and Christine arrived at the premises of Dignitas, they were met by two accompaniers, one of whom, Erika Luley, takes the situation in hand. As Christine wrote to the association three weeks after Peter died, in response to their "feedback form," from the moment Peter was greeted, they "felt assured." Erika Luley makes her excuses for the administrative paperwork they have to fill out and also that she will have to ask Peter at several points about his volition:

"Are you sure you wish to die?" she asks him, somewhat apologetically.

"I feel that I have very little choice, in the grand design," he says. It is a curious statement for a person about to end his own life: the "little choice" disturbs the opposition of freedom and obligation: a neutralization of the discourses and demands to be either in favor or against or to be either sure or uncertain (and hence disqualified) or either scared or steadfast.

PETER'S DEATH

Peter and Christine traveled from their hotel to the assisted suicide venue. It was snowing in Pfäffikon, 20 km from Zurich. The venue is a two-story pre-fabricated building in an industrial park. Dignitas was restricted to operating in an industrial zone after a campaign by neighbors to stop their work from taking place in an apartment in Zurich, which had been rented for the purpose. The administrative court ruled that the company could not operate a business in a residential area. The police attempted to stop Dignitas from setting up in the industrial zone, but this was overruled by the court on the grounds that Dignitas's work does not significantly differ from other businesses in the area. The cantonal authorities' legal judgment stated that the building did not need specific authorization given its particular "ideological emissions" (*ideelle Immissionen*) a category of "pollutions" recognized by law, which covers negative "ideological" externalities, such as the "pollution" of living near prisons and brothels. The ideological emissions of Dignitas were considered within the bounds of legitimate affective externalities and, moreover, were in keeping with the area, which is reported to host the largest brothel in Switzerland.[8]

A gravel path leads toward the simple apartment. Clean white plastic tables and chairs are in the front garden. A bamboo screen has been placed to fill in for any gaps in privacy left by the trees. The accompaniers from Dignitas, (another) Erika and Horst, met Peter and Christine outside and helped them to navigate the snowy path to the entrance of the Blue Oasis, as the apartment is called. Peter and Christine were dressed smartly—Peter wearing a pressed blue shirt and light trousers, Christine wearing a white roll neck with a black cardigan. In the film we see Christine sitting at a table with Peter. They are served tea and coffee. Terry Pratchett and his assistant, Rob, wait in the kitchen. Erika, the accompanier, sits with the couple. Peter sips his coffee. The accompaniers work through a voluntary death declaration with Peter and Christine. A short time later Peter looks over to his wife.

"Shall I take the, the initial . . ."

"Don't ask me darling."

"Well you know . . ."

"It's your decision."

"Yes, no no, no, I'll take it, but I mean, it's just the timing. I am quite prepared to do it, now."

Christine exhales loudly, clearly frustrated. "When you are ready . . ."

"Yes. Yes, yes."

"So I will go and prepare the drops?" Erika asks. Peter nods.

"And I will be back in a minute."

"Yes, thank you Erika." Erika goes to prepare the antiemetic solution and brings it to Peter. He drinks it swiftly.

"Right."

"Yes. Ok. The taste ok too?" Erika asks.

"Yes, it's not bad."

"You want a cup of tea or something?

"No, no, I've had my drink. That'll do me." Peter and Christine chuckle together. There is a moment to wait before Peter can take the lethal solution.

"Well that was fairly innocuous. Yes, it's the next one that is the . . ." Peter pauses.

"The killer?" Christine offers Peter a word, looking straight at him.

"Oh yes." Peter looks up and makes a grimace, acknowledging Christine's refusal to metaphorize. Both Peter and Christine are extremely composed but not relaxed. A calmness seems to be expressed through an intense determination and strain. Christine told me that she had taken a pill to calm herself down. She begins sorting out the different flavors of chocolate to be taken after the lethal medication. "Now, tell me which ones you like."

"I don't think it will matter a great deal."

"Praline?"

"No. That one and that one." He points to the chocolates.

"Not the praline?"

"No. (*Impatient*) How long have we been here?"

"Nearly twenty-five."

"I was going to say it's about a quarter past."

"So ten minutes more."

"What time is it?"

"It's twenty-five past."

"Oh. It's funny how time has different values at different occasions. Not that I am in a hurry, but I am just interested to know how long we have been here." Christine helps Peter up and over from the table to a two seat couch. Erika helps position him to one side.

"Should I be away from . . .?"

"No no," Erika and Peter say in concert, with Erika gesturing toward Peter.

"I'd rather you—" Peter half states.

"Well, if you'd really rather be away from him?" Erika begins to say, making sure that everyone's wishes are respected.

"Well no, I just didn't want to appear to assist him."

"No I don't think that would be the case," Peter says reassuringly. The couple is sitting next to each other; they look at each other very tenderly and kiss.

Erika is holding a plastic cup with a solution of pentobarbital. She kneels next to him.

Erika enunciates Peter's full name slowly, ceremonially. In addition to the camera from the documentary team, Horst is filming Peter with a small digital camera, as part of Dignitas's protocol. They submit a film along with the death record to the police.

Erika continues. "Are you sure that you want to drink this medicament with which you will sleep and die?"

"Yes I am quite sure that is what I want to do."

"I will give you the medicament." Erika gives Peter the cup but does not let go as Peter reaches for it.

They are both holding the plastic cup.

"You are sure?" Erika asks.

"Yes quite sure. Thank you," he says. She lets go. Everyone looks on. He looks down at the glass, which is just above his lap. He waits a few seconds, looking at the cup before lifting it to his mouth. It takes about five seconds to drink. He reaches for the chocolate and then puts it down having noticed the glass of water. Erika stops him reaching for the water and insists he eat the chocolate first.

"Hoooooo, that's the taste," he exclaims. Erika holds a tissue under his mouth and then hands him a glass of water.

"Bye-bye," she says softly.

"Bye-bye Erika. Thank you for looking after me," Peter looks up at her.

Erika shakes her head, "No, nothing."

"I would like to thank everybody else," he says waving around the room, to Terry, Rob, the camera man, and Horst. "They've been first-class too."

Terry gets up from his chair. "Peter," he said, extending his arm. The two men shake hands.

"Goodbye, and thank you very much."

"Goodbye, Terry. It's been a privilege. And speaking of privileges, my wife is very good at putting me to sleep just by rubbing my hands."

"Be strong my darling," Peter says, looking at Christine. Erika passes a box of tissues to Christine in preparation.

"I will. Just relax." Christine continues to stroke Peter's left hand. Peter is sitting upright with his right hand on his chest. Peter leans toward Erika, coughs violently and begins to groan loudly.

In a desperate voice he calls out, "Waaater." Erika embraces him gently, stopping him taking the glass of water. Christine looks away, covering her mouth out of shock.

Peter repeats: "Waaaater."

Erika holds his head against her, and Christine grasps his right arm. Peter gasps again making deep coughing sounds. He then begins to snore heavily. Erika has put a travel pillow around his neck. "Sleeping now. Very deep. No pain at all. He's snoring; he's sleeping very very deep. In unconsciousness. And then the breathing will stop and then the heart." Erika narrates what is happening in parsimonious terms, which give a feeling of protocol and procedure. Erika takes off the travel pillow, and Christine continues stroking his hand. Peter is not moving. Nobody says anything.

"Are you all right, Terry?" Christine asks.

"I'm fine," he says softly and shakes his head.

"Good."

"Well . . . for a given value of 'fine.'"

"Yes, well, it is what he wanted, and he was ready to go."

Terry cannot contain himself. He begins to weep.

"Yes, now you are allowed to cry," Erika says with her hand on Christine's shoulder. "Let it out; it does you good." Christine begins to weep. "Everything you kept inside and now you can let it out."

"I don't think I can do that."

GESTURES OF DYING

It should be remembered that the film, in addition to being a personal and ethical reflection for Pratchett, was also considered by Peter to be an intervention in a public debate in the UK about assisted dying: a way of dying that is relatively quick, usually taking fewer than forty minutes, when ingested orally, or a couple of minutes when administered intravenously, as well as being clean, as the body usually remains integrated with no liquids or solids leaving it. I stress that this is usually the case: there are, however, exceptional cases in which there are variations, such as it taking many hours for the person to transition from unconsciousness to death or, more rarely, complicated consequences if the person vomits the lethal solution, despite the antiemetic routinely taken to prepare the body for the lethal dose of barbiturate prior to oral ingestion.

To emphasize and to try to understand the gestural motion that is presented in the case of Peter's death, I extracted three images from the documentary, three moments from the time Peter ingested the lethal substance to his death: a process that took only a few minutes. I juxtaposed these images and then sought to describe them.[9] I considered that through such description it is possible to grasp both obvious and lateral significations in the scene. In what follows, I will describe the three moments, and the movement between them. The movement between three scenes is organized by way of a conceptual pair, diastolic and systolic movement,[10] a pair of terms that are useful for grasping the overall transformation and transitioning of the movement of the three bodies within the sequence of images. I then reflect briefly on the fact that I found with the identification of movements in these images a connection, perhaps what art historian T. J. Clark might call "tone," which links the images described to traditions of iconographic figuration of gestures of lamentation and compassion. It is a connection that has helped me in observing, and considering, the form given to such a visceral experience: a form for pathos.

There is an initial diastolic movement in the first moment after Peter ingests the lethal solution, in which the effect of the barbiturate takes hold in his body. He gasps. He is held by the accompanier, Erika, who pulls him toward her, her right arm around his neck, her left hand cupped under his mouth and chin, holding a tissue, just in case, with her cheek bone resting on his forehead, her gaze connected to his hands, which are on his lap, in symmetric opposition to Christine, who turns away from them both. Erika, to Peter's left, is containing Peter as Christine (to his right) contains herself and pulls away. Christine covers her own mouth with a tissue, containing her dread, in symmetry with Erika's placement of the tissue under Peter's mouth. This first movement, which is short and dynamic, is then contained and followed by a systolic movement in which the configuration narrows and closes in, as Christine turns to hold Peter and Erika clasps his head, her gaze fixed at a virtual point, a pivot at the center of the trio of bodies. Christine squeezes Peter's arm, her gaze fixed at that same virtual point. Peter is doubly embraced. Erika holds Peter's right hand with her left hand, the tissue grasped together and lowered to his lap. Christine no longer holds hers.

Finally, Peter has now lost consciousness; Erika, looking at Christine, is explaining in clear terms what is happening to Peter's body, that he will soon die, while Christine gazes past her: an air of "awayness"[11] in this last image. We see the entourage move to an upright position, as Peter's posture is now supported by an airplane pillow that has been put around his neck: he holds himself up, with the aid of the pillow, supporting his neck. The viewer now sees Pratchett for the first time since the sequence began, looking on. No one holds any tissues, although the box is placed close by in case. A calm has taken hold as each person waits for Peter to die. Christine's memory of this sequence was twofold: her initial effort to keep control as Peter gasped, and then of Erika walking over to the door and opening it as the snow fell, with cold air streaming in, so as to let Peter's spirit out.

Observing these scenes makes for difficult viewing. Most people today die in hospitals or care homes. The last day of life in a hospital often means supporting the body with the assistance of medications delivered through tubes, as the person lies on her or his back or side, assisting vital functions to slowly break down. In the course of many different forms of dying, there are gestures of care and compassion, by loved ones and medical staff.

A counterpoint to this sequence can be drawn from Frederick Wiseman's incredible observation, nearly six hours long, of the intensive care unit (ICU) at the Boston Beth Israel Hospital, given form as the 1989 documentary *Near Death*: an elderly woman has been transferred to the unit and will shortly die. Her son, who wanted her to receive everything in terms of treatment, endeavored to make it to the hospital from Chicago. He does not get there in time. The doctors have discussed what is reasonable in terms of treatments, given her intubated and semiconscious state and given her son's wish. She is visited by Rabbi Bard, who tells her that she is not alone and that they are there for her.

A striking image is of the lady, lying on her back, her face barely visible with her hospital bed sheet pulled up to her chin, and a tube obscuring her lower face. The nurse stays with her, clearly aware that she is dying, and does not want her to die alone. The nurse stands, gazing slightly up toward a machine, her gaze bisecting the length of the person, the slow bleep of the machine a signal of the end, her stethoscope neatly resting on her shoulders, one hand flopped over the bar of the bed, the other resting on the mattress. Assisted suicide practices, as those within and outside of the associations all insist, of course, do not have a monopoly on dignity or on compassion.

Nevertheless, observing Peter's death allows us to specify several aspects of its form in this particular situation. He was sitting upright. The posture has a functional as well as overtly symbolic dimension: functionally speaking, in order to prepare the body, an antiemetic is taken before oral ingestions of the barbiturate. The risk of vomiting is high owing to the fact that Natrium (Na) (Sodium) Pentobarbital is alkaline and has a bitter, unpleasant taste, and in its concentration (15 grams dissolved in a small quantity of tap water) can lead to nausea. The upright posture helps the barbiturate to flow more easily into the stomach and to minimize the likelihood of vomiting. Vomiting is a very rare occurrence, which can cause major problems, such as the person falling into coma and not dying but rather waking up again after many hours if not days. Second, there is the symbolic character of the position: a doctor, who is both a palliative care specialist and assisted suicide accompanier, described to me how she and other accompaniers consider the posture to be more dignified. Gesturally, assisted suicide provides something specific: the possibility of dying in a position and manner that adherents qualify as dignified, including the possibility (frequently the case during my fieldwork) of actually being held during dying. The specific manner in which Peter is held and holds himself configures the symbolism of dignity (uprightness) with a gestural index of compassion and lamentation, Giotto's *Lamentation* comes to mind (ca. 1303–5), heads tilted toward and touching one another. The cry of the angel is a call to those moved by Erika's gesture of opening the door. Beyond the specificity of the configuration of Peter, Christine, and Erika, the form of this held death, from the accounts of accompaniers and family members with whom I have spoken, and in the situations in which I have been present, is often composed of the holding of the head, hands, and/or feet. Such a form partakes partially of a long durational gestural survival: that of compassion and lamentation. One sees a gestural resonance in the *Lamentation*, which could be grasped as nonisomorphic (neither identical nor opposed) in terms of signification.

We can contrast the scene of leaving life, with its compositional signifying elements of both dignity and tenderness, with a scene of medical compassion, the *Self-portrait with Dr Arrieta*, by Goya from 1820. Rather than the held death in the second moment of Peter being contained, postures and faces turned to one another, we have in this painting Dr. Arrieta embodying the care and vital quickness of early nineteenth-century medical practice: rallying the sum of forces resisting death, imposing remedy as the patient, Goya himself, ready to acquiesce to fate, turns away.[12]

Assisted suicide partakes of these long durational gestural survivals, of lamentation and compassion, yet is equivocal in two key respects. On the one hand, as described above, the systolic motion is the second phase in a movement in which the trio is first split, the composition opening outward and away from the center. The second movement closes in around the body, as in the core iconographical gesture of lamentation, to then open upward, to an upright, neutral, position, as the body holds itself. This third, last, phase is crucial for ongoing indetermination of any possible judgment—judgment in the sense of the attribution of a mode of being to the scene and not attribution of one side of a binary value: lamentation in Christian iconography has as its ethical end a state of redemption, just as Arrieta's compassion had its end orientated to cure. Peter's final posture, in the sequence of dying, is oblique to these salvational stakes.

Regardless, he escaped.

Fabienne and Sylviane

I first contacted Exit *Association pour le droit de mourir dans la dignité* (Exit ADMD) in late 2013. In 2014 I began to meet with some of their volunteer accompaniers, as well as their members, and the families of people who had ended their lives with the help of the association. My aim, however, was to follow individuals from the beginning of their request, through to the end, whatever that might be. During 2014 and 2015 I decided to try to focus uniquely on Exit ADMD and on requests coming from people in the cantons of Vaud and Geneva. I excluded inquiring further into Dignitas on practical grounds. Being based with my family in Paris, I was unable to move to Switzerland, and the distance between Paris and Zurich was difficult to cover. Focusing on Exit, and principally the cities of Lausanne and Geneva, would, I hoped, help me delineate the perimeter of a more or less stable object of inquiry: one association (Exit), one language (French), principally active in just two cantons (Geneva and Vaud), which were relatively accessible, and with at least the veneer of sociological coherence—the members are all Swiss residents. This endeavor proved difficult to fulfill.

Living in Paris, I was an irregular, although persistent, visitor. I was able to get into initial, superficial contact with many people, but the goal, to follow a request from beginning to end, eluded me. To get in touch with people in the process of making a request, there were, essentially, only two options: (1) for the accompaniers to facilitate entry directly with individuals in the process of making a request or (2) for the association to make available, in one way or another, information about the project, such that people could, if they wished, contact me in order to take part in the inquiry. I hoped that over the year I would get to know one or two of the accompaniers and that that confidence could turn into trust. This did not happen. One of the accompaniers, a former cantonal medical officer, did facilitate a little announcement in the biannual bulletin for the association in the autumn of 2015: "An anthropological researcher, conducting work on assisted suicide, based at the CNRS in France, wishes to enter into contact with members who have made a request for assisted suicide, in order to be able to discuss with them about their undertaking. If you are able to dedicate a little bit of time to Mr. Stavrianakis, please do not hesitate to contact him."

I had several responses from members who were not yet in the process of making a request and several whose wives and husbands had recently died with the help of Exit.

And, I had one response from a person in the midst of the process.

FABIENNE

"Ah here he is. Bonjour Monsieur."

"Bonjour Madame."

"This is Romaine, and Hélène, from Exit, whom I think you know. You are just in time for the aperitif." It was 11:30 in the morning. I stood in the doorway of Fabienne's apartment in a small town on the outskirts of Sion, in the canton of Valais. Fabienne and Hélène were holding highball cocktail glasses, filled with bright blue liquid, topped with orange slices. Romaine had a shot glass. "It's a Blue Lagoon; invented at Harry's New York bar," Fabienne said. I tried to get my bearings. We stood together in the kitchen-cum-living room of her three-room apartment. "When you move from a sixteen-room house to a three-room apartment, it's hard to fit everything in!" Fabienne said, waving her long arms around.

The small table between the kitchen and living area was set for lunch. Hélène, I knew, was the accompanier from Exit. Romaine was the housekeeper whom Fabienne had spoken of on the phone. It was clear that her work, and their relationship, went far beyond this. When Fabienne's husband became very ill, she effectively became a home nurse, although that was not her profession. Romaine promised him that she would not leave Fabienne. It became clear, although never expressly stated, that for Romaine, an Orthodox Christian from Ethiopia, Fabienne's decision was, to say the least, difficult to accept.

"Sit down, sit down," Fabienne said to Hélène and to me, as she and Romaine went to prepare the lunch. We were ordered to drink more quickly.

"I'm driving," Hélène said.

"It's mainly pineapple juice," Fabienne said, with a big smile.

Fabienne was tall and seemed quite well, considering she had recently had a second surgical intervention for breast cancer and that she was suffering from renal failure. We had spoken on the phone twice prior to the lunch. I had understood that she had become a member of Exit ADMD in 2005, after her husband died: he had a cancer of the face, which destroyed him. He was her only family, she said, despite the fact that they had had two children together. Their son was killed by a car at the age of thirty—"murdered," in her words, even though the authorities had said it was an accident. I asked her what she meant by *murder* and she changed the subject. "You know, when Romaine doesn't come, I just stare at the ceiling. There's no reason they won't accept me. I've been a member for over ten years. In thirty years it [assisted suicide] will become normal."

I asked her about her family. She hadn't seen her daughter since 2009, although she was just twenty kilometers away. Her mother had married five times. She hated her, she said. Fabienne didn't have any brothers or sisters. A half-sister, yes, but she didn't know her: she was twenty-five years younger. Fabienne had studied biochemistry at Columbia University and "worked at NASA before it was NASA," in Chicago. She was a Catholic until her husband died, and then she lost her faith, a statement narrated simply as fact, with no interpretation or surprise, or justification. He too was a doctor, like her grandfather and father. She has no one now, she said—"no family, and no reason to do a third surgery."

Despite the Blue Lagoon, I was trying to grasp the character of Fabienne's request and especially to try to grasp Hélène's approach to this request for assisted suicide given that Fabienne seemed to be doing okay physically but was clearly isolated socially. Specifically, I wanted to gauge Hélène's approach to Fabienne given my own growing discomfort with her garrulousness. Given the discomfort that I felt in the situation, to what extent was this affect shared or not by other observers? It was not the alcohol per se that bothered me, or made me uncomfortable, and the party atmosphere in itself was not a problem; that she was verbose was useful to the degree that she was willing to narrate things about her life. Rather, it was Fabienne's flippant manner of talking about her request that bothered me.

This was my problem, not hers. Who was I to impose a standard and form for a discourse about someone's upcoming death? This is not a rhetorical question. I was a person who was seeking to find a position from which to follow and understand, I hoped, how it was that another person came to the judgment that it was appropriate to leave his or her experience of illness and of life through a voluntary assisted death. What I had understood about my own work to try to occupy such a position was that, minimally, there had to be some openness to discussing aspects of biography, of prior experience, that could help me to connect the practical aspects of the request to the specificity of the life, of the person, the one making the request.

Not everyone wants to do this of course. One particular exchange instantiates in exemplary fashion how my wish to occupy such a position of exchange has been rebuffed for the simple reason that the person seeking an assisted voluntary death not only doesn't want to engage in such exchange but considers it beside the point—which is to say, irrelevant. Here is an extract from a letter I sent to a person, following up on an initial discussion by telephone regarding her request to end her life, a request that had been accepted, in principle, by the association. My letter is followed by her reply:

> Dear Ruth, I hope you are doing ok after what I imagine were difficult first weeks of treatment. I didn't want to write straight away after our conversation for a number of reasons, one of which was that I thought it was important that I give you sufficient time to think about whether talking with me is of any interest or use to you. As I intimated on the phone, one of the things I would like to know more about is how people decide that an "insurance policy," as you called it, such as the one the association is able to provide, is something that individuals wish to pursue. As you put it to me, as long as you can remember, you have been in favour of people being able to have a choice. My job, as an anthropologist, is to try to put that conviction into a context, within the life of the person and within the network of relations in which the person is ensconced. As you said on the phone, you are a private person and this kind of exchange is necessarily exposing, to the degree that one is talking about personal matters. From my side, I want to be sure not to be a bother to you, and if talking with me is either troubling, or inappropriate then, obviously, I would not like to insist on us talking again.

Her reply was direct:

> You are correct in your assessment of me. Talking again to you is not really of any interest or use to me. History, in the normal meaning of the word, is of little interest to me; my own personal history, whether that be of my life or my ancestors, far less so. I have no wish to analyse my thoughts on the past. Yesterday is history,

today is good and tomorrow will be fabulous. Perhaps that last sentence tells you more about me. Does that make me superficial? I don't know. What I do know is that I look forwards, not backwards. My ongoing chemotherapy is a fortnightly rollercoaster of ups and downs. I go into what can only be described as "chemo black holes" for about five days in the middle of each cycle. I slowly emerge and rediscover my brain and some energy in time to accomplish a few things before starting all over again. This will go on until Christmas after which the hope is that it will give me three months or so of good life when I can travel. Will I consider this a sufficiently good "return on investment"? Time will tell. In the meantime I am content in the knowledge that I have the insurance policy from the association. I am a hugely optimistic and positive person. It is this which enables me to look forward to the end of this round of chemotherapy. Perhaps I will get a better than expected improvement for more than three months—who knows? In that case, perhaps I would decide to repeat the whole chemotherapy process in the hope of a further extended good period. Eventually, as things go downhill as they inevitably will, there will be a point sometime next year at which I decide that enough is enough and I will go. Anthony—I can see very little point in us speaking again. If you feel from this email that there is some point, then please feel free to ring me.

I thanked her for her reply and said I would not call again. In many respects her manner of thinking about her request resonates with both Peter's and Fabienne's. The difference with the story of Peter, though, is that I had the narrative point of view of his wife as historian to disrupt the uniquely "obvious" character of his request, which gave me a position, albeit a position based in retrospect, from which to think (about) the obvious.

With respect to Fabienne and Hélène, I wanted to see whether Fabienne would be willing to contextualize her request in relation to her own history and whether or how such "context" mattered for Hélène. "So you have already met Fabienne?" I said to Hélène.

"Yes. We already met twice last month. As you know, Doctor Sobel [Jerome Sobel who was the president of Exit from 2000 to 2017] receives all the requests, and he makes the judgment as to whether they are accepted or not. When he accepts a dossier, he telephones the office to suggest an accompanier to take on the case based on the nature of the case and on the location. Then the office phones us and asks us if we would be willing to take on a new case. Me, for example, I have a lot of trouble with the category 'age related illnesses'" [*polypathologies liées à l'âge*].

"Is this not the case with Fabienne?"

"No, she has renal insufficiency and breast cancer."

"Had her dossier already been accepted when you met the first time?"

"Dr. Sobel had approved it and then it is always for the accompanier to see. The first time we met, it was clear she was not very well. We saw each other a further time, with a documentary team, which Fabienne agreed to. In fact it was her suggestion even to allow a film team to follow her situation." This announcement was news to me. I was not necessarily alarmed but concerned as to how the situation would unfold with this added element.

"They will follow everything, right to the end," Hélène said.

"I see."

"The second time we met, she was as she is now, talking a lot, making jokes, laughing. She was so well, in fact, that I was wondering whether I could really accept the dossier. You know, we all have different styles of accompaniment. Me, I try to push people as long as they can go. This is a point of disagreement on the committee."

"You are on the committee?"

"Yes. There are twelve of us. We meet every two months to discuss difficult cases and other matters. Most people on the committee think that I am too concerned with social factors [dans le social]. I started this work by volunteering with the Red Cross and the Ligue contre le cancer. There was so much needless suffering that I decided to get involved with Exit. My approach is based in part on my experience and in part from the person who inducted me into the practice, Suzanne. For example, I always phone the doctor who provides the medical report. I visit people a lot, which isn't the case for all accompaniers." Indeed, Hélène's style of accompaniment can be contrasted with others, such as Daphné, who explained to me that she made it a point of procedure, also an ethical point, that her accompaniment consists in only two visits, the first visit to discuss the request and the second when the person is ready. Anything more than that would be to trespass the limits of her role, as she conceives it.

Fabienne then joined us and said that she had been worried Exit wouldn't accept her file. "When I first talked to my doctor, I was talking about ending my life, and it was he who suggested Exit; he reminded me that I had been a member for years. I thought that one had to have a terminal illness, but he said not. Still, I wasn't sure they would accept. Although I've been a member for eleven years. That's got to count. I've thought about it." Fabienne's "thinking about it" included an oscillating narrative of misfortune, fortune, achievement, and loss: a childhood marked by illness, with a mother she hated, who remarried five times; academic and professional success; a marriage that she considered fulfilling; the loss of two children, albeit losses of different kinds, and in different ways; the emptiness of life once her husband died; then breast cancer and renal failure. "Five husbands my mother had! I have the name of the first, I'm the progeny of the second, and it was the third who raised me— wonderful man. My mother sent me to boarding school at seven; he wanted to adopt me but she wouldn't let him. Her second husband was a nobleman; he got two women pregnant at the same time and said he would marry the one who had a son. When they announced my sex after the birth my mother said, "Little beast!" (*chameau!*).

"That's sad," Hélène said.

"I was unwell until age seven. I stayed at home, basically in bed, and I was allowed to eat only broth. I used to hide little packs of sugar under the table legs, which had feet like lion's paws. One day, the maid found them, and that was that. I had asthma, but this was the 1930s; there was only one doctor in Europe who knew about it." I thought about the fact that Fabienne was born in the 1930s, in Boulogne, just outside of Paris: the sickly child, with a watchful maid, who went on to become a French biochemist who had studied and worked in the US. She met her husband when she was a second-year student, a man who had studied both at the École Polytechnique and at medical school, a gastroenterologist who worked for Sanofi. They had wanted to go to a scientific conference together, but in those days it would have been impossible without being married. He proposed. She thought he was joking. "He slept around of course, a month at a time in Japan. It wasn't like he was going to be alone, but he's a man; it's normal. Any man that is normally constituted is like that. He was an amazing husband. We agreed on everything. But six months after his death, all the friends I had disappeared. Because a single woman could steal the husbands of others, so no one wanted me around. At the dinner table, we don't know where to put a widow." I looked around the table as we were talking and suddenly felt the weight of the four different portraits of her husband that were encircling us. I then noticed a portrait of her son behind her in the kitchen.

I wasn't uncomfortable. It was rather a mild boredom and irritation that had settled in me: bored by what I took to be a facetious discourse and annoyed that my efforts to get Fabienne to talk in terms other than those of the obviousness of her request were being rebuffed. "So will you discuss it with your daughter before the date for your assisted suicide in August?" I asked.

"Don't talk to me about my daughter! Ah. All she is interested in is money, uggggh [grimace]. She's just like my mother!"

"So you won't let your daughter know about your plans?"

"No. She can find out from the television. She didn't even go to her father's funeral. Cancer of the face. He was taken care of by our GP. Wonderful man. Very caring. He provided him with enough morphine at the end so that he could die peacefully."

"Is he the one who will write the prescription?" Hélène asked, referring to the doctor who will act as the authority taking responsibility for prescribing a lethal dose of pentobarbital. The association prefers it if a doctor outside of the association, who knows the patient, is willing to prescribe the pentobarbital, but this is relatively uncommon, and as such, a doctor from within the association often has to write the prescription.

"No," Fabienne said.

I looked at Hélène, who looked at Fabienne, concerned. "Can I call this doctor?" Hélène said.

"No. Why would you want to bother him with this? It's not necessary."

"So who is the doctor who wrote your certificates?"

"He's a gastroenterologist—weight loss and that sort of thing."

"I would like to call him; would you let me?"

"Please don't bother him. So the date is fixed for August?"

"Yes, the tenth, but you know that you can always change it, or tell me to go away, even on the day itself you can tell—"

"Certainly not! That's all I would need. That's really not my thing, to change my mind. If I didn't have Exit, what would I do? Overdose on medications, and then what? They'd find a way to wash my stomach." Fabienne was getting agitated, imagining all the horrible ways in which she could end her life, ways that are, it must be said, analogous to how her son died; "or else there are those bloody ways, like crashing the car into a wall, or else going under a bus, it's horrible! What a horror. Who wants to do something like that? So, what was left for me to do? Eh? Since I have Exit I feel free."

Once the lunch was finished, Hélène quickly wanted to leave, and I wanted a ride to the station. As we drove, she said that unlike some other accompaniers, she tries to make sure there aren't too many unresolved issues and that she encourages people to try and repair ruptures before they die. Hélène said she would try to contact the doctor who wrote her certificate, as well as her daughter.

I wrote to Fabienne after the visit, asking her whether I could return to visit her again before her death and also whether I could be present on August 10. A few days later, she called me saying that although she doesn't have a problem with it, she asked Hélène, and, in fact, Exit doesn't want me to be there. She didn't want to insist in case it put in jeopardy her assisted suicide. I said that of course I understood. An hour later I received an email from Hélène explaining further that she was aware of my request to Fabienne, that she had discussed it with Jerome Sobel, and that they would prefer it if I weren't there, since there will be "the television present": "it would be a lot of people and there's a chance the police won't be too happy about it." I said that of course I understood.

In fact, I didn't understand. I wondered whether it was a strategy to block the inquiry. I thought that perhaps the wish to facilitate a documentary team but not an anthropological inquiry might have something to do with the manner in which the association considered "documentary" to be a medium in which an *"effet de réel"*[1] could be assured, perhaps to a degree controlled. In particular, it concerns not documentary film per se but a particular subgenre of documentary, the short TV documentary (thirty to fifty minutes) aimed at stirring "public debate" (as with Terry Pratchett's film). Such a hypothesized reality effect is not isomorphic with the literary reality effect named by Barthes, in which description of supports and objects has no functional purpose other than to establish that narrative expresses a reality. I thought, rather, that the prevalence of documentary as a medium for capturing assisted suicide—it was both my initial entry point (with Peter) and will reappear within the fieldwork on two occasions here, with Fabienne and again with Florian—was a consequence of the imaginary link that is sought to be created by those who facilitate making documentaries on behalf of the subject who is ending her or his life, in relation to other subjects who observe the act.

What I mean by this is simply that documentary is considered a "self-evident" way of making other subjects (viewers) see reality in the way the documentary form proposes that the subject (of the voluntary death) sees it. There can be discord, of course; viewers are capable of making their own judgment, but the function is to establish the range of images that can count as part of the reality of the situation. I wondered if the concern of the association, the reason to block access to the unfolding of the practice, was that an anthropological inquiry, an anthropological narrative, would render uncontrollable the range of images through which the reality of the act would be narrated, a countereffect, or countereffectuation of the real, and the kinds of consideration that might emerge from that range of images.

It had taken a very long time to get Exit to agree to put my research advert in their bulletin; it finally appeared in September of 2015, asking members to get in touch if they were actively undertaking steps toward an assisted suicide. Exit had been very happy to facilitate my meeting accompaniers, and for me to conduct interviews, but had been reluctant to mediate my access to their members, concerned that it was not their position to propose an encounter with a researcher to their members, especially since what I wanted was to follow a request from beginning to end. I had had only four responses to my notice, all of which were either massively prospective—the person wasn't ill—or else pertained to a family member who had recently died. Fabienne was a late contact who, six months after the advert appeared, got in touch with me. It had been clear that the association was not particularly at ease with mediating my contact with members, and I worried I wouldn't have another chance.

FABIENNE ON TV

An off-camera interviewer asked Fabienne whether anything could change her mind.[2] "Nothing will change my mind; why would I change my mind? I'm already dead: I'm eighty-five years old, I'm ill. What more do you want? Eh? Frankly." She laughed. Fabienne wore a rose-patterned dressing gown. White roses were on the table. She sat next to Hélène.

"You're all calm you; you're all good," said Hélène.

"I'm not bothered by it. I slept well!" Fabienne burst out laughing. Romaine stood by the doorway, right hand on her hip, left elbow against the wall. Her look at odds with the gleeful smile on Fabienne's face. "This one didn't sleep a wink last night! Hahahahaha!" Fabienne says, pointing at Romaine. "At least I slept like an angel." While Fabienne carries on laughing, Hélène looks away, takes a breath, and then looks back to her, introducing a transition or break by way of a change of tone.

"So you're really decided."

"Ohh, Hélène!" She taps the accompanier's knee.

"I'm annoying you with this, I know."

"How many times is she going to ask me this? 150 times?"

"Yes, yes," Hélène said. Fabienne went into the bedroom and sat on the bed. Hélène came in after her. "There we are Fabienne; look, this is the whisky.

But you drink this, perhaps, if you are really sure, because you have the right to not—"

"Now look here, it's not possible! How many times [are you going to ask me this]? I am *def-ini-tel-y* sure, *I am definite-ly-sure, IamdefinitelysureIamdefinitely sureIamdefinitelysure*hahahahaha!!!!!!!!!!"

"Ok ok," she said, handing Fabienne the whisky.

"Drink just a drop of the whisky; it's just for the taste you know."

"Because it's that bad? [the taste of the lethal dose of barbiturate]"

"It's very bitter." After swallowing the drop of whisky, she made a grimace, and reached to take the other glass.

"This is the potion [*la potion*]."

"Yes I suspected that.... The other one is for after [looking at the whisky].... Errrgh," she says, making a theatrical grimace to the camera]." Fabienne quickly drinks the barbiturate solution. Romaine goes to give her a hug.

"No no, you shouldn't cry silly goose," Fabienne said to Romaine. Romaine ran out of the room in tears, covering her eyes and forehead.

"She's worrying."

"It's natural for her to be worried," Hélène stroked her arm.

"But there's no reason."

"It's natural [*c'est normal*]. They looked in each other's eyes.

"*Aller,*" Hélène said. They kiss goodbye.

"I hope I am going to fall asleep."

"Yes, don't you worry . . . *aller.*" Fabienne got under the covers.

"You are going to gently fall asleep." Hélène stroked her arm and looked down. The camera focused away from Fabienne's face and on Hélène caressing her, putting her hand on her heart.

EXIT TOWARD *LIFECIRCLE*

I was disappointed with how the interaction with Fabienne ended: it seemed to me that Exit had been excessively cautious, and controlling, in not allowing me to be present on the day of Fabienne's death. At the time, I came up with an interpretation that the real reason behind the refusal to allow me to be present was that it was very important to Exit to be able to control the terms of narratives that are rendered public about assisted suicide. The documentary films made on the subject limit themselves to a brief interview with the person, in which the reasonability and self-evidence of the request is outlined, and then show to one degree or another the process through which the person dies. My sense was that an anthropological narrative, even a very minimal beginning of the sketch of some elements for such a narrative, as outlined above, would ruffle and disrupt an easily consumable story about individual choice: what place would there be in a documentary film for telling the story of Fabienne's son's death, her hatred of her mother, her estrangement from her daughter, the fact that she told us that her daughter "could find out from the television" about her death, her experience of loss and isolation after the death of her husband: not that any of these elements undermines *that* she made a choice. If adequately presented, however, these narrative elements could enrich an understanding of the request. None of these elements were in the short segment of the television documentary that showed Fabienne's death.

To get toward such a narrative form, however, I would need to be able to follow the story from beginning to end, and I would need to find a position from which to narrate it. I took the blockage from Exit as an occasion to try and contact Erika, the doctor who had evaluated Peter, and her relatively new association, *lifecircle*, based in Basel, which I knew assisted not only Swiss but also French and English people (among others).

One of the raisons d'être for forming *lifecircle* as a new association in 2013 was explicitly political: to be able to work with others in order to legalize assisted dying in other countries so that people will not need to travel to Switzerland to die. The association helps approximately eighty to ninety foreigners a year to die but not more: the limit is necessary not only because it is a massively consuming and challenging engagement, especially for a small association, but also because the association does not wish to become the solution to a problem that other countries externalize.

In addition to Erika the association is staffed by an administrator and a few collaborators, including the physicians that she requires, so as to have an independent check on the process. The association has forged networks, in particular with documentary makers, with social scientists, with journalists, with activists and politicians, to try to reverse the power relations and political effects of the movement of those seeking assisted dying in Switzerland. The association thus becomes not only the container for the externalities of contemporary medicine but also a node in which the effect of the contained can be returned—an intervention, in Europe and beyond, from the parazone of the practice of assisted suicide.

When I contacted the association for the second time in early 2016, it was as I prepared to resubmit a funding proposal to the Swiss National Science Foundation. The project was in collaboration with anthropologist Marc-Antoine Berthod, an institutional figure in the anthropology of death and dying in Switzerland. I was surprised with the rapidity and strength of the response: the association was willing to write to all French and British members on my behalf, explaining that I was seeking to follow people in the process of requesting and carrying out a voluntary assisted death and to describe their undertaking.

Twenty-two people contacted me in the days following the request, of which one was Sylviane.

SYLVIANE

Thursday, 14 April 2016. An email from Sylviane to Anthony.

"Together with the association *lifecircle* in Basel, you have solicited my participation in your research about accompanied suicide, which I willingly accept, because I want to contribute to this project. Please call me back quickly, preferably at 11:45am, or after 3pm."

On reading the message for the first time, I thought I had detected an urgency, an anxiety in Sylviane's tone. When we spoke, at 11:45, her affect was cooler than I anticipated; it was discerning. With good reason, she wanted to know who I was, what exactly I wanted from her, and what the purpose of this inquiry was. I more or less repeated what I had written in the letter that had been sent to the members of her association. It explained that I wished to follow a series of people as they requested and possibly carried out an assisted suicide. The letter specified that I was concerned with how a person's request is accepted (or rejected) such that they can (or cannot) end their life—how different experiences and evaluations about the realization of an assisted suicide are lived and negotiated, through the entire process, as well as afterward.

I asked her about her situation. She began to explain. It was a complicated narrative. I understood that she had multiple sclerosis, but the chronology was confusing. I mixed up thirteen years of illness, what I thought, with illness since she was thirteen, what she meant. She got annoyed with me for having misunderstood; it became clear to me at a later date that aside from being annoyed with someone who did not understand a fact, my misunderstanding reflected, repeated perhaps, the experience of a teenage girl whose mother refused to believe that she was ill. "Can we meet face to face?" I asked her. "I see you are near Strasbourg. I could come to visit on Thursday." She sounded pleased about this, even a bit surprised.

I arrived at her public housing block, not far from Strasbourg. I began typing in the door code and before I could press the final digit, a woman opened the main door. "Who are you looking for?"

"Madame Borg."

"The lady in the wheelchair?"

"Yes," I said, spontaneously, although I didn't know.

"Third floor, it's on the right."

Sylviane opened the door, seated in her wheelchair. She remarked on the fact that I was exactly on time: "not a minute early or late"—just as when I called her on the phone. At the time I thought this was merely a remark on how people these days are typically careless with timekeeping, but now, with hindsight, I think that my being exactly on time was a marker, a small sign, that perhaps I was being seen as a person who could be counted on, counted on to keep my word and perhaps not to disappoint.

She showed me around the apartment telling me about the evolution of the layout: she had moved here in 2007, and the works were completed in 2009; the layout is circular so she has easy access to all parts of the apartment with her wheelchair. Her mood was upbeat and chatty, and it remained constant even as the topic of our discussions turned to the recent difficult phase of her illness. "What has changed is that it has really gotten worse in the last three weeks. I can't bear it any longer. . . . Do you want a coffee?" she asked, interrupting herself.

We sat at the kitchen table, and she began to tell me a bit more about her illness: she began to have symptoms when she was thirteen, including moments of paralysis. Her father took it seriously; her mother did not. No one wanted to speak of it. Even after the diagnosis, her mother would not allow her to speak of it. Suffer in silence. "My mother thought I was malingering. One suffers in silence here. And then I married a man who treated me like a piece of shit. Cooking, washing, cleaning was all I was to him. Even when I was lying down, after having a bad moment, he would knock on the door and ask when dinner is ready."

"Did you divorce him?" I asked, preemptively.

"I did. It took a long time for the divorce to be finalized, from October 2004 until January 2009. In 2005 I made a request to Dignitas. They would have accepted my case, but I wasn't ready to do it straightaway and you had to pay up front. My daughter was ten. I thought that I have to hold on a bit longer; otherwise, she'd have had to live with her father. She's grown up now. She's almost twenty-two. Then I met someone after putting an advert in the local paper. I was upfront about having the illness. He comes and sees me in the morning and puts me to bed at night. He has traveled the world. He grew up in Mulhouse but has lived in so many countries. He knows you are here. He doesn't want to talk about it. He can't talk about it. He will be very sad."

I asked her how she became aware of the possibility of assisted voluntary death. "I became a member of ADMD [the French association for "the right to die with dignity"] in 2003, after having seen it on television: Nathalie Baye [a French actress] on Michel Drucker's Sunday afternoon program was talking about it and why she is a member. ADMD has said they would accompany me [from France to Switzerland] if necessary. Someone from ADMD even came to visit me at home. In August 2015 I made a first contact with *lifecircle*. I had found out about *lifecircle* by googling around suicide assistance."

I asked whether she will need to send in medical certificates: she went to make me copies of the last ones she had: 20 July 2015. It was a report from the hospital stating that since last year, her situation had been more or less stable but that she increasingly feels the effects of her illness. The report described her as "active" and "courageous," participating in a group where she can meet others and talk about everyday problems.

It was about midday, and Sylviane asked if I'd like to stay to eat something. I had left the house at 6 a.m. and hadn't eaten anything. I accepted her invitation of eggs and toast and offered to make the lunch, which she gladly accepted. I didn't think it was an odd thing to do until I found myself looking around her cupboards for the right-sized frying pan, wondering whether olive oil is for cooking with—or only for dressings—in this house.

As I cooked, Sylviane talked. "I have discussed it in the past. I have talked a lot about ending my life, but no one takes me seriously. My best friend doesn't take me seriously. When I talk about it, she just says, no no, you're fine; and then she starts complaining about her own life; she says to me, you think it's all peaches and cream in my life? I have to go to work; I have to do this and do that. We all have problems. She comes over once every two months, when I have my hair done; she stays for lunch, and that's all. I live in solitude. I never go out. My daughter lives in Strasbourg; she is in the law faculty, doing an M2 [an advanced master's degree]. She has exams and a job interview in May, so I won't talk about my plans until she has taken them. She works really hard. I don't think she will want to come with me. I haven't explicitly asked. My brother understands the decision, as does my sister-in-law. If I asked them, they would come but out of obligation, and that is not what I want. My uncle always said to me, when you become dependent on others, that is not a life. I have become a heavy load for others."

I took the occasion to ask about her parents. Was her father as tough as her mother?

"No, my father really took the illness very seriously, but after some time I stopped going home. He never really understood why. I provoked his death; he died of a broken heart."

"What did he actually die of?"

"He was old; he was 82. Have you seen other cases, and how did the family react?"

I explained what I had seen and heard and underscored that I hadn't yet been present at an assisted death. I wondered, and asked her, why she was so insistent about her family, her daughter, her brother, and her boyfriend not being willing to accompany her. On the one hand, there seemed to be a concern for being strong, for not needing anyone else and not burdening anyone else. On the other hand, she needed her suffering to be recognized and expressed a wish that the suffering end. I must have heard the expression "I can't bear it any longer" (*j'en peu plus*) at least fifteen times during the day.

Sylviane took out her *lifecircle* folder and began to read the explanation of how a request is made. It seemed to me that this was in fact the first time she had really read the information provided by the association. I become increasingly uneasy and uncomfortable sitting at the table with her. I thought to myself that my letter and my presence was clearly a testing ground, a support even, for her reflection on ending her life. I wondered how I, and the apparatus of the inquiry, was in fact facilitating this person's movement toward a decision to end her life, under conditions in which apparently she was unwilling or unable to talk in a serious manner with family and friends.

She read aloud the information booklet sent by *lifecircle*. When she got to the part about the death itself, and the procedure for dealing with the body, she started to laugh. "You will be cremated and the ashes can be returned. . . . Oh that's not necessary . . . hmmm but perhaps my daughter or my family might . . . I will talk to her first." She carried on reading aloud. "Two nights in a hotel. If there is no medical bed, I cannot stay there. They will have to come to me for the first visit and then we take the train for the second meeting. You or you and your team could come here, and we can take the train. We would go to Strasbourg, or actually we could go [in] the other direction, from Mollkirch to Basel." She narrated the hypothetical situation. I nodded along, wondering how to express my growing discomfort.

"It's important to find out what your family thinks, depending on how *lifecircle* responds to your request," I said.

She ignored me and continued reading. "I need a medical report dating no more than three or four months. Hmmm . . . perhaps I will need to keep the appointment after all with the professor at the hospital." She rolled off into the other room. I heard some tapping for a minute or two, and then she came back, telling me that she had sent a message to the professor at the hospital asking for an appointment sooner than her scheduled one." Or else, I could also write to my neurologist, perhaps that would be sufficient?"

"Will you explain about your intention?"

"I think so. Perhaps that way he can provide the report more quickly. Otherwise, he takes a month to produce the report, 25th June and that will mean delaying things." Different elements had started to get mixed around. "I can't talk to my daughter until after her exams. I will have to wait. I can buy sleeping pills on the internet, of course, and I can take them and put a bag over my head, but I don't want her to come here to find me like that." The telephone rang. "I've eaten an egg. Yes come up." I understood that it was her boyfriend. "I didn't tell him you are here. He will see that." Sylviane then shouted out, as the door closed, "We're in here. How was the restaurant?" He entered the kitchen with several bags of shopping. He didn't introduce himself to me.

"Can I help you put away the shopping?" I said to him.

"No that's fine."

Eventually I tried to break the awkwardness. "You are Francis?"

"Yes."

"I'm Anthony."

"I brought you desserts," he said to Sylviane.

"Will you make us coffees Francis?"

"Ok. It's not that complicated. Press the button," he said, which I understood as a command. I tried to use the machine; it sputtered and burst, making a mess.

"Not that easy," she said.

"Let me do it; there's a trick." He continued, "This is the specialty of the region, and this is the specialty of the patisserie." We sat at the table with coffee and cakes. We did not talk of why I was there, nor was there discussion of Sylviane's illness or her reflection on assistance with dying. We made small talk. "You are English?"

"Yes. You are from Mulhouse?"

"Yes."

"I spent a year in Basel. Very nice city," I said. We talked a little more about food and languages as we ate the cakes.

"Let me look up your train times," he pronounced.

"Thank you; that's very kind."

"See you again perhaps," Sylviane said.

I headed to the train station, and as I waited on the platform, I sent a text message to my wife, Laurence. "16:36: I will take the train soon, in half an hour. Trying to write notes. It is quite complicated. It is clear the person I met feels she needs me in order to accomplish her suicide. Very difficult. There are legal parameters that I need to take seriously."

What I had in mind was how in the encounter with Sylviane, a steady affect of, what I'd like to think was, composed attentiveness gave way, slowly and surely, to creeping disquiet, accompanied by a slightly sickening feeling of having gotten into a situation that was quickly getting to be beyond my control, a feeling stemming in large part from the clear fact that my request to meet individuals who were in the process of requesting assistance with suicide was being taken up as an offer of just such assistance—in other words, the feeling of having made a mistake.

"So what happened?" Laurence asked at dinner.

"She can't talk about it with her family. She wants me to accompany her to Basel."

"You can't do that. Regardless of the legal stuff. That's not your place. You are not her family. It's unethical. Did you promise her anything?"

"Well, let's see: I nodded as she was imagining and narrating how it would go, and I didn't contest her imagined scenario when she said that I could come to Mollkirch and that we could go together from there. I was uneasy, though, and did make the point several times about how important it is that she talk it through with her family, but I didn't explicitly say, 'If no one from your family accompanies you then I cannot either.'"

"Don't you think you should?"
I said I was not sure.

DÉNOUEMENT

A few days later, I talked with Marc-Antoine. I felt completely ill at ease and as though I had made a big mistake. Marc asked me whether I'd be prepared to go with her alone. I didn't know. I said it depended on what her family said. While we talked, Marc looked up the letter the association had sent on my behalf: ". . . I would like to request your participation in this research. If you agree, we could first meet to discuss your situation and your reflections on it; in the event that you would be interested, I could then accompany you to *lifecircle.*"

"Yes there is room for interpretation: someone could read this and think, that person can help accompany me. You need to find a formulation to clarify your position without having an a priori position, *if* for you it depends on the family."

I wrote to Sylviane, thanking her for her goodwill and for having forwarded me a copy of the letter that she had sent to *lifecircle* two days after we met. The letter explained that she was a member of the association and wished to begin steps toward organizing the assisted suicide. I asked her, in my email, if the first step of the request is accepted, if it would be possible to return to see her, after May 10, that is to say, after her daughter's exams, to discuss her request and *lifecircle*'s response with her and her family, in particular with her daughter and her boyfriend. I expressed in the message that it was indeed very important for me that her relatives and I have the chance to talk, if I am to be part of the unfolding situation.

She replied shortly after, telling me that her boyfriend had left her and that she was now alone. She told me that she had invited her brother and sister-in-law to lunch, to discuss it with them, and she explained that she would wait until the end of May to discuss her request with her daughter. She invited me to get back in contact with her whenever I would like. I decided not to contact her, leaving it up to her to contact me again.

About a year later, I received an email from Sylviane, addressed to me, and sent also to *lifecircle*. In the letter she expressed the fact that she now felt she was ready to die, given that her state of health had degraded further. She asked me practical questions as to whether there would be a medical bed available for her on arrival in Switzerland; whether the number of nights in Switzerland could be reduced to one, so that everything could take place over two days; whether a nurse would be available to help with her catheter, and how much a nurse would cost; whether I would accept to contact her again; whether I would accompany her; what further documents would need to be sent to the association.

I replied, saying that I would be willing to get back in contact with her but only on condition that I could meet with her and her daughter. As for the practical questions, it was for the association to reply to her.

The association replied to her practical questions and then asked her directly whether "your daughter would be willing to accompany you? Or else perhaps with Mr. Stavrianakis?"

I said nothing and I have heard nothing since.

Clément

Like Sylviane, Clément contacted me in response to my letter, sent by *lifecircle* to its French and British members, which explained my request to meet people considering assisted suicide in Switzerland. I met him at home for the first time in early April of 2016. His son, and eldest child, Pascal, met me at the station in Cherbourg early in the morning. He took me to Clément's apartment in the center of the town, telling me a little bit about how his father was doing: fragile, but still with a surprising capacity to engage in discussion, when the subject interested him. He had been very frail since having been hospitalized in September of 2015 for heart failure. Clément and his late wife, Odette, had moved to Cherbourg about a decade earlier to be close to their youngest daughter, Marguerite, a family doctor in the town. Their elder daughter, in Grenoble, had restricted and limited contact with her family over the last twenty years. The distance started when she changed her given name from Natasha to Clara. It wasn't clear why. As we sat down, facing each other, Clément handed me a writing tablet: "What would you like to know?"

He had explained to me already on the phone some of the reasons why he made a request for a voluntary assisted suicide: they pertained mainly to his medical history, the cancers he had had—bowel cancer and a lymphoma—and his recent cardiac and respiratory failure, which seemed to be giving him the most trouble; so I asked him, if possible, to situate this request within the context of his life. He paused for a moment and then began telling me about his parents (Jewish Polish communists), their flight from Poland, his childhood, and their deaths. They left Poland at age twenty and went to Germany.

They were fleeing economic misery, and they were expecting revolution; they were communist militants, and Germany was where it was going to happen. The extreme right, however, was rising in Germany. Rosa Luxemburg was assassinated, which would have been 1919. They left for Paris. His brother was born in 1926, and Clément was born three years later. The family was spread out. He didn't know his grandparents. They were killed in the Shoa. His paternal grandfather was very religious, in contrast to his parents, who were atheists but who nevertheless maintained a great respect for the tradition. They left Germany for France because of an image of the country as a place of liberty, equality, and fraternity. They lived in the twentieth and the eleventh arrondissements, continuing their activities as militant worker organizers, specifically in the Jewish section of the Communist Party (founded in 1920), teaching Polish culture, but not religion, organizing meetings at home. They spoke Yiddish in the house, and Clément answered in French. Both seamers, they had two machines at home, which helped to make ends meet. He went to primary school, and the idea, generally, was that at age fourteen a child would get a *certificat d'études* and start work. After winning a prize for his studies, Clément was able to carry on at the Lycée Voltaire. His father joined the resistance in 1939, under the name "Thomas"; he was arrested and sent to a concentration camp in France and later deported to Germany.

Clément and his mother were in Paris. She carried on with meetings at home. It would have been May of 1942 when they had to wear the yellow star. The stars came from the Police Commissariat. They had to go down to get them, and it cost him a point, a ticket. Clément explains, in case I didn't know: just as there were tickets for food, there were also tickets for cloth and clothing. It cost a point. He paid his point and got his star. Then, shortly after it was sown on, he ripped it off so as to move about freely. Clément's voice is steady, neutral, then changing to a doleful tone, as images of others emerged through his speech. The transformation of the status of Jews would have been in 1940, which pertained to an anti-Semitism that predated the war. There were fights in the school, Avenue Parmentier: Jews vs. anti-Semites. It left its mark.

Clément explained to me that a little later, his mother was taken during a roundup by the French authorities, which I inferred, later confirmed for me by Clara, that it was during *La Rafle du Vélodrome d'Hiver* (The Vel' d'Hiv Roundup) of 16 July 1942. His mother told him to go and hide in the cellar until they were gone and then to go and find his aunt. With the help of one of his mother's sisters, Clément got to Arcachon. His brother had already been sent away to the Sarthe, to go and work on a farm. From Arcachon his aunt told him to sneak through the border to the free zone: he snuck through in the firebox of a train, coming a hair's breadth from getting caught, then went to a Lyon suburb to live with friends of his parents. The Germans then invaded the free zone, and he had to go to Isère to live with other friends of his parents; taken on as a farmhand, he worked for a year and to that day still received a retirement pension of twenty-nine euros a month, a fact told with a composite affect of pride and aloofness. His mother had three sisters, one of whom, the youngest, took him under her wing; she was the one whom his mother told him to go and see when the meeting was raided. Another sister left Poland for Australia in the early 1930s.

And his parents, did he hear anything about them after 1942? Clément replied only indirectly. After the war the Hôtel Lutetia, which had been the Nazi Kommandantur during the war, became the center for welcoming back those who had been interned in concentration camps. He left alone for Australia in 1947.

As I was listening, I was mainly, simply, trying to follow the story that I was being told; nevertheless, as I listened, I was noting how this narrative was a response to my request for Clément, as a man in his late eighties, to put his request in the context of his life. He was the one who found the starting point: the violence of not knowing his grandparents; the loss of his parents, which he never stated directly, showing rather than telling me of their murder through the juxtaposition of facts and narrative elements; the evident presence of ambiguous knowledge about his parents' deaths; their absence from the Lutetia and his subsequent departure.

Clément explained to me how he became a doctor in Sydney and then specialized as a psychiatrist, returning to France in the late 1950s. I listened as he narrated his career as a psychiatrist, in particular his role, thanks to his fluency in English, of bridging French and Anglo-Saxon movements. Of crucial importance is that he went to work at the St. Alban psychiatric hospital in the Lozère. He narrated this without special emphasis, but it seems to me to be far from a random chance that he found a job there: during the war it had operated not just as a psychiatric hospital but also as a sanctuary for a number of resistance fighters, conscientious objectors, intellectuals, and surrealist artists.

The hospital at St. Alban was well known as a setting in which *psychologie institutionnelle* was developed and, in particular, under the leadership initially of Francis Tosquelles and the participation of Jean Oury, who would then found La Borde; it was a setting in which experiments with transversal forms of responsibility were encouraged, and the dynamics of the entourage and the ill person were taken into account. Clément explained the general approach of the institution, namely that the mentally ill depend to a great extent on their milieu, and by acting on the milieu, one could try to render the milieu more humane and give people responsibilities, banal quotidian responsibilities: "It's a school of thought."

Did he recognize himself in it?

"Not totally. It's heavily psychoanalytic. Psychoanalysis is fine for people who are well but not for the mentally ill. Psychoanalysis invades everything now," he said, looking at me pointedly, "including anthropology." American psychoanalytic authors influenced him, though, people such as Eric Fromm, Harry Sullivan, Milton Erikson. French psychoanalysis, as he put it, was really not his cup of tea.

We discussed his implication with the ADMD (*Association pour le droit de mourir dans la dignité*). He had become a member in 2001 and organized and animated a *"group d'entre-aide"* (support group) for ADMD members, first in Bordeaux, and then when then they moved to Cherbourg to be closer to Marguerite, his eldest daughter, he set up a new group in the region. The idea was for these groups to be practical support networks: a space to talk, certainly, but also a practical network, if any one person needed help to end her or his life, among the members the idea was to procure enough of certain medications to enable the person to die, as she or he would like. In fifteen years of its existence only one member of either group ended her life, and it was not with the help of the group; she was a doctor and had her own supply, and she did not discuss the decision with the group.

Clément's wife, Odette, had been a member of ADMD as well. She was diagnosed with a primary liver cancer and was cared for at home; she did not end her life voluntarily. The process and timing of her death was marked by a particular event, which Clément returned to many times subsequently. Odette was being visited by a home palliative care team. Once it became clear to them that she was dying, they sedated her. The next morning the nurses came and woke her out of the sedation in order to bathe her. Years later Clément is still disgusted by the memory. Marguerite and he had angrily demanded that they sedate her a second time, up the dose, and not wake her again. She died thirty-six hours later.

Given the story of his wife and the active role his daughter took, recalling that she is a medic, wouldn't Marguerite be willing to help him as well, if it came to that, at home? Yes of course, he replied. Marguerite had said as much, and she said that she didn't want him to go to Switzerland. She avoided discussing it beyond that, except to say that if he stayed at home, she promised to make sure he died peacefully. I asked Clément whether he could imagine dying any other way than through assisted suicide. Yes, of course, he replied, in his deadpan tone, he could; but he didn't want to.

I tried returning to this question a number of times, trying to understand what the specificity of dying in this way was for Clément. For example, I asked whether there was something specific about the mechanism, the fact that it was a suicide and not an act that is ultimately performed by another person, say a doctor. Or else, whether the gesture mattered, the position and posture in which he would die. He waved his hand, dismissing the idea, telling me that it's a "fetishization" of the act, "like with the obsession about final words." What is important, he said, is what happens before and after.

ANNOUNCING THE LINK

In the evening Pascal walked me back to the station, telling me that he was pleased that Clément had agreed to my request, that I could follow him until the end. Clément had gone as far as to say he thought it would be good for Pascal not to be alone on the way back. In Pascal's view my visit had allowed Clément to tell certain things that he hadn't said before and was a means of objectifying and thus rendering more manageable some of Clément's anxiety.

I told Pascal that I didn't really understand how, on the one hand, Clément could be so insistent that he wanted to die in one way and one way only and, on the other hand, claim that the actual gesture, the actual mechanism, is of no importance. Pascal replied quickly, offering an explanation for the slow anthropologist who after nine hours still didn't get it: Clément's parents were captured and sent to Auschwitz. It's marked his whole life and will mark his death.

What kind of a statement or speech act is this? How to integrate it into the endeavor to try to understand Clément's search to give a particular form to his death? The narrative of Clément's parent's death, his subsequent escape, journey to Australia, and return to France is transformed from a narrative of "context" to an active element in making sense of the present.

We have in this scene three positions: the narrator (Clément), the receiver of the narrative (Anthony), and the interpreter (Pascal). The interpreter "announces" the link between a search for a form given to dying and a prior death. Pascal, it seems to me, in the position of announcing the interpretive link between two deaths, makes a claim to an interconnection in the imaginary of his father, an imaginary in which he shares and participates: Pascal's image of his grandparents' deaths, and of the signifying link to his father's own search for a form to give to dying, was produced through talking and listening to his father, to what was said, and perhaps also not said, about his paternal grandparents; but then also, necessarily, this imaginary also comprised the images he associates with the word *Auschwitz*, a word never uttered by Clément to me.

Perhaps more to the point, Pascal was incited to produce the series of images, of his father's wish to end his life, relative to his parents (and his grandparents) in this way, in reply to a question from an anthropologist who had failed to enter that "imaginary." I use the term *imaginary* in the sense of a "type of apprehension" through homeomorphism, which is to say, apprehension through topological transformation, or topological equivalence, that can take the form of repetition with differentiation. Put a third way, to enter an "imaginary" as a way of apprehending an action is to be able be to see how two events separated in time transform the arrangement of a set of shared elements.

My own capacity to understand what I was participating in became tied to a range of images and their arrangement in narrative—images that included a kind of fantasy of Clément's parents' deaths, but not only. It included also a range of fragments, partial images: the image of Clément as a thirteen-year-old boy, who to move about freely as a Jew in Paris in 1942 paid a point to get his star but then ripped it off—ripped off "the sign," the signifier—to move freely; an image of someone who, when he was about my age (mid-thirties), was explicitly opposed to psychoanalytic theory yet worked in a highly experimental setting, drawing on some pragmatic aspects of *psychologie institutionnelle*, such as work on the milieu, work in and on groups, as well as family therapy, while also rejecting the form and language of "French psychoanalysis"; an image of someone who within the psychiatric field had helped bring Anglo-Saxon approaches to family therapy into France and whose eldest daughter had for the most part cut off contact with him; images, moreover, of someone who for fifteen years, in his seventies and eighties, organized discrete discussion groups first in Bordeaux, where he and Odette lived, then in Cherbourg, for people who wanted to choose the timing and manner of their death; the image of a person who did not want to die any other way.

As such we have the observation of a heterogeneity of images within which to consider not only how Clément wished to lead and leave his life but also what it was that he was leaving—a question relative to which a purely medical or physical answer is inadequate.

SEARCH FOR A GREEN LIGHT

Typically, when a file is received by *lifecircle,* the file is reviewed first by Dr. Erika, who gives a general assessment; for example, if it pertains to a terminal illness with a relatively short prognosis, as is the case in ALS or advanced cancers, then the "green light" is usually given automatically, and the person then needs only to write to the association, pay the relevant fees in the case where the person can afford to do so, and agree on a date. The association allows for assistance in cases where individuals cannot afford the fee, paid for by a counterpart foundation, Eternal Spirit.

For people who are not automatically given a green light on the basis of their initial application, continuation of the process can happen in one of two ways: either the go-ahead is given on the basis of further written exchanges (email), with further explanation of the nature of the person's suffering, sometimes expressed by way of medical reports—the physical situation, for example, may have deteriorated—or else the person is given a *provisional* green light on the basis of the documents exchanged, which gives the individual the possibility of asking for a date. In practice, the distinction between being granted a provisional green light and a nonprovisional green light on the basis of documents is moot to the degree that the medical file and narrative must in both cases be sufficiently convincing for the association such that a date is given to the person. Then, regardless of which kind of green light has been granted, there are two medical interviews: one with Erika and one with an independent doctor, either of whom can veto the request if the person does not fulfill the basic legal criteria, to wit, having mental capacity, having the physical capacity to perform the act, and ensuring that the choice is not the result of external pressure—that is, that any of the people who are helping are doing it for selfish reasons (e.g., reasons pertaining to getting money).

I returned once again to Cherbourg at the beginning of May, and again Pascal picked me up at the station. He looked worried and tired. His first concern was what he considered a lack of clarity about the procedure at the association: at what point is a decision made as to whether Clément can do it or not? Pascal said that as the threshold approached, it was getting more and more uncomfortable for him. He was worried about whether he was doing the right thing, helping his father with this: "We're like pioneers. This is uncharted territory."

Clément had written to *lifecircle* to ask "for a date" and was given one: 23 May 2016. But what was the date for? What had he asked for? What did he want? This was as much my question as Pascal's and Clément's himself. They were just as uncertain as I, as to what would happen on the 23rd.

We went into his apartment, and Clément was standing, waiting for us. The first thing he asked me was, "What actually happens? Have you been to Basel before?"

I told him that I had not yet followed a situation to the end. He was surprised and looked disappointed. As he understood it, there were two possibilities: "One is that we have this meeting with Erika; then in order to do the voluntary assisted dying, I need to see two more doctors. The other [possibility] is that we have this meeting with Erika; then I see one more doctor."

I replied that, as I understood it, meeting with Erika on the 23rd is the first meeting with a doctor. Then if he is ready, he has a second meeting with the "independent doctor." Then after that, if all parties are in accord, it is the meeting for suicide. The *lifecircle* brochure explains the following:

> The Member of *lifecircle* presents a request for Assisted Voluntary Death [AVD] to the trustees of the Eternal SPIRIT Foundation. They will decide whether the reason for the application meets the guidelines of the foundation and they eventually forward the documents for further assessment to a Swiss physician. This Swiss physician will assess the request on the basis of medical reports enclosed, and after two personal discussions with the member. For a person from abroad two detailed discussions with a Swiss doctor are compulsory, during which will be clarified whether the death wish meets with Swiss guidelines. A person from abroad must therefore expect to stay in Switzerland for at least 3–4 days before an AVD can be realized. As soon as the Swiss doctor gives the o.k., an appointment can be scheduled for an AVD within one or two days.

What was thus unclear to Clément and Pascal was which roles Erika, the person with whom he was in contact, the president of the association, fulfills. Based on what I knew about the association, it was relatively clear to me that Erika is the internal doctor at *lifecircle*, and she collaborates with only one or two doctors external to the association. The limited number of collaborators is not willed but imposed, since very few physicians are willing to collaborate, although many send her their patients.

A key concern for Clément was about being able to arrange the suicide at very short notice. In early May he had asked for a meeting with Erika not because he was ready to end his life but because he was anxious to know how it would happen, with whom it would happen, where it would happen, and what it would look like. At the same time, at least discursively, he was weighing risks: the risk of hospitalization against the risk of not being able to get a date for suicide fast enough. This was the knot that he wanted to untangle with Erika. When I expressed this to Pascal, Pascal insisted that if this is the first meeting in which he would (potentially) get the official green light, then it was possible that Clément would decide then and there to die, which is to say to have the second meeting with the external physician and to request an assisted voluntary death. He was apparently capable of rash decisions, Pascal told me.

Although I didn't know Clément very well, I thought it unlikely he would request to die as early as May. I knew that Pascal and his partner were finishing building works on their house in order for Clément to be able to move in with them, and I could see that Clément was principally concerned with clarifying his position in relation to at least three elements: his own feeling and judgment of his own vital capacity, the association's judgment about his case, and the possible timing of the suicide.

I talked with Marc-Antoine a few days later, summarizing the situation, and I took note of his thoughts: "You say you are 90 percent sure he won't do it, but isn't it more like 50/50? This isn't the normal situation. The normal situation is where the person says, 'I'm sure,' and then the first meeting is to test the reality of that assuredness. This could be the reverse situation: that he says he is unsure and that in the situation the doctor will see/hear that he is ready. Perhaps he is waiting for Erika to announce what he desires?" We agreed that one of the things to look out for would be attention to relief or disappointment on the way back from Basel, if he came back with us.

TO BASEL, FOR THE FIRST TIME

I took the train an hour or so southeast of Paris, toward the Dourdan forest, *ma campagne*, Pascal would say. It was misty and raining. Pascal picked me up and drove me to the house where he lives with Caroline—a five-centuries-old farmhouse, passed down through the generations of Caroline's family. We passed his neighbor working in the allotment that adjoins the stables. Entering the house, I noticed that the ground floor was still under construction; Clément's room was to be the one to the left, as we entered—the same room in which Caroline had held her mother in her arms, as she died from a long illness. We walked up the narrow turning wooden staircase. Clément was sitting at the table. He took a little coffee and some juice. There have been a few problems: the nephrologist doubled his diuretic dose. He felt terrible and frankly wasn't sure he'd be able to make the trip: the drive from Cherbourg to Paris, and then Paris to Basel. The nephrologist didn't say anything, but clearly the size of the dose was not a good sign. Clément maintained that a doctor is always more optimistic than is warranted. He begins to fiddle with his hearing aid and puts in a new battery. He went to get ready.

While he was out of the room, I was told that Clément had met Caroline's three-year-old grandchild for the first time the previous day, and her children asked Clément for more time, a few more months, so as to be able to spend time with him and to say goodbye properly. Everyone was worried that he would leave quickly. He promised nothing. We packed the car, and I suggested Clément sit in the front, as it is more comfortable. Pascal intervened: "One of you has to go in the front, I'm not a taxi." Clément went into the back so we could talk; otherwise, I would be talking into his left (deaf) ear. We talked for most of the seven-hour journey. I kept glancing back to check on him, expecting him to fall asleep, but he was awake. We stayed in the same hotel, about 10 km outside of Basel on the French side of the border. We had dinner together: the mood was not tense but not joyous either.

There was a neutral calm. In the morning I went for breakfast at around seven; Clément was asleep in the armchair in the lounge. Pascal joined me, and we talked; he was anxious and said that all he wanted was just to go home. "I wonder if Erika is going to be able to provide him with what he is looking for?" Pascal said.

"What is he looking for?" I asked.

"Well he is anxious, and I think he hopes that Erika can reassure him." The anxiety seemed to stem from not knowing what the situation would be, meaning what sort of rapport there could be between Erika and Clément, and what she would be willing and able to say to him.

Clément woke up and looked over toward us. "I would like to go shopping. I would like to buy a Swiss army knife for the children."

"Ok. I don't know if we will be able to find that," Pascal called back, annoyed. Clément went off to the front desk to find out. "I told him before we left: no tourism." We followed.

Holding a blue Post-it note, Clément turned toward us, looking very pleased. "It's in Basel," he said smiling.

"We have to get petrol first," Pascal replied, dry. "It's now 10:30 a.m. or so. The meeting is at 3 p.m." We got into the car and drove to Basel.

"It's a funny present to give, right? From someone who is considering ending their life?" I said to Clément.

"Don't get started with interpretations," he cut me off instantly.

Getting into Basel in the morning turned out to be easier than getting back across the border to the hotel so we could eat something before the meeting with Erika in the afternoon. We found somewhere to eat with just enough time to go straight to the meeting. A tense edginess had set in among us.

We eventually arrived at the address. Quickly it became apparent that this was Erika's home, which Pascal and Clément had not appreciated. She greeted us at the door, and an awkward moment ensued in which Erika confused me for Clément's son and Pascal for the anthropologist.

We stood in her hallway, while she thought about what to do. I saw an elderly man in the kitchen, shuffling about. "This is the father of my boyfriend. My boyfriend, Marco, will be doing some works, so perhaps it is better if we go downstairs. English is ok?"

"Yes English is ok," Clément replied.

Pascal and I approached the stairs together. "After you," he said.

"No please, he is your father."

"I am only the driver."

I went ahead, and I whispered in Clément's ear, "Would you prefer for us all to speak in French? He nodded and I told Erika. Downstairs we sat, the four of us, around a table in the laundry room, clothes hanging to dry, while the sound of drilling drifted in. Pascal and I presented ourselves briefly.

Erika explained quickly her background, as well as how she began the association. "Now I am going to take notes: you are going to tell me why you wish to die," she said to Clément.

"Ok. There are principal reasons and ones of secondary importance. Since September of last year, I had heart failure, which manifested as exertional dyspnea, and thus my capacity to walk has been severely reduced; [I also have] bilateral pleural effusions and chronic renal failure. Here are my laboratory reports from last week. Since September, I have had a cardiac marker, which should be 5,000, but it was at 10,000. With diuretic treatment it went to 4,000, and two months later [i.e., ca. January, when Clément began seriously inquiring into the possibility of doing an assisted suicide] it went back up to 8,000. Last Friday the nephrologist upped the dose again, but after two days I couldn't bear it any longer, and so I stopped. So, I also have intestinal problems: the descending colon was removed following a cancer; the operation was conducted in time, but for reasons of vascularization, more was removed than anticipated. This was twenty years ago. In 2000 everything was going fine, but then I had a lymphoma. I was really in bad shape. I was well treated at the St. Louis hospital in Paris, but the Cisplatine [a chemotherapy medication] damaged the kidneys. I had several relapses in 2007. I wanted to bring you the nephrologist report, but they haven't prepared it yet. . . . So there we are, in four days, since Friday, I lost 3.5 kg—it's water—clearly with all of this I have low blood pressure. I can't walk straight: one would think I'd had a little too much schnapps to drink!"

"Do you have pain?" Erika asked.

"No," Clément replied categorically.

"So for you the main issue is the renal problem."

"And lungs and heart failure."

The pair began to discuss advances in the medical field around the use of diuretic for treating heart failure. As was then often the case with Clément, he took the occasion to explain the research that he had engaged in on the subject of euthanasia and assisted suicide, the works he had translated, and the relations he entertained with key figures in France and the Netherlands.

"We're going to give you a date. What do you think? When do you want to come?"

"It's difficult to say. I live alone. My daughter lives in the same city, but I see her only once a week, on a Sunday. She works a lot. She gets home late. She has a handicapped daughter. I have friends who come by every now and then, but the evenings I am alone. Her daughter is a little bit more autonomous now. She learned to walk a few years ago—she is eighteen now—but it is a lot of work."

"So you are saying that you still have obligations?"

"What do you mean?"

"Ummm, making the most of the grandchildren," Erika said, a little unsure.

"No, not really. . . . I can't look after the handicapped child. As for the other children, one is in Paris, studying in a *Grande Ecole*, and the other is thirteen. I don't see him very often either. Pascal visits me regularly."

"It's difficult then for you to say when is the right date?"

"That's for sure."

"No one else can tell you when is the right date."

"Yes. The reality is—all week I am alone. Now, I tried to find solutions, for example in senior residences. Materially it's fine, but I came to the conclusion that these are places for people of the third age [the young old] as opposed to the fourth age [the old old]. I tried living in one of these residences, but the affective connection was difficult to establish. And then I had the cardiac problem. And since September my son drives 400 km each way every other week to look after me. He is doing works to the downstairs of their house, so I can move in. The works have been going on since . . .," he trailed off.

"January," Pascal piped up.

"What?" Clément asks.

"January," he repeated.

"You saw the two old people upstairs; they are the parents of my partner, ninety-one and ninety-four. They began living with us three years ago; they were much less in shape then. Now they have the garden. But he fell twice, so we're doing works so they can stay here with us."

Turning to Pascal, Erika continued: "Since you have the opportunity to welcome your father to your home, it will be all the more difficult for you when he leaves?"

"No."

"No?"

"No. It's a passage. We are very pleased to be able to welcome him and to be together, but when the time comes, I will drive him [here]."

"From the moment that you give me the assurance that it suffices to call you, then I am reassured," Clément said.

Erika gave him an example of a woman in Paris whom she had promised to help, and when it got very bad toward the end, she phoned her, worried that it was too late, but Erika helped her organize an ambulance and she was able to go to Basel and ended her life there. "That way you can carry on living for as long as possible. Rest assured that we can always find a solution."

The pair shook hands. Clément had gotten what he came for: a promise.

EVENT AND GESTURE

Clément was given the "green light" by Erika on 23 May 2016; his request had thus been accepted, and he could then subsequently ask for a date when he felt ready. Pascal and his wife, Caroline, had been renovating the downstairs portion of their house since late 2015, after Clément's turn for the worse, so that he could move in with them. The plan was that he would do so as soon as the works were finished, with the idea of spending *la belle saison* (summer) together, in the countryside of the southern region of the Ile-de-France.

In fact, two weeks after his request was accepted, Clément asked for a date to end his life; the first available was Monday, 27 June. I had no contact with Clément and Pascal during these two weeks, and I was surprised, when I wrote to him to see how he was doing, that he had just made the request. When we talked, it was clear that Clément was concerned about his multiple major organ problems, liver and heart in particular, and that he was very concerned about the possibility of stroke, which would render him, in his terms, at the mercy of the medical corps, which he did not want.

Yet there was another factor that seemed to be tied up with the request for a date, and the seeming rush.

After Clément's meeting with Erika in May, we left her house where the encounter had taken place and we all got into Pascal's car. Clément, sitting in the backseat, took out his phone and called his friend Alice. On the phone he learned from Alice, a very old friend, that she had a metastatic cancer that was spreading rapidly. He was distressed, pointing out the injustice and what he called the "irony," that he had just been able to travel to Basel to have a meeting where he had been promised a way out, when Alice would need the same much more urgently than he would.

Clément then immediately wrote a message to the association to inquire on behalf of his friend whether she might be able to be assisted by the association, a request whose difficulty was compounded by the fact that Alice's husband suffered from Alzheimer's disease and was completely dependent on her. Clément, fearing that the association would not be able to help, set about trying to get hold of the necessary medications for Alice to be able to take control of her death if necessary. It was a week of great stress, and amid this stress Clément contacted the association to ask for his own date. I would learn when we met again in Cherbourg that, in fact, Alice was a friend from childhood, whose parents had helped him escape from occupied Paris. He felt he owed her his life. It seemed to me that he wanted to help her escape just as her family had helped him escape.

I also later learned that after returning from Basel to Cherbourg, Clément and Pascal had become worried that there was something fishy with the association: what had initially been taken to be signs of Erika's commitment, that the meeting took place at her home (with laundry drying around us) became worrying signs that perhaps it was a scam. Pascal explained that Clément had written to Erika and that she had not replied for a number of days, and during that period there was a great deal of anxiety about the authenticity of the association, assuaged, he told me, only to a degree by the fact that a researcher from the CNRS had accompanied them. Fears were allayed, finally, when Clément was given his date.

Clément, Pascal, Caroline, and I agreed to meet at a hotel just outside of Basel on the evening of 25 July. On arrival I went straight to the restaurant and saw Clément and Caroline sitting together: I asked where Pascal was. Clément had forgotten his passport, so his son had to drive the 1,000 km to Paris and back. "He forgot one of the bags," Clément said, laconic and smiling. "He will be back here tomorrow afternoon." He smoothly changed the subject: "You know, the one thing that would stop me going through with my project on Monday is if Erika hired me, to work with her to put in place a method for the psychological preparation of assisted suicide; to find methods to help prepare those involved, members of the family as well." I took the occasion to ask about how his final conversations with his daughters went. "With Marguerite it went well. With Natasha, well, as I've told you before, what happened is that we saw each other two years ago. I wanted my three children together with me, so I invited them to Italy; she came but did not say very much. The distance began with her changing her name. There was no "event." One day she changed her name. The only thing I could think of was a cult. I gave her the name of my mother, you know." I had not known this.

Caroline leaned over and touched Clément's arm. "You shouldn't reproach yourself Clément," she said.

"This has nothing to do with reproach. I didn't shove anything down her throat, repeating stories about my mother; on the contrary, if there is a reproach, it is of myself, for not having said more about her." We finished dinner and said goodnight.

The next morning, Clément and I were sitting together, waiting to see a doctor sent by the association. He wasn't sure what to expect. "How do you feel?"

"Not bad, but I have to play the role of the patient. I can't tell him that everything is fine. I will say as little as possible. I am surprised to be so calm about it. If something happened to the doctor and he wasn't able to come today, if it had to be delayed, it wouldn't have to be now. But that doesn't mean that I'm indifferent. It's normal to have doubts. My parents lived until age forty-two. I am in a special situation now; it is paradoxical. I want to die in good health, and pursuing this possibility, I find myself becoming creative, and this itself would be a reason, if there wasn't a negative side, not to do it. [By 'negative side' I inferred he meant the risk of stroke or of vital organ failure that would mean hospitalization.] It's a test [*épreuve*]: listening to myself, it seems weird [*incongru*]; at one time I would have found myself weird [*incongru*]. But it's a question of preparation: I am so well prepared that it has no effect."

Minimally, let me pick out several elements: the range of images I have already narrated (of Clément at different moments in his life); of the bag left behind; the question of reproach vis-à-vis his daughter, and Clément's self-image as well-prepared to die but also of his qualification of his decision as paradoxical, given that he both wants to die (in good health) and feels creative, that there is work for him to do with respect to this practice.

We arrived at the premises of *lifecircle* in Liestal, a rented apartment in an industrial zone: "romantic," Clément joked, deadpan. A metal staircase ascended to the entrance of the apartment: a corridor faced a kitchenette and led to the right toward a room with a bed and a salon area, further along, where the paperwork was signed and a few more jokes were made. Clément took off his sunglasses and gave them to Pascal:

"No need for these where I'm going."

"You don't know that," Caroline said.

"Nor for this," he handed Pascal his hat.

"Well, Pascal, thank you for being there since September. . . . Try to put things . . . with Natasha . . . tell her that it is what I wanted."

"Yes papa."

The intravenous drip was set up; Clément sat back into the reclined medical bed. Erika inserted the needle and tested the apparatus with saline solution. Clément was quiet, smiling. I felt a slightly numb neutral affect in the room.

Erika explained that her brother would make a little film of him, for the police. She asked him to state his name and to say what will happen if he opens the tap: I will fall asleep. She asked him to say more explicitly what will happen. He told her that he will die. Pascal took a picture. Clément waved him away, to say, stop that.

"You asked me to do it."

"A last word?" Clément said to Erika.

"Yes."

"Thank you Erika, very much. I would have liked to do what you do" [*j'aurais aimé faire ce que vous faites*].

Clément was sitting on the bed, lying back into the pillows. He was serene, smiling. His left arm extended, perpendicular to his body, out of which the intravenous drip (IV) spiraled. His left leg was extended, his right leg bent at the knee, his right arm relaxed behind his head. Erika and her brother sat on a small couch near the intravenous drip. Pascal and Caroline stood by Clément's legs. Erika told Clément that if he is ready to die, he could open the tap on the IV, which he did. I stood a meter behind Caroline and Pascal. Looking on, I thought he looked an image of *otium*.

"I'm leaving" [*je pars*].

Pascal went to hold and stroke his left foot, and Erika stroked his head.

DESIRE FOR INTERPRETATION (IS NOT AN INTERPRETATION OF DESIRE)

Five months later, in November, I returned to Pascal's home. He showed me the downstairs area of the farmhouse, still unfinished, where Clément would have stayed. "He could have waited, you know." Pascal did not look in great shape:

> These last months, I've been haunted by the last words of my father. He didn't even tell me that he loved me. The first two months I slept really well, better than I'd slept in years, but during the day it was awful. I felt terrible. Now I'm better during the day, but I can't sleep at night. The big event was that I saw my sisters, and after seeing them, I was worried about what I would tell you: you had affection for my father; that's why I'm worried. Marguerite insisted on the fact that he didn't need it; he didn't need to do an assisted suicide [*strictement aucune nécessité*]. He could have just stopped taking his medication, and it would have been the same effect. As she said, it was his malign pleasure to stage his end of life [*un malin plaisir de mettre en scène sa fin de vie*]. It was the final element in his perverted game, just as when we were children, there always had to be one child excluded, always secrets.

As I understood it, the way to apprehend that two children were excluded was that Marguerite was the excluded one, the counterpart to Pascal's inclusion—good son / bad sister, a narrative which was heavily present leading up to the death; Clara / Natasha by contrast figured as the child who had countered the transference of her father by refusing, and thus escaping, the supposedly perverted game. The proof of the transference, in the sibling narrative told by Pascal, was precisely that they only found out the name of their grandparents by chance, as adults, when Pascal had to make a copy of the *livret de famille* [official family record book] for an administrative reason. Pascal thus confirms what his father said at dinner with Caroline and me, that he hadn't said much about his parents, and this then became evidence, for Pascal, of the problematic transference that led to his sister fleeing the family circle. "He chose a death that resembled that of his parents but which he controlled," Pascal continued. "Even down to forgetting his passport: this was something that would happen every time we tried to go away, go on holiday, cross a border. There would be some problem; he'd forget something, his passport or wallet, which meant we'd have to go back." As Pascal talked, I had in mind the image of the boy hiding in the firebox of the train, the child who was almost caught.

At the same time, the traumatized boy was also the experienced psychiatrist and the activist for choice at the end of life, and precisely the creativity and the paradox that Clément described was the desire to help others escape from situations that they don't wish to be in, to work on methods for helping prepare families with the event of this kind of death, the conditional tense of his last statement to Erika—I would have liked to do what you do—inflecting hope with his own principle of reality, that not leaving life at that moment would risk dying in another way; indeed, one could push the interpretation further and say not only was it an expression of gratitude and a wish to be able to repay the gift in kind but also even a critical reflection on the work that remains for the future of this practice, that precisely because of the difficulty of preparation for dying, not only for the person concerned but for those left behind, he wished he could live to do what Erika is doing.

The difficulty of preparing oneself and one's friends and family is, furthermore, all the more pressing given that (as Clément knew as well as anyone) words and images live on and necessarily get reinterpreted. He knew that he couldn't control whether we were to remember the child in the firebox or the figure of the incongruously prepared father, ready to leave life. Desire has its interpretation and each interpreter his or her own desires and fantasies.

Florian

A little after meeting Clément and Pascal, I came into contact with a young man named Florian, from Rouen. When I say he was a young man, what I mean is that we were born the same year, 1983. Our encounter began in May of 2016 and ended in late October of the same year, before he then ended his life with the assistance of *lifecircle*, in Liestal in the canton of Baselland in February of 2017.

Without knowing exactly how, I have felt that this encounter was a disappointment in that I tried without success to live up to an image or standard of both ethical and scientific conduct within the confines of the situation with Florian. There was a tension between these two kinds of injunction that led me to break off contact with him, precisely for ethical and scientific reasons, letting him down, while simultaneously continuing to follow his story through the work of two others: Dr. Erika and Françoise, a journalist who had begun in early September of 2016 to make a film partly about Florian.

Unlike other encounters I have had, the one with Florian, and the way it unfolded, has left me with doubts about my conduct, the conduct of this inquiry, and the conduct of others, including Florian himself, specifically in terms of what relation between knowledge and care is called for in an inquiry such as this one, as well as in a request for assistance, such as the one Florian made. The character of these doubts and disappointments can be better specified, I think, in comparison with what I thought I had achieved in relation to Clément. There are two aspects to the "understanding" that I considered I had achieved with Clément and its character as a contrasting case: I entered a situation in which Clément, in his late eighties, suffering from multiple health problems but none necessarily life-threatening in the short term, was requesting assistance with ending his life. He was undertaking the request with the help of his eldest child, Pascal. Entering the situation meant that I was able to visit Clément and Pascal, at Clément's home, over a period of three months and then travel with them on two occasions to Basel, where Clément ended his life. Subsequently, I would visit Pascal several times, at home, over the course of a year, as he tried to integrate the event of his father's death, albeit with great difficulty. Yet, and this is the second aspect, it was not only the fact of being able to enter the situation and follow it to its end that characterized what I have considered, whether correctly or not, to be the success of the episode of participant-observation; it was, moreover, that in participating, I found myself in a situation in which there were three positions that Clément, Pascal, and I were able to variably occupy: the narrator of a story about Clément's life and his request, the receiver of the narrative, and the interpreter.

In the first place, as a person attempting (wanting) to understand the search for a specific form of death in relation to a narrative told to me by Clement, Pascal was incited to make an interpretation of things his father had said to me, when we were away from him, to help me understand not the narrative per se but rather the undertaking, to die in this particular way, assisted suicide—an undertaking that cannot be explained uniquely by reference to a particular kind or stage of an illness.

Reciprocally, in relation to Pascal's difficulty with and confusion in the aftermath of the assisted suicide, I found myself in a position of wanting to make an interpretation of what had transpired, during the event, in particular an interpretation of something Clément had said before dying, in relation to his prior narrative and Pascal's prior interpretation. In both cases our interpretations turned on the significance of the murder of Clément's parents in the German death camps in 1942 as a way to try to make sense of his determination to die in this particular way. The incitation to interpret was the result of our having been able to occupy variable positions—receiver of narrative, interpreter—then, in turn, in writing about it and talking about it, I have become a narrator of this death, itself subject to reception and possible interpretation.

I use this countercase as a way of trying to determine a difference in my encounter with Florian: to put it succinctly, Florian, a young man then in his early thirties—we were born just three months apart—wanted me to accompany him in his assisted suicide, yet he actively blocked opening a space in which I could take a position in relation to him, a position in which I could receive and think about his wish to end his experience of suffering: he did everything in his power to short-circuit interpretation, while at the same time insisting on being observed.

He wanted me present as an instrument for the realization of his willed death, as a technical means to carry his voice out to others but, perhaps also, simply in itself, to carry his voice, a gesture that might show that he was cared for, that he was loved. What was unacceptable for Florian, however, it seems to me, was for me to be a subject capable of thinking about him and his undertaking. What I think was unacceptable to me was to open myself to his demand for care, a demand that unlike with Clément felt like a consuming and overwhelming demand. In relation to this blockage I refused to comply and refused to accompany him.

In the case of Clément, his son, Pascal, after his death, was preoccupied by the question of whether he had done the right thing. I, however, and I state this as an observation, not as a self-justification, have not once put in question my participation in Clément's death, even though, as Pascal put it to me months later, I was part of the reason his father was able to go through with it, that I facilitated, rendered possible, the *mise-en-scène* of his self-centered drama, as Pascal's sister put it.

The same cannot be said of my relation to Florian. Did I do the right thing, in refusing to accompany him, and was it for the right reasons? In asking this question of myself, I am then led (like Pascal, who asked it of me) to ask it of others who participated and through this basic question to try and understand the variable dynamics and qualities of care, as well as its absence, present in the unfolding of Florian's request for, and ultimate realization of, an assisted suicide.

TO GET TO KNOW

It began with a surprising email. In mid-May of 2016 I was cc'd on an email from *lifecircle* to Florian asking him to contact "Dr. Stavrianakis" so that he can understand that young people, too, are caught in situations of great suffering. The email stated that if he wanted a date, he would need to explain more specifically the evolution of his situation, then to specify his ideas about timing, and how he would make the trip. Underneath, I saw Florian's message from the day before:

My very dear Erika, Never would I thought to have fallen to such a low level of human dignity: torture, this is it, and I live it every day. I have cannulas on the colon, which are sticking out and are visible, and it is unbearable: it hurts physically and mentally, why so much unnecessary prolongation and torture?

I want this to end.

Scrolling further, three emails were below, from the course of April in which Florian explains some technical aspects of the surgical interventions he has had on his bladder and intestines, the nature and degree of his suffering, and Erika's specification of what he would need in order to be able to end his life with the assistance of *lifecircle*, in particular, the presence of "a trusted person" who will be able to accompany him to Basel.

Soon afterward, I received a message from Florian asking me to call him. I inferred that he thought, perhaps with good reason, that Erika would help him only on the condition that he talk with me. On the phone I tried to resolve this by explaining that I have nothing to do with Erika's judgment about if or when she would give him "a date." We spoke four times that first week, in which little by little I both thought I had a clearer idea of what his situation was, and then also felt what little I had thought I had understood slipped away from me. Medically speaking, the name Florian gave to his suffering, and his medical condition, was spina bifida. The elements that he narrated to me, nevertheless, were far from clear. Spina bifida is a birth defect of incomplete closing of the spinal cord and backbone. It basically has two forms, a covered form, which is hidden under the skin, which is usually asymptomatic, and a protruding form, in which the newborn's spinal cord pushes through an opening, resulting in severe health consequences from birth; moreover, in the severe form spina bifida is associated with learning difficulties. As a child Florian had had problems with his spine but did not have a protrusion of the spinal cord out of his back; he had a corset and had multiple periods of hospitalization, leading to several operations on his back and, in particular, a major operation in 2004, at the age of twenty-one. It was then in 2011 that his physical state began to degrade seriously; he had to stop working as a special needs teacher and began having to use a wheelchair, although not uniquely; he could also still walk. The evolution of the illness did not, and still doesn't, make sense to me; neither of the two usual forms of spina bifida seemed to correspond. He had the physical problems associated with the severe form, but emerging very late in life, and moreover, Florian, in my experience, was very intelligent, extremely well-spoken, and erudite, as well as curious and clearly caring. He was also very isolated, angry, needy, and manipulative.

He had first contacted Erika in 2013, and then a year later, his mother was diagnosed with pancreatic cancer. He had been living in Cantal, near Aurillac, with his partner, Olivia, and after his mother's diagnosis decided to move back to his hometown in 2015 to care for her. Olivia decided to move back to the island of Reunion, where she is from. In Florian's terms she left him, but it was a topic he refused to talk about other than to say that she couldn't bear to live with a handicapped person anymore.

I asked him if we could meet at his home and, if possible, talk with his mother about his request: he demurred, saying that his mother was already very fragile and that he didn't want her to have to hear "heavy things"; "besides," he told me, "Erika already called her," back in 2013, which had been a shock to him. "If you come to the house, I will have to explain why you are here," he said. Florian insisted, nevertheless, that she was 100 percent supportive of his wish; it was just that she loves him so much, and cannot tell him to stay, and cannot bear to let him go either.

What seemed to be clear was that he was taking care of her. His time was spent between caring for himself and caring for her: getting ready in the morning could take him two or three hours, principally the irrigation of his ostomy—a hole in the stomach for the removal of body waste—a procedure that for him was extremely painful, owing to what he characterized as a poor outcome of the surgical procedure—something the surgeon agreed to orally but denied in writing, much to Florian's anger.

He had had eight intestinal obstructions over the year, each one resulting in a hospital stay of a month: add to that the regular visits with the neurological team and urological team, as well as occasional other visits, and visits to accompany his mother, and the impression was that Florian more or less lived at the Rouen hospital. He was frequently angry on the phone, rendered through narratives of utter humiliation at the hands of a medical corps that, in his terms, were uncaring, incompetent, and ultimately indifferent. Phone calls were also an occasion to demonstrate suffering: I would systematically be asked to wait a little bit while he did a treatment (*un soin*): this would be accompanied by groans and gasping. At the time it seemed to me important to be able to listen to it; I was probably trying to show him (or was it myself?) that I could withstand his suffering, as well as his anger—that I wasn't made of sugar.

Having said that, by the fourth call that first week, I found myself using distancing devices, which themselves had effects. On Sunday he called me at midday. I didn't pick up. He called two more times within five minutes, and on the third call I decided to pick up. Our young son, three at the time, was on the little balcony in our apartment messing with the plants; as I spoke to Florian, I was also telling Marcel to be careful, to not do this or that with the flowers. Florian understood that I was latently telling him that I have a life, that this is Sunday, that yet another hour and a half on the phone with him comes at a cost to me: this was the starting point for his observation, true in my own judgment, that I am a fortunate person: "you have a life" (*t'as une vie*), he said; "I am a remnant" (*une survie*).

He agreed to meet me but not at his home: we could meet in the foyer at the hospital after one of his appointments; we met in person only twice. The first time we met, I was surprised at how he looked: having been sure that he was one of a series of fragile wasted bodies that passed by in the waiting area, none of whom stopped to see if I was the anthropologist they were expecting to meet, it was a plump, charming, sad person who rolled up in his wheelchair next to me. The affect of sadness, the lilting pathos in his voice, I think, was only partly accounted for by the double patches of fentanyl he wore.

At this first meeting in person, I heard several things repeated from previous talks on the phone and then heard things for the first time that would then be repeated. There was with Florian a sort of discursive repertoire of topics from which he would construct narrative: "Staring at me in the face a urologist dared to tell me: 'Go home, wait until this rare progressive disease eats away at you, grit your teeth and you will know that it has reached its peak when you have your nose in your shit.'"

+ "You probably think I'm exaggerating."
+ "They're proposing another surgery for me, what should I do?"
+ "No matter how humiliating the tests and the interventions I go through, I cry in the car and then I come in the house with a smile on my face."
+ "How can I tell my mother? She understands, but I can't tell her."
+ "I hate going out and going shopping; with my shit bag; I've had enough, enough of all this shit."
+ "Don't you know any vets? You could get the barbiturate solution for me."

This range of things said, moving from anger to self-observation, to a call for care and counsel, for love, recurred over the six months that we spoke, reaching consummate form in a letter he sent to the president of the republic. Initially, I tried to receive the statements, to work with and through them, to give them back to him in a way that might produce some movement in his own thought, something that would then allow me, in return, to understand him better and specifically his wish to end his life in this way. But there was no such movement. I thought that perhaps the only way to produce such movement, and such understanding, was through a third person—hence, my wish to meet his mother.

ACCOMPANIMENT

I explained to Florian that I could go with him to Switzerland only if he had a friend or relative with him as the primary accompanier and in relation to whom I could try to understand his request. He began to talk about a friend, Marc, who would be willing to go with him. They had met in hospital and had had rooms next to each other. The friendship seemed tenuous, something that would later be confirmed, but he needed some placeholder, someone, anyone, who would be able to help him make this happen.

As the summer progressed, the ambivalence and the contradiction, the bind he was in, and that we were in, only deepened. Despite his increasing gastrointestinal and neurological problems, and despite the sequence of requests for a "date," several of which had been agreed on and organized, he nevertheless subsequently decided, each time, not to go through with them, in order to continue to look after his mother. Nevertheless, he insisted on the fact that the only thing he could look forward to was the day when he could end his suffering. Clearly, Florian was ambivalent—and caught.

It seemed to me that Florian thought that the bind he was experiencing, of wanting to end his life, of not wanting to do it alone, and not knowing how to resolve the ties that still bound him in life, could be resolved, or at least held at bay, by my participation.

I made it a condition of our continuing telephone conversations that he understand and reflect on the fact that I could not be the person to occupy the position of the loved one or friend, the person of trust, to help him end his life. He said he understood and then asked me to take him on holiday to London over the summer: the last wish of a dying man. I refused. He must have asked me ten times over two weeks. He was persistent and obstinate to the point of irritating—in his own estimation he had alienated the majority of the medical staff at the hospital in Rouen.

Moreover, his seeming incapacity to "hear" what I was saying was then paralleled by his reductive and closed way of thinking about others. In all of his accounts each character he narrated, with the exception of his mother, and Erika, could really only be grasped as uniquely ethically deficient, sometimes bordering on evil: he narrated the near total isolation of both he and his mother and the near total indifference of neighbors and supposed friends; his ex-wife; a maternal grandmother in Bordeaux so completely indifferent to her kin that she hasn't visited her daughter since her cancer diagnosis; as well as an absent father (who left the family when Florian was a baby): added to these miniature portraits of human beings' ethical shortcomings were those of the medical corps, for whom Florian reserved his ire and contempt.

I would be the first to admit and concur that human beings are capable of significant ethical shortcomings, yet I also know that we are incomplete and inconsistent beings. With respect to each of these people—the doctor, the wife, the grandmother, the friends in Rouen, the father—as I pressed for clarification from Florian, I received only further layers of fog. Even the exact nature of the illness, the diagnosis, and the evolution of the disease began to seem strange and unclear.

I became suspicious: is he lying to me?

Yet all the while, in the fog, Florian was asking me to occupy a proximate position, with a form and degree of care that I was not prepared to give, and he was unprepared to tell me more than a thin story of personal suffering in an evil world. I wanted more than this—care for him would come at a price, a cost of knowing something about him, a price he was unprepared to pay.

The only solution was rupture.

(YET ANOTHER) FILM

In August Florian transformed his bind and the problem of accompaniment: he decided that his death should serve a purpose and decided he wanted media coverage of his death: "I don't want my death to be in vain; things have to change," he would say, indexing the growing political and social problem in France around end-of-life issues. Through Erika he contacted a documentary team and a journalist, Françoise, who was in the process of making a short film about assisted dying. The documentary team had already been following a Belgian Paralympian who was considering euthanasia, and they wanted a second figure to complement and perhaps contrast with her story.

The documentary team became the invested target of Florian's attention from September. At the end of the month he asked Erika for another date, this time in mid-November. His mother, it seemed, had taken a serious turn for the worse. She had several heart attacks after the documentary team and I saw him in mid-September. According to Florian it was the doctors' fault that she had taken such a bad turn, as they had given her an antibiotic contraindicated for her anticoagulants.

Françoise had the impression that if she died, he would want to leave quickly. Indeed, the sense was growing that between Florian, his mother, and Erika, they were managing the timing of his death in relation to his mother's: that it was only once she died that he would be able to leave. But Florian could never articulate this; he did not (could not?) say that he was waiting for, wishing for, his mother's death, and at the same time he insisted that for him, his limit point was 1 May 2017, his thirty-fourth birthday, by which time in any event he would go.

I told Françoise that if Florian could envisage waiting until May, then I saw no reason to accept precipitating the assisted suicide on the basis that his mother would have died, especially since the two things seemed to be so linked. What place is there for his grief?

"What place is there for the fact that once she is gone, he is really alone?" Françoise replied. "He has no one other than this supposed friend, Marc." We agreed that if he got a date, it would be imperative that we meet him. Françoise then asked me if I had considered her request that I be in her film, to be present with Florian during his death, and to be filmed. I refused: the situation was, it seemed to me, becoming close to absurd, arguably perverse: a documentary team, an anthropologist, all ready and waiting to observe but no one to hold him as he dies, assuming his mother either could not or would not go. Moreover, my own initial concerns about the veracity of Florian's narrative were beginning to be echoed by the documentary team: things were not quite as they seemed or, at the least, were opaque.

By October we had been informed that Marc was now an "ex-friend." I made it clear to Florian that if we were going to continue this work together, I would need to talk with his mother, as well as whoever else would be the one to accompany him; I knew to a degree that I was exacerbating his bind. When he demurred again, I told him that I wouldn't be present with him and that I didn't see on what basis we could continue to talk. He then turned his full attention to the documentary team. Françoise would check in with me to let me know how things were going, and Florian still cc'd me on his written communications.

On 23 December Florian wrote to Erika: "I have all the documents necessary and here is the ID card of the one who will accompany me." Marc had made a surprising reappearance. "May I have a date for a voluntary assisted death as soon as possible? Before the end of April I beg you." The same message was present on Christmas Day. The next day, Erika replied that there are no more dates for January, but she was sure that she would be able to arrange an emergency date.

On 29 December Erika replied, asking whether he really wanted to end his life in January, explaining that there is one date left and that he must send her the required documents. She then asked him if he would inform his mother of his decision. He confirmed that this was what he really wanted, but he did not answer Erika's question about his mother. A date was ultimately fixed for 23 February, which gave Françoise and the documentary team time in January to visit Florian and to film him at home.

Things then started to get weird in the first week of the New Year of 2017. Florian wrote to Françoise, explaining about the procedures for the event of the death in Basel, asking her to read the documents sent by *lifecircle*, specifying that the process requires two nights in a hotel, to have enough time to go through the medical visits—"two nights in a hotel, who's paying for it?" he asked. Erika intervened in the barrage of emails from Florian to Françoise, asking him to stop bothering her, as his behavior was generating concern from the team. Finally, a rumor emerged that Florian was, in fact, in the hospital and was about to undergo surgery. Neither Erika nor Françoise seemed to understand what was going on, and certainly, no one had had any news of his mother.

Françoise and the documentary team then visited Florian at home on 15 January to film him. Françoise called me the following morning:

> Are you sitting down? We went to Rouen: turned up at 3 p.m. He then announced that he had a doctor's appointment at six, saying that it was probably not enough time to do the film. We managed to do the interview but still. And then he asked us to drop him at the doctor's appointment, wait for him and then go and pick up some shopping. He is pulling us around by the nose. When we were able to film, one minute he'd be walking up the stairs fine; he would then ask us to film again and then put on a performance of someone in immense suffering and difficulty. After a while, we asked where his mother is, as we'd agreed that we could talk to her; he said she was out, at a physio appointment—physiotherapy for someone with late stage pancreatic cancer?

This only confirmed my earlier suspicions: "What did I tell you, I was 100 percent sure that it was impossible he would let you see her," I said.

"Just wait: you'll fall off your chair: eventually, at around ten, he finally admitted that his mother is dead."

"What?"

"Yes. He only told us after we demanded a telephone number to call her, threatening to get Erika involved if he didn't give it to us. She died on the 18th of November."

"This is insane. What did Erika say?"

"Only one thing: 'I need a death certificate.'"

"He's mad [*il est fou*]."

This last two-bit judgment, of which I am certainly not proud, is nevertheless important because it reveals the degree that I, as a figure at this point on the outside of this configuration, was genuinely troubled. I said as much to Françoise and questioned how *lifecircle* could accept the request of someone who had not told the truth about the death of his mother ("she's at physiotherapy"), especially given its importance in relation to the timing of his own death? For me, to the degree that calling him "mad" was something more than an inappropriate statement, it underscored that I thought, and still think, that his capacity or incapacity to come to terms with his mother's death should have been taken into account in the timing of letting him go.

LETTING FLORIAN GO

The assisted suicide was still supposed to go ahead, and Florian was to be accompanied by a man called Franck, who had been his mother's lover. His mother had asked her lover to make sure at all costs that Florian's supposed friend Marc was kept away from Florian; it transpired that Florian had agreed to give his house to Marc in exchange for accompanying him. Her lover promised to take care of Florian and to make sure that Marc stayed out of the picture. Her lover had been reluctant to get involved as Florian's accompanier, but he was forced to as the only means of keeping his promise.

Florian then had to explain to Erika about his mother's death:

"Erika, I have always been frank and I will continue to be. My mother passed away on November 18, 2016, but the causes seemed suspicious. They were hesitating between her pancreatic cancer or some other reason. They did several autopsies to determine the true cause that turned out to be a cardiac arrhythmia. During all this time, they did not tell me anything because I myself was operated on during these dates, and they did not want to disturb me as soon as I woke up and especially that I had had complications, they preferred to wait and tell me that she was being examined so as not to worry.

I only knew it on the 5th of January when all the steps had been taken and I was in home care, so I believed them. Today, I have a double sadness: my suffering that makes me no longer able to go on, and this long, brutal and sudden grief. I can send you a death certificate if you want. I beg you that this will not change anything. Until that date, I always believed that my mother was alive but was doing medical exams. Is it possible that you can call me because it's important and I've always been honest with you? I need to talk to you and it's so important. It's very important that I talk to you for a few minutes. I hope you will understand."

AN ANTHROPOLOGICAL LIMIT

There is no moral to this story, although there are ethical subjects (a point I will come back to): I've wondered at times whether I should feel vindicated, but I don't. I've wondered whether I should be suspicious of Erika, but I'm not. I've wondered whether I should have scorn for Françoise and the documentary team, to the degree that they knew that what was going on was strange but wanted, needed, to come through with the film they'd been commissioned to make, but again I don't. To the contrary, Erika, Françoise, and Franck, as a configuration, were willing to participate in the act of breaking the bind that Florian found himself in. They were ones who attended to Florian, in the way he demanded.

Did he really not know for seven weeks that his mother, the only person really dear to him, was dead? Was his denial of it part of the bind that this configuration was mobilized to break? Did he keep his mother alive in his mind in order to sustain the bind of his ambivalence? Was it the right thing to do to break the bind and let him go? Perhaps these are the wrong questions to the degree that they are analytic ones. And in any event, I don't have the means to make an interpretation and no position from which to make it. Descriptively, it is the case that Florian, in the end, was able to create a space that corresponded to what he wished for: someone to give him the instrument, someone to watch him without interpreting him, and someone to hold him.

An anthropologist was surplus to requirements.

PART THREE

Ethos, Three Studies

Part 3 is made up of a trio of studies, each of which takes up my experiences in the practice of assisted suicide and configures them with a knowledge domain of the human sciences: first psychoanalysis, then sociology, and finally anthropology. These exercises are not theoretical; that is, they are not in the service of "theory." They have, rather, a dual aim: on the one hand, a conceptual aim, which in a strict sense is part of a search for, but, arguably, not an arrival at, understanding: a testing of the source of concepts (stemming from different knowledge domains), in relation to experience (empirical knowledge), with the aim of seeing whether these concepts can enrich understanding of that experience. On the other hand, there is an aim at the level of the concepts themselves, an aim that can perhaps best be situated within the larger endeavor to forge an anthropology of the contemporary. Given Paul Rabinow's diagnosis of the contemporary as a moving ratio of the recent past, the present, and the near future, a diagnosis that observes and takes up the historicity of an ethos of modernity, two questions follow: what is the modern manner of gauging the ethos at stake in this practice, and, if it is already becoming historical, what is the position from which to take up that manner of gauging ethos "today," a position that produces a relationship, or ratio, between the modern legacy of these knowledge domains and the contemporary problem space of illness, care, and the critical question of the limits to living? I pose this question by taking up two sets of older concepts, the psychoanalytic and the sociological, relative to which the work of an anthropological account can be made visible. This is not to say that this is a battle of the sciences; it is not an argument against or in favor of a specific set of reasoned discourses. As I hope and trust the reader will see, I have a kindred feeling for both psycho-analysis and sociology. The question is rather the Weberian one, already cited at the beginning of the book, of what use a science is, with its concepts, given that science can give no answers to the anthropological questions that ulti-mately remain, for the author and reader alike, questions that pertain to their judgment of such a practice, in the cases presented. In each study I affirm the pertinence of concepts and problems that stem from these disciplines, and then I endeavor to bracket a totalizing discourse about assisted suicide on the basis of the knowledge domain in question. I qualify this undertaking as contemporary to the degree that it is a refusal of the modernist task of both making new and of binding together the contradictory poles of fracture and totalization, the modernist split, whilst claiming that there are elements to be recuperated, cared for, and taken forward from these modern early twentieth-century human sciences. These elements include what became for me a truly fundamental problem, one I did not anticipate at the beginning of the inquiry, of desire: both my desire and the desire of the other, correlated to the concept of narcissism, as a heuristic device for better discerning the phenomenon of repetition and the discourse of control with which I was frequently confronted. A second problem was the sociological one of account-ing for the nonindividual character of virtue, without falling into the trap of having to decide between the cardinal modern vices of egoism and anomie, which by way of a rereading of Durkheim's *Suicide*, allowed me to give a social and sociological sense to the counternormative character of the conduct at stake in the practice. The third and final problem was the anthropological one of how to account for the ethics of the practice without falling into the blind spot of values and ideas, both of which cover over the actuality of ethical work engaged in by the subject, and the place of others in the configuration of that work. Through mobilizing Foucault's problematization of the genealogy of ethics and Barthes's concept of the Neutral, a suspension of semiotic commit-ment, I found a form for my anthropological effort to capture the obstinacy of those who had given me a place from which to contemplate the manner that they sought to give to leaving life, as well my desire to know it.

Desire | Narcissism

In "Contributions to a Discussion of Suicide," a short text published following a session of the Vienna Psychoanalytic Society in 1910 dedicated to the topic of adolescent suicide, Sigmund Freud (1856–1939) summed up the fundamental puzzle of suicide from a psychoanalytic point of view—a view that, at that time and up until the publication of "Beyond the Pleasure Principle" in 1920, considered the problem of suicide in terms of a disruption to the "life-preserving drive" and to "libido," a term that is difficult to define briefly but that can be understood schematically as the dynamic manifestation of mental energy or investments with a specifically sexual character: "We were anxious above all to know how it becomes possible for the extraordinarily powerful life drive [*Lebenstrieb*] to be overcome: whether this can only come about with the help of a disappointed libido or whether the ego can renounce its self-preservation for egoistic motives [*Ichmotiven*]. . . . We can I think only take as our starting point the condition of melancholia, which is so familiar to us clinically, and a comparison between it and the affect of mourning."[1]

If it is the case that from the point of view of psychoanalysis there is a fundamental drive that strives for the preservation of life, what happens such that an "ego," the coherent organization of mental processes, to which consciousness is attached, can go against such a drive? It is worth recalling for the discussion that follows that a basic distinction of mental life between "what is conscious and what is unconscious is the fundamental premise of psycho-analysis."[2] Moreover, while consciousness is attached to the coherent organization of mental processes ("ego"), these processes are also, in large part, unconscious, just as both repressed and latent elements are also unconscious.

As Freud indicates in his remarks from 1910, his reflection on this question will turn initially on the indetermination as to whether going against a drive that seeks to preserve life requires a disruption to, and withdrawal of, the psychic investments that people have made into "objects" (i.e., libido), investments that are sexual in character, or else whether such renunciation can be understood aside from any question of such investments (and associated losses). The question, in other words, is whether the overcoming of the life drive in suicide is ultimately a matter of desire, and the elusive question of the cause of desire, or else whether it could be understood uniquely in terms of reality and pleasure principles, an acquiescence of the ego, and its critical agency, on the rational grounds of the reality principle, to the demands of the id, the psychic entity ruled by the principle of the avoidance of unpleasure.

The question was relevant to Freud's own life, given that he, suffering from advanced cancer of the jaw, asked his friend and physician Max Schur to end his life—a request to which Schur acquiesced. As Schur recounts in his biography *Freud: Living and Dying*, by September of 1939, "it was becoming more difficult to feed him. He was suffering badly, and the nights were miserable. . . . It was an agonizing experience not to be able to alleviate his suffering, yet I knew that I had to wait until he asked me to do so."[3] This turning point, in Schur's account, was marked by Freud's reading Balzac's *La peau de chagrin*, whose hero, Raphaël, like Goethe's Faust, makes a pact with the devil. "Raphaël is given a magic but fatal skin of a wild ass. All his wishes will be fulfilled—but with every fulfilled wish the skin will shrink, and along with it, his life. Raphaël cannot master his wishes and tries in vain to deny them. He cannot master his fear of death, and dies in hopeless panic."[4] The day after finishing the book, Freud took Schur's hand and said, "My dear Schur, you certainly remember our first talk. You promised me then not to forsake me when my time comes. Now it's nothing but torture, and makes no sense anymore."[5] Schur said he would do what was necessary and narrates (a narrative whose veracity has been contested)[6] how he injected Freud with two 20 mg doses of morphine at twelve-hour intervals, soon after which Freud died.

A significance of the timing of the request, and the relation between the request for assistance with dying and the story of the last book that Freud read, *La peau de chagrin*, was laid out by Schur through his investigations in writing Freud's biography. Schur linked the significance of the story of wish fulfillment and its connection with a shrinking skin to a description Freud had made of his dying father in a letter to his friend Wilhelm Fliess, forty years earlier. At that time Freud had written that his father was "steadily *shrinking* towards a fateful date."[7] The tone of Freud's letter to Fliess was one of acceptance, and Schur implies, although he does not expound, that his acknowledgment and acceptance of his father's impending death, his father's shrinking, was of importance in Freud's own acceptance of his death, and his request to Schur.

Perhaps this request is to be understood "merely" as a renunciation of life for egoistic motives, an acquiescence by the rational mind to the "reality" of the situation, impending death, a motive of the ego that has made a rational calculation about the relative costs and benefits, and the unpleasure that is to be experienced by seeing things through to the end. Given what we know about Freud—precisely his obsession with knowing the date of his death, an obsession facilitated by the numerologist Fliess, who himself had predicted (incorrectly) the date of Freud's death through one of his bionumerological calculations—such a claim is not really credible, just as Schur's claim that Freud "had overcome all of his fears, as far as is humanly possible" seems a little too hagiographic.[8] Roy B. Lacoursiere points out that "both Schur's and Anna Freud's reports of Freud's reaction to the novel omit two noteworthy events from the last pages. First, trying to avoid his approaching death, Raphaël asks for and receives from his physician an opiate that renders him unconscious except during a daily meal; and second, Raphaël's death is due to the presence of the woman he loves because he cannot suppress his desire for the childlike, yet maternal, Pauline. If the first event prefigures the manner of Freud's death, the second reflects the role played by Anna [Freud, his daughter]."[9]

Precisely the reason to dig into the psychoanalytic literature is that it has tools for going beyond hagiographic or restrictively rational explanation and sentiment. Peter Gay cites the now well-known letter from Freud to Oskar Pfifster, wondering what he would do when the day came "when thoughts fail, or words will not come." His response: "No invalidism . . . let us die in harness as King Macbeth says." Gay reads Freud's image, no doubt rightly, as the prefiguration of an "old stoic, in control to the end,"[10] a hero in harness, riding onward, toward an end, a determined one at that. Yet it is an open question whether and how such an end, an exit, such a way out, such a death, exemplifies fight or flight, for the person concerned, and those who participate and observe: heroism in b-flat.

Without having anticipated it at the outset of this inquiry, I realized as I listened to people that frequently the phenomenon of requests for assistance with suicide cannot be grasped without entering into the formative experiences of a subject, particularly his or her family relations, losses, and in particular relations to the deaths of family members. It was not that I didn't think that there was a "psychological" aspect to such requests but rather that I had thought I could somehow bracket it.[11] I found myself fascinated by the question of the cause and the truth of the *desire* (to use a term to which I will return) to die in this way. The question of the person's desire, and its sources, was a way for me to think about people's requests, given that the character of the narratives of request for assistance with suicide indicated things about the person's character and biography that could not be restricted to a rational calculation based on the actual or projected medical trajectory of an illness.

PREOCCUPATION

Where did this preoccupation come from? Although people frequently refer to the "obviousness" or "self-evidence" of their decision, sometimes, when they talk a little more, there would be a connection with some *other* event, or *other* person, often a story of loss. Their requests to die voluntarily with the help of others provoked in me a desire to know their desire, the cause of which, I became convinced, has little to do with the frequently expressed reasons in terms of needs. The character of their request or, more accurately, the character of the one who was making the request, I became convinced, was only to a limited degree connected with physical suffering. Such stories of loss were clearly present with Clément, to whom we will return, but there were also intimations in the stories of Peter (his father's death), Fabienne (her son's death, her relation with her mother and daughter, her three fathers, her husband's illness), and Florian (his mother's illness and his father's absence). It was also repeatedly present, however, in many other encounters I had with people to talk about their requests. This repetition indicated to me that I could learn something from psychoanalysis.

From my position as receiver of narrative, as a person in an intersubjective relation with someone narrating her or his life, her or his search for a form to give to leaving life, I frequently had the impression that I was being given elements to understand, or perhaps even *interpret* (another term to which we must return), the request to leave life in this way and hence to interpret that desire. Given the nonreducibility of such a "choice" to utilitarian reason, bio-medical or otherwise, given that no one can "need" a voluntary death, I had the impression that these stories that linked the search for death in the present, to a prior death, was one way in which a person's undertaking of a chosen death, their choice, could be understood rather than merely accepted (or rejected) as a self-evident statement or act.

In what follows, I will first outline two basic psychoanalytic framings for interpreting suicide; these are not mutually exclusive. I will then narrate a series of encounters that seemed precisely to call for something like "interpretation," perhaps even an interpretation that could draw on psychoanalytic tools and yet that seemed to capture perhaps more about my own endeavor, my own desire to grasp their desire, than the person's desire itself. This is not to say that the latter is absent. Rather, it is to say that the contribution of psychoanalytic reflection is, in my view, less an explanatory tool of an individual psyche than a means of grasping the position and practice of the observer, or analyst—not only the anthropologist—in relation to those people he or she is endeavoring to apprehend.

In the encounters that I will narrate, I want to underscore two things: (1) to insist on how by talking with the people who were seeking a voluntary death, their undertaking of the steps toward such a death seemed to turn on the narration of a prior death, of the production of images of a prior death, among other images formed through words and gestures and affects, and shared through language; (2) since the origin or source of "desire" or "wish" will always be open to interpretation, what seemed to require more thought, and analysis, was the role of my (and others') interpretation of the narratives, and hence of the images, connected to the search to die in this way. Rather than seeking to focus on explaining or understanding the desire itself, that is to say the truth of the interpretation, what seemed more important was to grasp why it was important for me, and others, to want to interpret these stories in relation to the wish to leave life in a particular way.

These encounters were moments in which I both saw that the wish to end life provoked interpretation of that wish but that I lacked the means to understand the place of that interpretation in relation to the unfolding arrangement of the practice of voluntarily ending life, a configuration that involved participant-observers (i.e., people who participated and made observations, not only the anthropologist), who sought to interpret desire and who found for different reasons psychoanalytic terms useful or somehow readily available. The point is not to make a judgment about the veracity of the framings, or the status of psychoanalysis as a science, but to share with the reader both the nature of the indeterminations I had about the materials I was receiving from persons I would talk to and why I thought that psychoanalytic interpretation could help me grasp that material and those indeterminations—even if ultimately I will dissent from affirming a strict psychoanalytic reading of the materials themselves.

To put it succinctly, I want to show the necessary but insufficient place of the desire-to-interpret-desire within the unfolding of the request for a voluntary assisted death. To not recognize that discursive and nondiscursive elements furnished by people call for interpretation would be deficient, as though the practice could be reduced either to strategies and power relations or else to self-evident biomedical explanations of pathology; but to propose a totalizing interpretation on their psychic basis is excessive. The challenge was of finding a mean.

The first interpretative framing stems from Freud's writing prior to his postulation of the death drive and pertains to the disruption of libido, characteristic of melancholia, a regression of libido into the ego, and the subsequent sadistic attack of ego on itself. The interpretation in terms of melancholia and sadism will then be supplemented with interpretations in terms of identification and separation that take into account the subject's desire by way of its position with respect to chains of signification, thus drawing on some of Jacques Lacan's reflections on drive.

MELANCHOLIA

Freud considered the psychological mechanisms behind suicide primarily in terms of the pathological condition of melancholia, a condition that could disrupt the life drives and their investments in external objects. His reflections on melancholia were themselves based on his understanding of the more fundamental mechanism of narcissism: "Freud presupposes a primary narcissism of the individual, through which the body is invested with libido, or sexual energy. From this body-reservoir of libido, are emitted secondary investments of objects, and what follows is an apparently reversible coming and going: in love, the object entices almost all the libido: in illness, or in the dream, libido returns to the self."[12] For Freud, in the course of normal life there is a primary investment by the child of libido into the ego, including investment into its "ideals," a source from which libidinal investments go out into objects in the world, and these investments come back to the ego at various times, disinvesting from objects on occasions such as illness and sleep but also on the occasion of disappointments, betrayals, and losses in the object world. The normal process is that some later cathexis (investment of mental energy) of objects takes place. Indeed, Freud pithily defined a person's "character" as "the precipitate of abandoned object cathexes."[13] We are, in other words, what we have loved and lost—including images, ideas, forms, and ideals about what we thought we should be, as well as critical evaluations of the gap between what we have been, what we have loved and lost, and what we thought we should have been (or how we should or shouldn't have loved or lost, or been loved and been lost).[14] Through the role of this critical agency Freud compares and contrasts mourning and melancholia as normal and pathological states, and it is with respect to the function of the critical agency that he can use melancholia as a model for thinking about the act of suicide.

The comparison between these two states or conditions is justified by Freud through the basic mechanism of narcissistic withdrawal of libido from the object world. Not only are both mourning and melancholia characterized by painful frames of mind; they also both index a loss of interest in the outside world, loss of capacity to adopt any new object of love, and a turning away from activity not connected with the (lost) love object. In melancholia, however, he goes on to specify, there is also "disturbance of self-regard" (*Störung des Selbstgefühls*).[15]

In conditions of mourning, detachment (*Lösung*) from the object is accomplished through hypercathexis of memories and expectations of the object. Once the object has been worked through, the ego should be unharmed and can continue to invest in new objects. In melancholia, by contrast, Freud explains the following process occurs:

> An object-choice, an attachment of the libido to a particular person, had at one time existed; then, owing to a real slight, or disappointment coming from this loved person, the object-relationship was shattered. The result was not the normal one of the withdrawal of the libido from this object and displacement of it on to a new one, but something different, for whose coming about various conditions seem to be necessary. The object-cathexis proved to have little power of resistance and was brought to an end. But the free libido was not displaced on to another object; it was withdrawn into the ego.[16]

As such, we have here a mechanism of narcissistic regression that from the mechanical point of view seems to be analogous with dreams and illness. Freud continues, however, specifying something particular about melancholia. Once withdrawn into the ego, this free libido

> was not used in any unspecified way, but served to establish an identification of the ego with the abandoned object. Thus the shadow of the object fell upon the ego, and the ego could be judged by a special agency, as though it were an object, the forsaken object. In this way an object-loss was transformed into an ego-loss and the conflict between the ego and the loved person into a cleavage between critical activity of the ego and the ego as altered by identification.[17]

Typically, a narcissistic regression, as in the example of illness, an example first suggested to Freud by his close associate Sándor Ferenczi (1873–1933), involves investment of the ego, after disinvesting from objects. In the case of melancholia, the point is precisely that object loss becomes a loss suffered by the ego because of identification with the lost object.

Ego loss accounts for the painful mood of melancholia, but in themselves the narcissistic regression and identification with the lost object characteristic of melancholia are not sufficient to explain how the ego can attack itself to the point of death. Rather, another part of object-cathexis, in addition to the part that identifies with the lost object "under the influence of the conflict due to ambivalence, has been carried back to the stage of sadism which is nearer to that conflict. *It is this sadism alone that solves the riddle of the tendency to suicide* which makes melancholia so interesting—and so dangerous."[18] Suicide was thus explained by Freud as a sadistic attack on a lost object identified with by the ego, the love for which was withdrawn onto the ego, allowing the ego to be taken up as an ambivalent object by the critical agency, and then attacked. It is crucial that from a strictly Freudian point of view the attack of the critical agency is a response to an *affect* consequent to loss: "If the love for the object—a love which cannot be given up though the object itself is given up—takes refuge in narcissistic identification, then the hate comes into operation on this substitutive object, abusing it, debasing it, making it suffer and deriving sadistic satisfaction from its suffering."[19] It is necessary to insist on the affective source of the attack, in a classical Freudian reading, as it does not lead necessarily to a discursive interpretation of what is going on within narcissistic regression, in contrast to the Lacanian view that I will lay out momentarily, a view rooted in the significance of (chains of) signifiers.

Although she didn't elaborate the point in this technical language, for one of Clément's daughters his suicide was, at least in part, a means of "getting at her," after she broke off contact with him. And recall his son reporting what his other sister had said, and with which he seemed to agree, that it was a "malign pleasure" that his father took in staging his death. There is thus a secondary question of the precise character of the lost object, particularly in a situation, for example in the case of Clara's interpretation, given that she first bore, and then refused, the name of Clément's murdered mother. On a more affective register, recall the example of Fabienne, whose hatred for her mother is perhaps echoed in the statement, apropos of her daughter, and with respect to the question as to whether she would inform her daughter of her decision, that "she can find out from the television."

Sadism here thus refers to satisfaction dependent on suffering inflicted on an object, but it does not necessitate aggression per se. As such, it is important to distinguish two aspects of sadism: that which pertains to satisfaction and that which pertains to an instinct to mastery, which takes no account of the pain inflicted on the other, characterized primarily by aggressiveness. At its most extreme this sadistic attack on the lost or hated object takes place in at least two possible ways—through suicide, the internalized relation of love is *destroyed*; thus, an aggressive attack on the internalized object, and also in the case of an unconscious relation of hate with an object, an attack on the ego is understood as a mechanism of *revenge*, inflicting suffering.

As such, Clément may not have been necessarily trying to "get at" his daughter; rather, it is possible that his suicide concerned the realization of a revenge phantasy. From a strictly Freudian point of view it would not be absurd as an interpretation of the last thing he said (before saying he was leaving), addressed to Erika, the Swiss German doctor who helped him to end his life: "I wish I could have done what you do." The expression, "I wish I could have done what you do," could be understood in terms of Karl Menninger's classic tripartite figuration of desire for suicide as the simultaneous configuration of the wish to die, the wish to kill, and the wish to be killed.[20] "I wish I could have done what you do" would figure Clément as the one who is looking on, facilitating the ending of life of the other. Crucial to make sense of his son's later statement, that Clément created a death resembling that of his parents but that he controlled, from a strictly psychoanalytic point of view would be a claim to mechanisms of introjection with displacement of the wish to kill, through identification with an external figure, which could be interpreted as revenge for the loss of his parents, an unconscious fantasy tied to dead or dying images in that unconscious.

As Freud's colleague Wilhem Stekel stated at the 1910 session in Vienna, "I am inclined to feel that the principle of talion plays the decisive role here.

No one kills himself who has never wanted to kill, or least wished the death of another."[21]

There are problems with such an interpretation: typically, concerning suicide, interpretation in a psychoanalytic sense is only possible in a situation of an "acting out," a "suicide attempt" as it is sometimes called, in which the subject remains in relation to the range of potentially signifying elements, not only signifiers but also affects, gestures, the unsaid. When the subject is no longer there to interpret, there is a serious indetermination as to what means psychoanalysis has at its disposal for understanding the event.

SEPARATION

In a collection of essays titled *Clinique du suicide*, published in 2004, the practicing analyst Geneviève Morel brought together analysts and commentators to reflect on the phenomenon of voluntary death; all of her contributors are predominantly oriented by the work of Jacques Lacan in their practice. One distinguishing feature of Lacanian work in general, and on the phenomenon of suicide in this case, is the orientation to the phenomenon as an "act" in which to be constituted as an act, and not a behavior, the subject of the act must reconstitute its signifying point. The signifying point, Lacanian analysts are at pains to point out, is accessible to the subject only with great difficulty. Indeed, Morel shares with the reader her experience as an analyst in which, systematically, individuals who have tried to end their lives, and who for different reasons were thwarted in the endeavor, all deny having wanted to end their lives, suggesting a variety of reasons that could render nonsuperimposable the thing done with anything approaching a supposed intention.

Thus, as an act, the endeavor to end one's life can either mean something, "*vouloir dire*"—i.e., want to say something—in which case it is a desire supported by a chain of signifiers; or if it doesn't mean something—if it does not want to say something—it is because the desire that subtends the act presents a structural incompatibility with speech. The incompatibility is structural for Lacan, or a Lacanian analyst, because regarding the chain of signifiers in relation to which the person's desire can be supported, Lacan takes as a basic premise that the locus of this chain, which is to say, in discourse, is located in what he calls "the Other" [*l'Autre*]: "The Other is the locus in which is situated the chain of the signifier that governs whatever may be made present of the subject—it is the field of that living being in which the subject has to appear.

And I said that it was on the side of this living being, called to subjectivity, that the drive is essentially manifested."[22] As such, desire, for Lacanians, is "desire of the Other," which means it is situated in discourse in which the subject must both realize itself and from which it is fundamentally alienated. Moreover, drive also is situated on the side of discourse, thus marking a radical and unequivocal distinction between the properly psychoanalytic concept of drive and the term *instinct*, a distinction frequently collapsed by Freud's heirs, in which drive has a fundamentally biological underpinning.

Lacanian analysts take as their basic orientation that the subject does not know the cause of desire, which is other than the intentional or stated object/ objective; the cause can be made to appear only in language, in interpretation. Concerning the realization of suicide, which frequently leaves those left behind searching to understand what happened and why, a Lacanian orientation would indicate that the successful realization of suicide actually *tries* to be misunderstood, short-circuiting the interpretation of desire. Either the act "slips" and thus leads to the elicitation of an interpretation (the act "wants to say something"), or it takes the position of remaining unknown.

To the degree that the goal (death) is not the cause (a desire for death), Lacan is in agreement with Freud that the subject does not believe in its own death: the unconscious, for Freud, has no representation of death. Lacan contradicts Freud's understanding of primary narcissism, however, to the degree that he insists on the subject's relation to language, a relation to the Other, even before birth and before becoming an ego. A consequence of this basic orientation, regarding the subject's relation to language and discourse, is that the subject's "desire" is desire of (and rooted in) the Other, and its interpretation requires pinpointing the signifier in language that could help to interpret the cause. As Lacan puts it, "The unconscious is the sum of the effects of speech on a subject, at the level at which the subject constitutes himself out of the effects of the signifier."[23]

To say that desire is desire of the Other leads to two questions: what is this Other, and what does it want from me? These questions lead to consideration of the phenomenon of identification and of Lacan's reading of identification through the concept of separation. A key moment in the formation of such identification, through the question of what the Other wants from me, occurs during the "mirror stage," a fundamental and constitutive moment put forward by Lacan in which the ego is constituted through an identification with an image of the body.[24] Morel explains: "The operation of identification with the image of the body sets up the narcissism of the subject, gives its matrix to the ego, and delimits the place of the ego-ideal, which will remain a point of reference for the subject. . . . The ideal-ego is the image designated as desirable, at the moment of the mirror stage, by the adult situated in the place of the ego-ideal. In the future, the subject will endeavor to make coincide his image, which is to say, his ego, with his ideal-ego."[25] We can draw five terms from Morel's exegesis: (1) ego, (2) image of the body, (3) ego-ideal, (4) ideal-ego, and (5) the actual body. In relation to any actual body (5) we have images (2, 4) and the counterpart positions in the subject (ego [1], and ego-ideal [3]). When the ideal and image coincide with ego and ego-ideal, there is jubilation, and when there is dissonance between them, there is melancholia, following the mechanism outlined in the previous section.

Although Lacan agrees with Freud that the subject has no unconscious representation of death and, as such, does not believe in its own death, the subject can imagine itself as mortal because of both the image and language (image of the body, ego-ideal, ideal-ego): the sign can separate from and even disappear from the chain of signification, and the body/ego can separate from the sign. To put it concretely, from this Lacanian point of view, an event of some type occurs that calibrates in a specific way the relation connecting body, image, and ideal. Following the first exposition from Freud, this will be some loss in the realm of objects. What is of note for us, following Lacan, is that because of his conception of primary narcissism as being an identification with an image in discourse, in relation to an ideal-ego, a loss in relation to that image, just like with Freud's loss in relation to an object, can function as an ego loss. As such, anxiety about death is better understood as an anxiety about separation, which is to say a desire to separate from the Other, from the chain of signification.

Thus, for example, when a person has some event in relation to illness, let's say a serious illness that puts in jeopardy their image of themselves as a person, they respond, in that separation, Morel suggests, at an unconscious level by asking what the Other wants from me, from the position of the ego-ideal. As such, a lack of separation from a damaged image/ideal can cause, through the anxious desire to separate from that damaged image, a new investment or identification with the image and a new ego-ideal.

At the level of the imaginary, within such identification with a new ego-ideal, an ego-ideal of control, mastery, there is a potential fantasy of overcoming the fundamental alienation of the subject, the loss of *jouissance* imposed on the subject as the price to be paid for its entry into the symbolic order, a fantasy of reconciliation that is transfigured, in line with Freud's fundamental thesis, into "mania." As Freud put it, "In mania the ego must have got over the loss of the object, and thereupon the whole quota of anticathexis which the painful suffering of melancholia had drawn to itself from the ego and 'bound' will have become available. Moreover, the manic subject plainly demonstrates his liberation from the object which was the cause of his suffering, by seeking, like a ravenously hungry man for new object-cathexes."[26] Critical for Lacan is that the "suicidal tendency" appears to function at the level of the "image" and of the imaginary, but its *signifiance*, its truth, can only be discerned at the level of the symbolic.

To put it succinctly, what looks like mastery, an overcoming, at the imaginary level is also at the same time, at the symbolic level, the repetition of a lack, located in the subject's desire to restore or recover the lost object.[27]

CASE IN POINT: REPETITION, CONSIDERED

I met Babette at her assisted living residence in an upscale Parisian suburb in April of 2016. A short elderly woman, with a piercing no-nonsense demeanor, Babette had replied to my request to meet people who were considering assisted suicide in Switzerland. She could neither sit nor stand for more than a few minutes. She lay on her couch, and I sat in a seat by her feet, diagonally facing her. In fact, Babette was expected to have died six months previously. Her daughter had helped her arrange an assisted suicide in Basel. As the date approached, her daughter changed her mind, telling her mother that she could not die like that and must have a natural death. Babette had to make a plan B. It would take place right here, a stockpile of medications hidden, an insurance plan, so to speak. Her granddaughter would like to stay with her, but Babette said she did not want to tell her the date, in case somehow there is an accusation against her. They are used to it here: opening the door in the morning, someone died. Then they put a little announcement downstairs on the notice board. We talked all afternoon, for hours, moving back and forth between her current state of physical degradation, her pain, and her family, including a lot of discussion of her daughter, who initially helped her organize her death and then refused to help, blocking her escape. We also talked about how she raised her family after her husband died at a young age and how, thanks to the fact that her parents were fluent in German and English, she herself had become fluent, allowing her to gain work, after his death, at the Paris headquarters of a big company.

It was approaching six o'clock, and I was worried about being late to pick up my son from the crèche. I began to fidget in my seat.

"You have to go."

"I'm sorry but yes, the crèche will close soon."

"She didn't want to tell people how I was going to die," she carried on, referring to her daughter.

"Why?"

"Shame. I told her, why do you care what anyone thinks? If I had to care about what people think, I would have gone a long time ago. Shame is very difficult. I had to work through a lot of shame."

I was rather confused. "Hmmm . . . I'm not totally clear on the nature of the shame you are talking about."

She sighed, waited a moment before speaking. "My father was a pilot in the First World War. Imagine, back then, planes were really something; you had a couple of lessons and then *op*, you were expected to get to it. And he was a very very good pilot. Flying with the Americans. In the Second World War he had to parachute behind enemy lines. He became a double agent [working for the Germans]. He was shot [by the French] in 1945. They were marched south and then executed." Babette lay in silence. I waited. "But now you have to go and get your son." I thanked her for telling me her story and left.

The image of Babette, on the couch, with her anger and disappointment toward her daughter, and the story of her father, lingered, and began to form a kind of contraction of elements, as I continued to think about the encounter. There was a sort of passive synthesis in my imagination, a synthesis of the story of the past death within the scene of "telling" about her present attitude toward dying, her orientation, her plan, for a voluntary death. Could we call the telling of that death a sign, a sign composed of the expression of her physical suffering, of her character, of her relation to her father's death? And might it be a sign of (i.e., conveying to my mind an idea about) her desire to die at her own hand rather than any other way? This is a shortcut, for Babette I could not, cannot, say—it is unearned.

A word is necessary, then, about the choice of this term *desire*. Laplanche and Pontalis's well-respected *Vocabulaire de la psychanalyse* is of help in specifying "desire" in relation to two other terms, *need* and *demand*:

Need aims at a specific object and is satisfied by it. A demand [*une demande*] is formulated and addressed to another; if it does still concern an object, it is nevertheless inessential, the articulated request being, at base, a request for love. Desire arises from the gap between need and demand; it is irreducible to need, because it is not principally in relation to a real object, independent of the subject, but rather to fantasy; it is irreducible to a demand, insofar as it seeks to impose itself without taking into account language and the unconscious of the other, and demands to be recognized absolutely by him.[28]

The definition, I think, is of use to the degree that, on the one hand, a request for assisted suicide cannot be reduced to a "need"; that is, you cannot "need" an assisted suicide in the way a person could be said to "need" heart surgery. Moreover, as Laplanche and Pontalis point out, there is something about the vitality of desire, which cannot bracket the subjective specificity of the one who desires, with reference to an objective reality, and this subjective specificity is also not reducible to a pursuit of recognition in language, a request for love, as they put it, or compassion, or grace, I would add, which is to say it cannot be reduced to the negotiation between subjects. When I began this inquiry, I specifically thought I could and would, and should, stay at the surface level of interaction. My encounters and the stories I heard made this impossible.

The specificity of desire brings up a connected term, one that is just as problematic: *phantasy*. Laplanche and Pontalis again: "Phantasy (or Fantasy): Imaginary scene in which the subject is protagonist, representing the fulfillment of a wish (in the last analysis, an unconscious wish) in a manner that is distorted to a greater or lesser extent by defensive processes."[29]

As the authors point out in their subsequent essay, *Fantasme originaire, fantasmes des origines, origines du fantasme* (1985), these scenes in the imagination, conscious and unconscious, which underpin what happens in the exchange between the analysand and the analyst, posed a problem for Freud in terms of their "psychic reality."[30] The fact that decisions to seek a voluntary death, and the wish to do so, cannot be explained or understood solely by need or by demand poses the very basic question of the psychic reality of desire and of the range of elements conscious and unconscious that make up the phantasy that underpins verbal and gestural material observed during the process of talking about, and fulfilling of, the assisted suicide, and of the potential "defensive processes" that constitute that phantasy and that desire.

To return to Babette: the presence of images in her scenario, the imagined form taken by the killing of her father, permitted me to constitute an active linking, if not yet an interpretation; namely, after the refusal of her daughter to occupy the role of a facilitator of her desire, she found in me a subject willing to listen to what *I took to be* the cause of her desire—her father's execution and the shame she lived with, and that she worked through, which could be said to be important in having formed her character and in having formed a desire, constituted through phantasy.

But, is it not too active, and too imaginative a link?

The problem here is that I have no way to grasp the configuration of her desire with elements within a temporally unfolding situation that could allow me to understand how and why I was interpreting her desire in this way.

As I began to think of this image narrated, and her desire linked to this element of what might be called her phantasy, it made me think of another contraction of elements, another image of desire that I had already encountered, in which a wish was bound to an image, through speech, that then functioned like a sign of that wish, which then, in this case, did produce an interpretation. I was beginning to make a series relative to which the question will be, What would constitute a test of the claim to have described elements of desire and to have grasped the assemblage in which it produces effects?

Juan, a vivacious man in his sixties, is not ill, but he has been a member of the association Exit ADMD for ten years. I visit him in his home in a small municipality between Geneva and Lausanne, where he begins by telling me of his experience at the main teaching hospital in Lausanne, concerning a cardiac problem: no one listened; it was a machine; it was a flesh factory putting broken parts back together, regardless of what anyone says. Juan resolved then and there that he would never accept a situation where technical machines keep him alive against his will.

This is a parameter of what could be called the counterexample among people searching for assistance to voluntarily end their lives. Such a parameter is intuitive. It served as a starting hypothesis for my work, as well as for many others who have worked on assisted voluntary dying: not wanting to die in a certain way, not wanting to die "like that," where the "that" indexes, frequently, a negative experience with the medical environment and practice. Such negative experiences are cited as a key reason why people join "right to die" associations: a bad experience shows individuals how they do not want to die.

Juan and I continued to discuss his situation, and I asked him after some time to return to what he had told me, whether it was his experience at the hospital that was the central parameter in his decision. I asked him about the chronology, about whether he had thought about the possibility of assisted suicide prior to his stay at the hospital. He considered the question and then began to talk to me about the death of his father, which occurred a long time before Juan's heart problem. As he began to narrate the death of his father, he also commented on the fact that he had never made the link but that it could well be part of how to make sense of his decision to join Exit: Juan came from a family of doctors in the city of Ciudad Real. During his adolescence he distanced himself from his family, and from fascist Spain, making his life first in Morocco and then in Switzerland. When he learned that his father was dying, he went to see him in his hometown. His father had been bedridden for months; he had almost completely stopped eating and was drinking little, seemingly drinking less and less. It was clear to Juan that his father was in the process of intentionally, slowly, ending his life, "like Buddha."

"He was doing an exit on himself [*Il était en train de faire un exit sur lui-même*]. Me, I'm not brave enough to do that. That's why I need Exit."

It seemed to me, as I began to constitute in my imagination a series of cases, and a series of repetitions, that what was being repeated was precisely not memories of past deaths but rather a form given to images of dying that bear, in one way or another, on a present desire toward the process of dying.

I have encountered many such images, but I will stop this sequence with one more: Maria, who is also Spanish and who grew up in Switzerland. She lived for many years in London, a successful businessperson, but then in her forties she made a decision to end her life through assisted suicide and had been given the green light by an assisted suicide organization. She suffers from a debilitating and severe form of bowel disease. She has had fifty operations since the age of thirteen. I asked her how she came to the judgment that she should die in Switzerland through assisted suicide and how she made the decision, in relation to thoughts about her illness. She narrated how her mother had not put her affairs in order, which was very distressing for Maria after her death—a big headache, she said. In order not to pile a bureaucratic burden on top of mourning for her brother, she wanted an orderly, clean death. "Control is very important to me," she said, reflecting a common trope among those who do, and who facilitate, this form of dying.

Maria's situation, however, is uncommon in my experience. Her illness is a chronic but not deadly disease. Moreover, the intensity of the affect of anger in the manner in which she narrates her decision stems largely from the way in which British social care services increasingly abandoned her (according to her), under well-documented conditions of austerity, retrenchment of funding for local care services. The local council progressively cut her social care, such that as she became more disabled, she had less and less care paid for by the council, leaving her to fund the increasing required care from diminishing funds.

Such a story, as complex and difficult as it may be, might be self-sufficient as a narrative for understanding Maria's decision to end her life. Chronic illness with a high degree of pain, repeated operations that would extend long into the future with no likelihood of respite, a growing sense of dependence and abandonment, even regarding basic care such a being helped with the preparation of meals, might be considered sufficient in order to understand why Maria would wish to leave her experience of suffering. Put in either economic or psychological terms, her choice could easily be rendered comprehensible through a cost-benefit analysis exercised by pleasure and reality principles: given the reality of a biological, as well as a medical-technical and social situation, avoidance of unpleasure (avoidance of the counterexample) could incite a person to look for a way out.

Nevertheless, over the course of repeatedly meeting individuals who are seeking assistance with suicide for reasons related to illness, I have noticed—and been surprised by—how, in their narratives, in addition to reasons that we could qualify as counterexamples, whose economy could be said to be governed by a ratio of pleasure and reality principles—not wanting to die "like that"—people frequently refer to images of past deaths that somehow have an "active" presence. I was aware, in the wake of Freud, that one can become attuned to dynamics "beyond the pleasure principle," which I considered to have heard in many of the narratives I received, as well as in what I have observed, in which a dialectic of mastery and repetition of loss were articulated.

In Juan's case his father's voluntary ending of his life was an active presence. Juan was reflective about not repeating such a death in the same way; nevertheless, in such reflection he introduced for himself, and thus for me, a connection between a prior death and his own search for a form for dying, what I had previously called homeomorphism. And then there was the shame that Babette says she lived with owing to her father's execution, which mixed with the clear admiration she had for him: in this case, unlike Juan's, in which it is he himself who announces the connection, the proximity between the prior death and the search for a form for dying, it is I, and not Babette, who made the connection. Her story, and the timing of the story, just as I had to go, not incidentally, posed the question of its function and of her intention: why tell me such a story at that precise moment? What is the connection between her pain, her search for a way to die, the shame she lived with because of her father's death, and the conflict she had with her daughter, who insisted on a "natural" death? In her case I cannot say, and I refuse to make a direct interpretation, since she refused contact with me after our meeting. I do, however, think it is crucial to my inquiry that I found myself with elements that I thought needed to be given a form, elements that on the one hand, through passive synthesis took a form as an image of a desire (not yet a sign with its signification) and, on the other hand, also demanded from me an active, and act of, interpretation.

With these encounters in mind, during the course of the conversation with Maria, I endeavored to explore the process of her coming to the decision that it was necessary to seek a way out through assisted suicide beyond the obviously important elements of her physical and psychic suffering and the social situation in which she found herself.

I asked Maria to go over again for me the chronology of her decision.

"So in about 2008 [which is when cuts were starting to be made to her social care], I made a living will, DNR [she signed a "do not resuscitate" order] and began to explore the possibilities of an assisted death."

"There were no other events at this time?"

"No."

"Really? Nothing at all?"

"Well that's not entirely true: my nephew, my favorite nephew, killed himself at the barracks in Switzerland during his military service. He was very intelligent. His death was traumatic for those of us who remained, but he showed me that suicide is a realistic way out."

DESIRE AND ITS INTERPRETATION

On beginning this inquiry, I was basically focused on the practicalities of how people request assistance with suicide. This concerned in particular how others, specifically doctors who receive these requests, make judgments about them and the different kinds of negotiations and processes people go through in order to accomplish it. As the inquiry continued, and I talked with more people, and as I came to actually participate in the event of an assisted suicide, in the case of Clément, I began to think that the real question, that which I wanted to know, was not actually about medical judgment. If the person in question has a significant illness, causing suffering, with little or no chance of amelioration and as long as the person is an adult of sound mind, then, almost always, the doctors connected to the associations agree to the request for assisted suicide. Aside from cases of requests pertaining uniquely to psychiatric disorders, I have never heard of an association refusing a request if the basic criteria are fulfilled and if the person lives in his or her own home. The question for me, that which was abstruse, was rather to grasp the desire to die in this way: that is to say, prior to the putting in place of everything required to do it, the will to enact it, there is a desire that, it seemed to me, was being expressed in these stories.

What had initially seemed obscure—the practice of medical judgment—with time appears to be relatively simple or, at least, not significantly problematic: to grasp medical judgment was a matter of tracing the network of material-semiotic associations through which a judgment is produced.[31] And what had initially seemed to be rather self-evident or unproblematic—the wish to die at a moment of one's choosing, in as nonviolent a way as possible, understood as a choice or a decision, premised on the judgment of a doctor who accepts the request—became less so. Following the work of sociologists such as Michael Pollack, I found that the problem is one of trying to find a way to account for a present orientation, disposition, or attitude, under conditions in which reference to a socially determined and determining "habitus"—the ensemble of predispositions, acquired during a person's life, notably in childhood, which function as a generative matrix of conducts—is dissatisfying.[32] That is to say, on the one hand, it is true that statistically the vast majority of people who request assistance with suicide are those with secondary or tertiary, compared with compulsory, education; those living alone, compared with those living with others; those with no religious affiliation; those in urban, compared with rural, areas; and those in neighborhoods of higher socioeconomic position.[33] On the other hand, when actually talking with people about undertaking or seeking assistance with suicide, things are said that are not graspable either as individual choice or through reference to the ensemble of predispositions that make up habitus.

For example, intuitively I understood that a person, such as Peter, whose story we followed from a distance in part 2, suffering from a motor neuron disease, might wish to avoid letting the illness take its course. That is to say, on the basis of a very basic principle of avoiding suffering in a situation in which there is little to be done in terms of slowing the progression of illness (although there are things that can be done to render life perhaps more manageable), I find it "normal" that a person might wish to and then choose to end his or her life (a combination of reality and pleasure principles) at a given time, before the experience of the illness got too bad, in the individual's own judgment. Nevertheless, in investigating Peter's request for assisted suicide, I noticed elements of his story that went beyond the self-evidence of the medical situation, the self-evidence of a doctor agreeing to such a request, and the fact that, sociologically, he fit the statistical norm of those who request assistance with suicide (well-educated, high socioeconomic position, no religious affiliation, urban environment): like with the stories narrated above, the specificity of Peter's story concerned things told about dying relative to his life. He had an ensemble of concerns around death and dying that included an obsession with submarines sunk during the Second World War (he could name every case of a sunken submarine); a persistent fear, an obsession even, from an early age that he would develop a locked-in syndrome (he had a library full of books on the subject); a history of joking with friends from an early age about ways he would end his life rather than live on with debilitating illness; and his suspicion that his father had ended his own life in relation to undiagnosed motor neuron disease, years before he himself was diagnosed.

The people that participate in assisted suicide, those that do it, that facilitate it, often have recourse to a simple narrative of assisted suicide as an obvious or reasonable response to a problem of physical or psychic suffering: a choice, a rational choice. Physical and psychic suffering linked to diagnosed illness is the means by which doctors and family members assure themselves that there isn't a reason to not accept the request. In itself, though, it doesn't tell us much, positively, about how they then understand that this is the particular form that a person would like to give to the search for a way to leave a situation of suffering—a positive form given to a desire, whose character is unclear, on the basis of a life: a life of experience, a subject with its subjectivity.

Attempting to grasp positively the character of the desire to die in this way is, I think, a necessary response to the deficiency of treating a choice to die as self-evident and as a matter of individual psychology. Taking up the question of the desire through which an assisted suicide happens, in terms of its assemblage, orients me to the practical arrangements that afford subjects the possibility of taking a position within a configuration of signs, images, gestures, and bodily and affective states—medical ones, biographical ones, historical ones—that refer to a multitude of elements, including pain and death, whose signification is open to and, I will claim, seems to require interpretation.

Trying to grasp a desire to die can only occur through that which is said, and the element of that which is said that I have been struck by is the narrating of prior deaths within a process of the creation of an attitude toward dying. Key to these narratives of prior death is the effect that they have: that they seem to call for interpretation and, moreover, an interpretation that can link desire for this form of death to the narrative told. We have seen it already: Babette's search for a way out was narrated by her in a way that juxtaposed the desire and the narrative, thus prompting a suggestion on my part as to their connection; Juan's self-interpretation of the repetition through the difference of his father's death in relation to his search to not die tied to technical machinery; and Maria's announcement of the significance of her cousin's suicide as showing her the real possibility of voluntary death.

If we return to Clément, his telling of a biographical narrative, a reconstitution in narrative of a set of experiences, solicits interpretations that operate as devices for making the desire for this form for death *cohere* with what has been said and what we know about this form of death, as an ensemble of material and semiotic elements. If you want to know about desire, you are obliged to take up those configurations of elements that make up "scenarios" and then to make an interpretation; the interpretation might (try to) produce narrative coherence (some version of hermeneutics), or one might try and see how the demand to make an interpretation, and the character and content of those interpretations of that psychic reality (thus of the signs being interpreted) is in a structured or structural relation with the reality being interpreted. I am dissatisfied by these two options, for reasons of trying to do justice to the reality of what I grasped as the heterogeneous elements that constituted the desire and fulfillment of the cases of assisted suicide.

The configuration of elements does not cohere in a single narrative of desire stemming from a subject. The person in question does not seek to instantiate a "synthetic unity," to use Paul Ricoeur's phrase. As such, the "imagination" in question is not that uniquely of a single subject, whose imagination functions as "schematizing a synthetic operation."[34] Nor are the significations of the elements and their interpretations reducible to a structural arrangement under a master signifier, one that would underpin the variable positions from which meaning is attributed, even though these narratives and these structured positions of interpretation are clearly present. To do justice to the assemblage, I want to both acknowledge the desire for interpretation and underscore the fact that a concern for understanding desire leads to interpretations that risk being totalizing: to postulate sadistic attack, narcissistic regression, identification, and alienation that strives to recuperate a lost object. To a degree, these terms make visible, perhaps too clearly, things that I have seen and heard. More than functioning as a diagnosis of those that have given me a place from which to listen to their desire, this psychoanalytic repertoire makes visible the desire of the anthropologist to grasp their desire.

Conduct | Obstinacy

Mrs. Milner was diagnosed with a glioblastoma, a kind of brain tumor, in 1993. She had it checked on regularly, and for fifteen years she went about her life—the tumor showing benign tendencies. In 2008 her eldest daughter had a child. Mrs. Milner looked after her grandchild five days a week while her daughter was at work. She refused more scans on the grounds that if they found something, then she would no longer be able to do this. She wished, in effect, to care for the child as long as she was physically able, without concern for her own medical situation. At the end of 2012 her husband, a family doctor in the small agricultural commune in the north of the canton of Vaud, where they lived, persuaded her to do a new scan. It showed that the tumor had grown considerably. She underwent surgery, but the surgeons were unable to remove it entirely. Two months later more scans showed it had grown back significantly. The couple had a friend who suffered from the same illness: "she spent the last years of her life as a vegetable in a local home," Dr. Milner explained to me, an effect of the tumor on the frontal lobe of the brain.

His wife's situation was followed at the major teaching hospital, an hour and half from where they lived. The medical team suggested she undergo a new form of chemotherapy, available only there. She refused. Too many side effects for a treatment whose aim, ultimately, was comfort care rather than cure. Also of concern to Mrs. Milner were practical things, such as the exhaustion of traveling regularly from the rural commune to the city to be seen at a "factory"—that is to say, the big, impersonal, teaching hospital. Mrs. Milner telephoned the hospital to explain that she did not wish to go through with the proposed chemotherapy. The neuro-oncologist did not react well, Dr. Milner explained: "He washed his hands of her, like Pontius Pilate. The oncologist said that if she did not do the chemotherapy, then he wanted nothing to do with her." This moment marked a turning point for Mrs. Milner, as narrated by her husband, a turning point in her illness and in her attitude: "Her behavior became more aggressive; she had incontinence and became extremely dependent. And then, soon after the phone call with the oncologist, she made a decision to contact Exit."

I returned to see Dr. Milner on several occasions, and we revisited together the event of her suicide: "It went very well: she even managed to sleep the night before. Me too. She didn't sleep *very* well, of course, but still she was able to sleep. We stayed up late that night confiding in each other. We had gone walking in the forest on the Sunday afternoon. We went and had a look where she wanted me to put her ashes. Holy smokes to think of that!! Then on the day, Mrs. Pinelli arrived. My wife wasn't allowed to drink or eat anything. She said again to my wife, if you don't want to do it, I will gladly go home; it's good weather, it's the summer. We'd be happy if you didn't take it, but the decision is yours."

Mrs. Milner had been resolute about the date. Once the accompanier from Exit, Mrs. Pinelli, had told her that there was the possibility of doing it in mid-August, nothing would change her mind. Dr. Milner explained that he himself, Mrs. Pinelli, the prescribing doctor, friends, and their two daughters had all tried to persuade her to wait until after the summer, but she would not consider it. They insisted on the fact that her eldest daughter was pregnant with a second child, to be born in September, but this did not shake her resolve: "I don't know why she was so stubborn about it," Dr. Milner stated simply. "Then she drank the potion [the barbiturate solution]. The potion is a bit bitter so I gave her a piece of chocolate. Me, I like *Ragusa*,[1] so I gave her some, for after the potion, and then, she shouted at me saying 'you know I hate it when there are nuts in it!' Then *pof*: she died. The last words she said to me. It's a bit tragic, but that shows the character of my wife. Even at the end, she made a scene: (Imitating her) 'No! You put nuts in the chocolate; right to the end you annoyed me' (a chuckle from Dr. Milner). You know, she was an aristocrat; her family was part of the Crusades. It's crazy, eh."

Although in many respects singular, unmarked by what is typically considered "violence," Mrs. Milner's death was nevertheless neither normal nor ordinary nor customary.[2] As a kind of prepared and chosen death, it exhibited the opposite hallmarks of practices ranging from Jains in Jaipur to Buddhists in Kathmandu—namely, in those cases, a valorized ritual practice of dying realized through the diminishment of attachment and desire in the world.[3] Mrs. Milner's death, on the contrary, exhibited many kinds of attachments, including attachment to the timing, to the form, and to the taste of her death. Her suicide was not the result of a lack or breakdown in "social relations,"[4] and the control she sought to exert did not lead it to be qualified as a "bad death."[5] As with the narratives presented in part 2, the form of control she was able to assert, as a subject, was precisely the *outcome of*, rather than a mere *baseline for*, such a form of death—justified, negotiated, and mediated with others.

It was thus, on the one hand, not a normal death, yet neither was it unique. She was one of a small number of people in Switzerland—a small number that is nevertheless growing—who, when faced with a situation they consider blocked and intolerable, choose to die rather than live on in available ways. One of the anthropological stakes in inquiring into this practice is to understand, beyond the contours of an individual choice, the social determination of such a practice, or the possible significance of the specifically "social" character of the practice, as distinct from the psychological aspect that we have just worked through. My approach will be to confront the observation of such a practice with prior manners in which the specifically social significance of suicide has been determined.

LE SUICIDE

Emile Durkheim (1858–1917) considered voluntary death a privileged phenomenon for indexing and characterizing the moral temper of society—an object that took on its specific reality through the long nineteenth century.[6] Not only did Durkheim claim that suicide rates could indicate the social (sui generis) causes of suicide, thus defying those sciences that would reduce acts of suicide either to mental pathology[7] or psychic imitation,[8] but furthermore and moreover, he aimed to establish sociology as a science of moral facts and thus a science of the normative orders that are given form under modern conditions of the organization of work and life. Studying suicide as a specifically social phenomenon was therefore a way for Durkheim, as exponent of what would become the science of the social, to study the moral forms of social life through their exaggeration in this specific gesture.

A central thesis of his 1897 study *Le suicide* is thus that suicides "are not an isolated class of monstrous phenomena, with no relation to other manners of conduct." Rather, they are "only the exaggerated form of ordinary practices."[9] As such, suicide is an ethically qualified social phenomenon not reducible to individual psychological reasons (or causes) because of which people end their lives. The originality of Durkheim's analysis was precisely his specification of its ethical character: "Every sort of suicide is thus only the exaggerated or diverted form of a virtue."[10] The sociological challenge for Durkheim was, then, to identify the moral forms and social causes through which these virtues are exaggerated and hence the standards and forms with respect to which such exaggerations (excesses and deficiencies) can be judged as vices. Crucially, the "exaggeration" of these forms of conduct can be judged as excessive or deficient in the individual, that is to say, exaggerated from a mean, only with respect to the social environment that encourages or demands the form of conduct and the virtue in question. Such a qualification should then lead us to specify these exaggerated virtues—hence vices—as "social" in the specific sense Durkheim gives to the latter term, that is to say, pertaining to a sui generis object, a standard, "collective representation," and a form for living, called society.

The presupposition of such sociological determination is that the articulation between societies and moral orders, although historical and subject to possible transformation, is nevertheless the outcome of what we can call a large-scale eighteenth- to nineteenth-century social, political, and juridical institutional solidification such that at the end of this "heroic" age of science,[11] sociology could finally be professionalized and authorized to pronounce truth claims about this object—society—and more specifically the virtues with respect to which the moral order of society is supposed to be regulated. Sociology as a science was able to occupy a discursive position so as to articulate the rapports between social structures and normative orders.

DURKHEIM, ETHICS, AND A PRAGMATIC ANTHROPOLOGY

The last decade has seen renewed interest in Durkheim's legacy and a question of the continued relevance of inquiry based on Durkheimian methodological and philosophical postulates.[12] For me, as an anthropologist, such readings have involved questioning what I thought I knew about Durkheim, to wit, a deterministic view of the isomorphism of social forms and normative orders. British anthropologist James Laidlaw summarizes a version of one such view succinctly: "Durkheim's conception of the social so completely identifies the collective with the good that an independent understanding of ethics appears neither necessary nor possible."[13] At stake in what follows is the question of how Durkheim's *Le suicide* can be read in relation to an anthropological endeavor to grasp the "subject of virtue,"[14] that is to say, the ethico-pragmatic variation in which people give form to their practices, their lives, and crucially, to the ending of their lives, specifically relative to modern institutions for the management of health and illness (hospitals, doctors, treatments, prognoses, etc.).[15] If Laidlaw seeks to valorize an anthropological attentiveness to a plurality of modes and forms of ethicality in human practice, practices whose domains are resolutely open and dynamic, an anthropological endeavor I wholeheartedly share, I would nevertheless like to confront Durkheim's text with an investigation into what Kant named as the core *pragmatic* anthropological problem: what the human being as a free acting being can and should make of itself.[16]

Simply put, I do not want to presuppose that a pragmatic anthropology of ethics has either no point of articulation or else a necessary connection with Durkheim's social science of moral facts and his modality of inquiring into virtue. Rather, the critical limits and possible fruits of such a confrontation for anthropological inquiry must be tested and shown. I am thus purposefully constraining the conceptual stakes in this chapter to an engagement with, and testing of, Durkheim's model, engaging in a stepwise reading of the significance of Durkheim's assumptions in order to better diagnose the critical limitations of his sociological model in the service of a more general anthropological grasping of plural ethical practices today, specifically in relation to the practice of assisted suicide.

I consider the organizational form that has developed in Switzerland since 1982 to be a significant morphological change in the form given to suicide, which Durkheim assiduously defined as "cases of deaths which result directly or indirectly from a positive or negative act accomplished by the victim herself and that she knew would produce that result."[17] Although often appropriately taken up in its connection and continuity with medical ethical questions of euthanasia and doctors' capacity and legitimacy to hasten the dying process of the sick, the invention of such a new form of assisted suicide can also be taken up in relation to the longer durational anthropological and sociological problem of the moral forms of acts of voluntary death. I thus use the inquiry from parts 1 and 2, in connection with the broader experiences, encounters, and observations that I have had over the course of this inquiry (2013–17), as a testing ground and conceptual gauge for clarifying the limits to (and hence also interest of) a Durkheimian sociological approach to inquiry into moral forms and practices, as it pertains to the question of voluntary death.

By confronting my inquiry with my reading of *Le suicide*, I probe the conceptual limits to Durkheim's conception of the relation between the sociality of practices and the moral forms they both imply and produce. Such a confrontation indexes what Paul Rabinow has posed as the demand for a contemporary anthropological reconceptualization of the breakdowns and remediations in the plurality of ethical forms that can be observed as modernity's *ethē* and institutions undergo change; in this case I take it up with respect to assisted suicide as a novel response to the question of how to die (in Switzerland) today.

The key point of conceptual breakdown and remediation, which I will outline in the section that follows, is a demonstration of the significance of the well-known lacuna in Durkheim's presentation of the social facticity of the moral forms that can be grasped with respect to suicide as a human practice. I will argue for observing Durkheim's conceptual blind spot as constitutive of the character of his modern, normative, scientific posture, which is crucially also a political one: that sociological science has the means to identify *the* political ends toward which social life should aim.[18] That is to say, Durkheim's normative political posture is a regulative one.

How can a pragmatic anthropological inquiry adequately take up social practices that are obstinate to regulation? As such, I am concerned with what Lisa Stevenson has called the "affront" of voluntary death to certain *specifically modern* forms of institutional reason, in her case "colonial" and "bureaucratic" forms, a practice whose obstinacy, in my case, consists in opposition to moral demands, an opposition "eventalized" in the opening scene of the chapter with the neuro-oncologist "washing his hands" of his patient and of the patient transforming her renunciation of treatment into an active search for a means to leave her experience of illness and to give that leave-taking a form.

I will describe how such social practices are a blind spot for Durkheim and all others who unthinkingly apply moralizing sociological reasoning (such as the ethicist Bertrand Kiefer from chapter 2), and as a counterpoint I will suggest how Durkheim's conceptual scheme can be opened up in order to adequately grasp and understand the multiplicity of moral forms and practices, including those that might be conceived as anti- or countersocial, without descending into the ideological trap of so-called "individualism."

A PROBLEM OF SYMMETRY: DURKHEIM'S TYPOLOGY

Durkheim's typology of moral tempers of modern society exaggerated in voluntary death is both canonical and incomplete: egoism, altruism, and anomie reflect forms of social life that are excessive or deficient along two axes, each with poles of excess and deficiency: (1) social integration and (2) moral regulation.

Let us briefly recall them. *Egoism* is a social condition of deficient integration correlated to an ethos and virtue of individualism. In his deductive account Durkheim links the egoistic etiology to a specific form ("morphology") of suicide, "melancholic languor."[19] *Altruism* as a social condition can produce excessive social integration and deficient individuation, indexed to an ethos of obligation and virtue. Although primarily conceived as archetypical of nonmodern societies, Durkheim shows that this virtue reemerges in excessive form with respect to voluntary death in modern arrangements around warfare. The corresponding moral form is "active renunciation"[20] of a self for a common endeavor or *telos*. Finally, *anomie* as a social condition is characterized by breakdown in moral regulation and practices indexed to unbridled desire for progress.[21] The subjective form that Durkheim associates with such deficient regulation of desire is "exasperated lassitude."[22]

For Durkheim, a balance must be established among the types of suicides. What is normal is the right composition of virtuous exaggerations, a normal rate of vice, expressed as a stable rate of suicide. The stability and regularity of the suicide rate across the plane of "the social" is indicative of the effectiveness and vitality of the corresponding virtues. The mean (i.e., virtue in Aristotle's sense),[23] for Durkheim, can be conceived only with respect to society and thus only through the judgment of someone authorized to pronounce in its name. Sociologically, what is problematic is when one virtue (and vice) is exaggerated at the expense of the others, which was the historical diagnostic concern of Durkheim—namely, that individualism was exaggerated at the expense of altruism with an accompanying effect in terms of moral deregulation under conditions of historical progress, hence an increase in both egoistic and anomic suicide. The vice of any particular act is conceived and judged with respect to the extraparticular plane of the social calibration of three ethical topics: individuality, obligation, and progress. Crucially, since duty or social obligation is characteristic of nonmodern societies, and modern differentiated societies tend to express exaggerations of individuality (egoism) and the desire for progress (anomie), the normative posture of the sociological scientist can easily be justified through the claim to a remediation of the lack of regulation or control in social forms under modern conditions and in modern institutions.

This nineteenth-century picture and model of social causes is clearly missing one type: excess along the axis of moral regulation. Durkheim is aware of this, of course. A footnote in the section on anomie explains the following:

> We see from the preceding considerations that there exists a type of suicide which is opposed to anomic suicide, much as egoistic and altruistic types of suicide are opposed. It is that which results from an excess of control [réglementation]; that type of suicide committed by those subjects whose future is mercilessly worn, whose passions are violently held in check by an oppressive discipline. It is the suicide of husbands who married too young, of the married woman without children. To be comprehensive we should therefore constitute a fourth type of suicide. But it is of such little importance today, beyond the cases we have just cited, it is so difficult to find examples that it seems needless for us to stop there. However, it could be that it would have an historical interest. Is it not to this type that the suicides of slaves are linked, which it has been said were frequent under certain conditions, all those, in a word, which can be attributed to immoderation of moral or material despotism? To render visible the unavoidable and inflexible character of the rule under which we can do nothing to change, and in opposition to that expression "anomie" that we just used, we could call it fatalist suicide.[24]

If, as Durkheim writes, his typology shows the exaggerated or deflected form of a virtue, then we must ask, what is the virtue of which the vice of suicide due to "overregulation" or "excessive control" (excès de réglementation) is the exaggeration? Furthermore, if, as he writes, in the late nineteenth century it was "difficult to find examples," we can nevertheless ask whether this fourth term, already present on the surface yet inactive at the beginning of the twentieth century, can be read as virtually opening a space of a future problematization whose significance, for us in the twenty-first century as observers in the present, can be grasped?

Said another way, if, for example, the social cause of "deficient regulation," responsible for a high rate of suicide (anomic), is connected to the exaggeration of the virtue of the "love of progress," then what is the corresponding virtue calibrated to material or moral despotism? How can "moral or material despotism," as a type of social environment, cause a particular form of suicide and as an exaggeration of what kind of ethical practice? Where could we look for cases?

My argument will be that from the point of view of dominant norms, exemplified in the first story with respect to the medico-moral injunction instantiated by the doctor who "washed his hands" of his patient, and from a strictly Durkheimian perspective, it is an exaggeration that should be qualified as a refusal to advance in line with a range of instituted expectations about how one should conduct one's life, in this case when ill. As Sharon Kaufman has demonstrated at length for the US context, "ordinary medicine" today is normatively oriented to proposing more and better treatments no matter what stage of life and illness of the patient. "Doing nothing," and certainly to refuse treatment at any point, has become, in the words of one physician, "nonstandard."[25] I will argue that Durkheim couldn't understand the social significance of such counternormativity, which from the point of view of those engaging in assisted suicide, and those facilitating it, is sometimes also a search for a virtuous manner of moving against stasis, including the stasis of those dominant norms. My aim here is to test this conceptual, general anthropological question with the case of assisted suicide in Switzerland.

I begin with the three examples Durkheim suggests: (1) "the young man who marries too early," (2) "the married woman without children," and (3) the historical example of "the slave." The examples should produce a set, if they are coherent. In what does their coherence consist? I suggest that each example gives an instance of a situation in which a person is aware of a normative conception of the appropriate conduct of life—a normative conception of married life for the young man, a normative conception of family for the married woman, and the normative naturalization of inequality for the slave—yet finds him- or herself blocked with respect to that expectation and seeks to challenge it, materially and morally.

These persons are subject to the "despotism" of social norms and the unwillingness or incapacity to fulfill the expectation. Such a distinction between being unwilling or unable is moot from a nonpsychological perspective. What is crucial here is that while there may be a biological determinant for the incapacity or unwillingness to fulfill a social expectation, for example in Durkheim's use of the case of a woman unable to have children, or closer to my own inquiry, an illness that is likely to take a particular trajectory, or that produces a particular experience of suffering, it is the normative expectation of a certain comportment, or qualification of such a form of life, that produces contestation. It must be underscored here that the cause of suicide is not the excess of regulation itself or the moral demand itself; we are not dealing with the case of social obligations that result in or produce voluntary death, as is the case with altruistic suicide (e.g., the obligation to end one's life when one is sick in old age without chance of recovery, an example Durkheim gives of an Old Norse custom among warriors). We are rather in the domain of the kicking against excessive regulation, judged as excessive by the person, in negotiation with others, and whose action in turn is open to judgment on moral scales of excess, deficiency, and appropriateness. As such, this is the only type of suicide in Durkheim's model that is expressed through a countermovement by subjects against social norms.

Aside from the empirical claim that this fourth kind of suicide barely existed in the late nineteenth century, we lack in Durkheim's account an understanding of the ethical character of it and its relation to social forms. Given the rapport that Durkheim constitutes among moral order, social causes, and juridical regulation (sanction), I think that regardless of his empirical claim, he cannot grasp the significance of this fourth virtue, which is crucial for a pragmatic anthropology of the plural ethical characters of living, particularly with respect to the case of assistance with suicide.

Whether he was unable to grasp the content of the "fourth virtue" because empirically it did not exist across the nineteenth century, or whether he was unable to grasp the empirical phenomena because of a blind spot in his conception of the relation of society and moral order, is a crucial question. The empirical question of the existence of the phenomenon in the nineteenth century greater than the examples given by Durkheim is, however, beyond the scope of the present analysis.

Nevertheless, logically, it seems to me, we can first take up the problem of the fourth virtue as a conceptual blind spot that closed the possibility of such an inquiry, for a modern such as Durkheim, at the end of the nineteenth century. Furthermore, the incapacity to grasp this fourth virtue is significant for showing us a historical transformation in moral forms from the point of view of today, based in an experience in the present (see parts 1 and 2). We can see the significance of this historical transformation, it seems to me, in the invention of new manners of suicide and in particular in the fact that this manner of suicide indexes the importance of intransigence against the social determination of moral forms—a kind of social activity that has no place in Durkheim's asymmetrical schema.

MRS. MILNER'S VIRTUE

How to name the virtue at stake in this fourth bracketed type of suicide? Taking up Durkheim's model, it should be a counterpart to "the love of progress," which in the anomic variant is the excessive exaggeration of the virtue of participating in sociohistorical progress. Let us characterize this fourth virtue as follows: the endeavor and effort of a subject to produce movement and motion toward ends, to act in a situation of the experience of stasis. Such a virtue is irreducible to that which is grasped under the term *individualism*, along the axis of integration, since here our subjects demonstrate many kinds of attachments, and it is precisely the character of the normative social relations they encounter *against* which they purposively act, with the assistance of others. It is also irreducible to political and psychological tropes of "resistance" (passive or active), or "rebellion," as I will later demonstrate. Let us for now state that the exaggeration of such a virtue is, then, perhaps appropriately described by Durkheim as "fatalist," as it is a countermovement that under blocked conditions and with a degree of obstinacy, produces motion toward death as the only movement judged as possible by and for a subject, albeit crucially, with the help of others. Such obstinacy, I am arguing, as a moral form of practice, is aimed at producing countermotion under conditions of stasis experienced with respect to normative injunctions.

Although there could appear to be an analogic rapport between the virtue I am trying to name and what Gilles Deleuze, writing of Melville's "Bartleby, the Scrivener," called "the formula"[26]—Bartleby's "I would prefer not to"—the latter is resolutely about *producing* stasis ("I like to be stationary"). As such, arguably, "the formula" is both "ironic," insofar as its mood endeavors to produce a static distance between characters as well as between the reader and the events narrated, and heroic, insofar as it is a political allegory of "resistance" read at the level of psychology.[27] Indeed, in relation to my starting point in *Leaving*, of trying to sketch out the terrain of a cramped situation in illness and the parazone in which alternative parameters are added, we are precisely not in a totally "thwarted" situation but rather in a situation in which subjects endeavor to keep going, despite restrictions on their action. What I am naming as the virtue of "obstinacy" is neither static nor heroic, nor modernist, and is resolutely "social" in Durkheim's sense, although not in a modern modality. It is rather a countersocial, contemporary manner, a manner that I argue Durkheim was unable to grasp.

The significance of this fourth virtue, hard to name as it is, emerges I think only under changed historical circumstances. Its significance, however, can be shown with respect to our starting point: that over the last thirty years a new modality and form of suicide has emerged, one that did not exist before. Grasping assisted suicide in terms of this fourth virtue is of interest with respect to how sociologists and epidemiologists have typically attempted to grasp the phenomenon. Statistical interpretations in the last ten years confirm an orthodox Durkheimian view of the social causes of this new form and practice: those living alone, educated, and divorced are statistically more likely to end their lives through assisted suicide.

We are given an image in these statistical studies of what should properly be called egoistic and anomic suicide, which is to say, among those who are experiencing serious illness, there are moral and social forms—a lack of integration and a lack of psychosocial or even moral regulation—that shape the fact that a certain percentage of these suffering individuals seek to end their lives. Indeed, this narrative is confirmed in studies today that characterize these suicides as "potentially vulnerable."[28] These studies are concerned with the social environment and the psychosocial causes of the increasing numbers of people who seek assistance with suicide.

Inquiry, however, indicates that the morphology does not fit the proposed causes: in *Le suicide* Durkheim writes that those lacking social integration inhabit a subjective form of "melancholic languor"; those lacking moral regulation inhabit a form of "exasperation and weariness." Durkheim characterizes these forms with specific kinds of motion: centripetal motion for the melancholy of the excessively individuated suicide, centrifugal motion in the case of the exasperation of the deficiently regulated person. Among those suffering persons who, together with others, come to the judgment that they can be assisted in the wish to exit their experience of illness, neither melancholy nor exasperation adequately captures the phenomenon of those engaging in assisted suicide, nor do the forms of motion proposed by Durkheim adequately capture the movement of their thinking and their steps toward that solution.

Melancholy associated with detachment from social relations fails to adequately grasp the phenomena of those seeking assistance with suicide given that, first of all, those seeking assistance with suicide must engage in making and maintaining a series of (frequently strong and intimate) relations with those willing and able to assist and often with the help of a particular family member or friend. It takes a lot of work of arrangement to go through the sequences necessary for assistance with suicide, as we saw throughout part 2.

Mrs. Milner, for example, was ensconced in different kinds of relations: kinship, friendships, and the demands of the hospital to be a "good patient." She refused certain kinds of obligation, including the projection of self as grandmother-to-be, as well as that of "the good patient" who should either follow the doctor's orders or else be left to her own devices. Mrs. Milner sought out a different support, from Exit and Mrs. Pinelli, as well as support from her family, to assist her in her endeavor to shape actively her experience of giving up on the hope of ameliorating her situation.

The result of such refusal was therefore not isolation or lack of attachments. Although initially she asked her husband to keep her decision a secret from their daughters, with the mediation of the prescribing doctor, who became a family friend, and with the intervention of Mrs. Pinelli, the family came to an open discussion in which Mrs. Milner's judgment was worked through collectively and shared. This is not to say that all were in total accord but that disagreement and thoughts about her suicide and her refusal to continue treatment and her positive decision to end her life could be reflected on together. Furthermore, it must be underscored that suicidal ideation due to depression ("melancholic languor") is a core criterion for exclusion by assisted suicide associations.

By contrast, it is more difficult to establish that "exasperation" is not part of the morphology of assisted suicide: anger, from accounts during my inquiry so far, is regularly seen as part of the affect field of those living with debilitating (although not necessarily "terminal") illness. Indeed, Mrs. Milner's last words were in keeping with what her husband called her "forceful character" and in keeping with the increasing anger she expressed through the last months of her illness, according to him. Nevertheless, as a morphological type, in Durkheim's model, exasperated weariness connected to a lack of moral regulation due to an excess of progress connects exasperation or anger to a centripetal motion, an outburst consequent to the lack of moral direction, standards, and forms.

The narratives of part 2 indicate to me that an affect of anger in the search for assistance with suicide is, on the one hand, clearly connected to the experience of illness but, on the other hand, and more pointedly, is directed toward those viewed as blocking the path to an assisted suicide, particularly those who uphold norms and forms against which the person endeavors to kick back. This results often in the creation of discrete dyads (discrete in the double sense of discretion and separation) so that those who are seeking assistance must turn to a medical third party for the realization of the suicide. Such a situation becomes all the more clear when we think of the perseverance and work required from Peter, Fabienne, Clément, and Florian.

In Peter's final letter, outlining his request and arrangements for an assisted suicide in Switzerland, he specified his antinomian stance with respect to the legally suspect nature of his action as seen from the point of view of the United Kingdom, and he specified the lengths he would be willing to go in order to subvert the blockages he experienced:

> In order to avoid any proceedings against anyone accompanying me on such a journey, who may be deemed to have assisted me, it is necessary for me to undertake my journey far earlier than I would otherwise do in order that I can still travel unassisted, other than with the usual assistance provided to all travelers at airports and on airplanes. This is manifestly unjust and unkind to be confronted with such an undesirable set of conditions at such a sensitive and distressing time. In the absence of our societies' abject failure to confront this obvious need, or to make any provision for those afflicted or indeed to fashion the law in a humane and caring way, whilst still retaining any safeguards required, creates a cruel and uncaring situation for so many people in similar situations such as mine.

With these specifications in mind, I would like to suggest that the force and directionality at stake in the fourth type of suicide seems to be best characterized neither as centrifugal nor centripetal but rather as obstinate: a refusal to comport oneself in line with a received normative injunction. The range of affect is vast, composite, and changeable: anger, serenity, assuredness, ambivalence. These passions are configured with thought and action, which manifests in this specific form of motion toward a highly determined *telos*: an ending of life that is considered a form of death in keeping with the normative orientation of the suffering person. What is important to characterize is the possible, and virtual, motion of a subject, consequent to the situation experienced, and to characterize the form given to that experience. The configuration of thought, passion, and action of this fourth type of suicide distinguishes its form and motion from that which could be grasped as either renunciation or exasperation, despair or melancholy.

The term *obstinate* has at least two senses that are of interest: (1) it is defiant of authority, and (2) it is difficult to overcome. For those whose experience of illness is that it is not responsive to treatment, or that they no longer wish to carry on with treatment, or that they no longer wish to live with a certain

experience of illness, there is a question of what to do. The question of authority is an accompanying one: modern medicine has, to a degree appropriately,
a normative orientation toward cure and sustaining life as long as possible.
There can also be excess, however, in modern medicine's normative orientation
to the sick and dying. In situations where medicine cannot cure, those who
are sick live under a dual moral demand: hope and courage, which as a discursive norm was institutionalized throughout the nineteenth century.[29] The
creation of associations in the 1980s for assisting with voluntarily ending life
was defiant with respect to such a normative orientation, experienced by some
as a form of moral and material tyranny. Some people would rather not participate in phase 1 experimental trials. Some would rather not be governed in
the ways proposed by modern institutions for managing sickness: they may
choose no interventions, or they may choose to end their lives.[30] Nevertheless,
as historian of medicine Harry Marks pointed out about his own experience
of illness and treatment, even for someone who "for a long time" thought they
didn't want an extended "medicalized death," there is the realization that "it
is hard to avoid once one starts the medical grand slalom."[31]

The motion of such a moral form of recalcitrance is neither centripetal nor
centrifugal: it is refractory with respect to the stasis-inducing combination of
exterior forces and the moral and material demands of the institutions in
which people are embedded. Such motion can indeed be surprising: I met the
husband of Gaby Mosa in December of 2015. Mrs. Mosa had ended her life
in April of 2014 with the assistance of Exit. She had begun to have speech
problems in late November of 2013, and she was finally diagnosed with amyotrophic lateral sclerosis in March of 2014. On hearing the diagnosis, the
prognosis, and plans for management of the illness—the need for an artificial
feeding tube, then an oxygen mask at night, and then intubation in hospital—
she turned to her husband in the consultation room, in front of the doctor,
and immediately said, "Josy, you will stay with me. I won't go to the hospital.
Not for intubation or anything else. When I can longer breathe well, I
will leave (*je m'en irai*). You will help me and will hold my hand." Joseph
Mosa promised her. He is, however, a devout Catholic who grew up in the
mountains around Sion. His wife was likewise a faithful Catholic. "It was
surprising," he explained to me: "we're religious: we don't do that around here."
Joseph made sense of this surprising spontaneous request, as well as his promise to her, with respect to her character: her courage and her formidable
decisiveness.

This fourth type of suicide puts in question the role of society or, more accurately, the professional groups and institutions dealing with specific problems, as legislators within society. It questions, furthermore, the authority and normativity of those who instantiate and attempt to regulate what they would consider *the* moral order relative to which persons give form to their lives. As such, it puts in question the nineteenth-century figuration of *l'homme* in terms of doubles, to wit, in the case of Durkheim, of that doubling between society and individuals. In attempting to grasp the social form of normative order, Durkheim presupposed his object in terms of a duality between two abstract general concepts: "In so far as we are at one with the group and share its life, we are open to their influence; but inversely in so far as we have a personality distinct from their own, we are refractory to them [*nous leurs sommes réfractaires*], and try to escape from them. Since there is no one who doesn't lead this sort of double existence concurrently, each of us is animated at once by a double movement. We are drawn in a social direction and tend to follow the inclinations of our own natures."[32] Within this figure of "Man and His Doubles," refractory motion is taken up, indeed can only be taken up, by Durkheim in terms of a remainder of socialization: rebellion, or strife, or courage, or decisiveness, as with Gaby Mosa, is reduced by Durkheim to the level of psychological experience.

Sociology becomes the moral legislator of order: the right mix of egoism, altruism, and anomie consequent to progress. Heterotopias of governing oneself and others differently are unintelligible in this problematization of modern society: "*Volenti non fit injuria.* This is an error," writes Durkheim: "Society is injured because the sentiment is offended on which its *most respected moral maxims* today rest, a sentiment almost the only bond between its members, and which would be weakened if this offense could be committed with impunity. How could this sentiment *maintain the least authority* if the moral conscience did not protest its violation?"[33] The moral conscience that seeks to maintain the moral authority that binds society is that of the sociologist. The sociologist, furthermore, takes on a figurative character, as we will see—that of the "hero," a figure with a long afterlife in the social sciences.

FRENCH MODERN, CONTEMPORARY SWISS

As Francesco Callegaro has indicated, Durkheim's scientific attitude is heroic, which is as much an effect of the social environment as any factor of personality.[34] His heroism, a mean form of the altruistic social etiology he diagnosed in *Le suicide*, is counterbalanced by the specificity of the individual sociologist-as-hero, who is able to remove himself from attachments to the relevant degree that he can "see" that to which others are blind (i.e., Bourdieu's critical distance). Moreover, the sociologist partakes of, observes, and contributes to the modernity that produced his own subject-position. The accelerated progress observed by the sociologist provides him with a counterbalancing aspect of irony: Durkheim the sociologist is heroic enough not to be taken in by progress; he is ironic enough to keep a fixed distance from this so-called progress, as well as his own heroism.

What is crucial in terms of this scientific and ethical position, as we see clearly in Durkheim's account of rebellion in "Man's" doubling, is that obstinacy is treated psychologically and thus externalized as a form of motion. Such a psychological rendering is an effect of what we must consider the jurisdictional counterpart to the sociologist's scientific position: the role as support for the figure of the legislator. As Callegaro points out (vis-à-vis Durkheim's criticism of Montesquieu), "Durkheim will not try to establish the laws of modern societies himself, but rather indicate the social institutions that would enable modern individuals to build themselves the new modern order."[35] I note and repeat Callegaro's use of the definite article: the new modern order, which requires the sociological hero to indicate the means to build it.

In contrast, for the more modest anthropological observer, the observer who seeks neither heroism nor irony, there is on the surface of Durkheim's own model of suicide a brazenly critical pivot point from the past, one that from our present position and with a contemporary ethos can index the movement of a future problematization of the object he has founded through his science: the fourth virtue opens a door to multiplicities of norms and forms of living and not an opposition of "collective force" to "individual personality"—not "Man and His Double" but rather a plurality of indeterminate norms and forms for governing oneself relative to others, a possibility Durkheim was unable to grasp. Moreover, he was unable to grasp it precisely insofar as it appeared as insignificant given the stability of the nineteenth-century historical configuration within which he was operating.

Paul Rabinow's nominalist genealogy of the emergence of "the social" explains how by the 1840s "historical development, statistics, and industrial and moral topography" could be elaborated for major urban centers (e.g., a study of the industrial and moral topography of Nantes 1835), contextualizing

Durkheim's sociological intervention as the outcome of rather than the starting point for a new science of society.[36] Indeed, it is only as the outcome of
this more-than-a-century-long development that the stability of the object can
be understood and hence Durkheim's inability to grasp its points of fracture
and rearticulation. Of critical importance in the emergence of this object is a
relation between norms and normativity. Rabinow quotes Georges Canguilhem in order to clarify the beginning of a type of normalization specific to
social arrangements at the end of the Enlightenment, "one that was more
dynamic, restless and expansive."[37] "Between 1759, the date of the first appearance of the word *normal*, and 1834, the date of the first appearance of the word
normalized, a normative class conquered the power to identify social norms
with its own uses and its own determination of content."[38] As Rabinow indicates, synthesizing Canguilhem's arguments, such a "power" was provided in
part through an epistemological intervention, the "metaphoric transfer of
concepts from a newly emergent physiology—function, hierarchy, and norm—
to the social realm."[39]

To seize the effect of such metaphoric transfer, we can revisit Durkheim's
observations in the chapter of *Le suicide* treating anomie and against which
fatalist suicide is opposed in his model. It is worth observing that the explanation of anomie as a type of suicide is the only one to proceed by way of analogy
with biological organisms. The chapter on anomic suicide introduces the
phenomenon in the following terms: "society is not only something attracting
the sentiments and activities of individuals with unequal force. It is also a
power controlling them."[40]

Anomie is Durkheim's manner of grasping an exaggerated phenomenon
of the way this regulative action is performed. As is well known, his first
scientific gesture is to use economic data to show that industrial or financial
crises increase suicides, not because they cause poverty but because they
disturb the collective order. How is it possible, he asks, that men are more
inclined to self-destruction when social readjustments occur, whether owing
to growth or catastrophe? Especially in the case of economic growth, he asks
himself how a phenomenon that could be considered to improve existence
increases the rate at which people end their lives. His answer begins with
biological reasoning: "No living being can be happy or even exist unless his
needs are sufficiently proportioned to his means. . . . Movements incapable of
production without pain tend not to be reproduced. Unsatisfied tendencies
atrophy, and as the impulse to live is merely the result of all the rest, it is bound

to weaken as the others relax."[41] That is to say, the more unsatisfied tendencies, the weaker the impulse to live. Animals, Durkheim goes on to reason, given that they depend on purely material conditions, establish the equilibrium between needs and means automatically: "This is not [the] same with man."[42] Clearly. "Beyond the indispensable minimum which satisfies nature when instinctive, a more awakened reflection suggests better conditions, seemingly desirable ends craving fulfillment. . . . How to determine the quantity of well-being, comfort or luxury legitimately to be craved by a human being? Nothing appears in man's organic nor in his psychological constitution which sets a limit to such tendencies."[43] It is here that the biological analogy is made operational: if nothing biological sets the limit to humans' needs, as pertains to other biological organisms, there must be something else, something social that sets limits to their wants: "A regulative power [*puissance*] must play the same role for moral needs which the organism plays for physical needs."[44] To think about the problem of the analogy and of the (lack of a) place of the fourth virtue in Durkheim's conception of the social, it is worth displacing our reading of Durkheim by way of the work of Canguilhem.

In a lecture originally published in 1955, titled "The Problem of Regulation in the Organism and in Society," Canguilhem offers an incisive intervention into the problem of biological and social analogism: "in the order of the organism, we commonly see the whole world debate the nature of ills [*mal*], and no one debate the ideal of the good," for the simple reason that the ideal of the organism is the organism itself. By contrast, "the existence of societies, of their disorders and unrests, brings forth a wholly different relation between ills and reforms, because for society, what we debate is how to know its ideal state or norm." As Canguilhem puts it, there is precisely a "multiplicity of possible solutions calculated or dreamt up by men to put an end to injustices."[45] Society, in Canguilhem's text, is a means for the pursuit of these multiple possible solutions. Thus, insofar as society becomes a medium for the administration of diverse solutions and to the degree that they are institutionalized, society is stabilized relative to the problematization to which it is conceived as the means of solution.

Canguilhem draws out a point implicit in Durkheim's view of society when he writes that precisely the limit of the analogy is that societies are not self-regulating, hence the need to institutionalize regulation and hence the need, as Canguilhem writes, drawing on Henri Bergson, for "heroes," the philosopher or sociologist included. The same point holds true for Durkheim as we saw: moments of social crisis, of too much disequilibrium, of pathos tipped over into exaggerated pathology is a moment that Bergson named "the call of the hero."[46] Durkheim, Bergson, and Canguilhem are moderns to the degree that they think the hero is the one whose ethos renders such a subject capable of grasping and resolving breakdown, even if they disagree on the correct configuration of life and the social in the reconstruction of those breakdowns.

Durkheim (heroically) assumes discursive responsibility for the ethical, and then juridical, character of the sociological judgments he claims: "the first and most important question which concerns the subject is to discover whether or not suicide should be classed among the actions permitted by morality or among those proscribed by it. Should it be regarded, to any degree whatever, as a criminal act?" Crucially, the persistence and legitimate qualification of suicide as immoral stems, for Durkheim, from the fact that "it has preserved something of its old criminological character. According to the most widespread jurisprudence, an accomplice of suicide is prosecuted as a homicide. This would not be so if suicide were considered an act indifferent to morality."[47]

Let us note here an important historical and sociological fact: unlike in France, which decriminalized suicide after the Revolution, many other European countries only decriminalized the act in the 1970s, at which point they reinscribed and insisted on the fact that assistance with suicide was still regarded as a criminal act. It is precisely a transformation in the ethical character of the human relations and social forms at stake in assistance with suicide that is increasingly in question today.

Durkheim notes two historical exceptions to the general interdiction: forms of legitimate suicide specific to city-states in ancient Greece and in Rome. The legitimacy of suicide in these cases turns on political-legal institutions administering the demands of citizens to end their lives. The relaxation of former interdictions against suicide, as well as the gradual lengthening of the list of "legitimate excuses," was, for Durkheim, consequent to "serious disturbances that afflicted these societies."[48] He thus poses two arguments to retain the distinction and distance between modern and ancient relations of power linking the individual, his or her life, and the state: on the one hand, the fact that these societies had political means of judging whether and how a person may dispose of his or her own life indicates the symptom of a morbid condition; that is to say, a state's legitimation of forms for suicide is, for Durkheim, in itself an index of breakdown in social and political life. On the other hand, and more fundamentally, the modern character of the rapport connecting persons, death, and political power is, in Durkheim's judgment, that "with the progress of history, the prohibition, instead of being relaxed, only becomes more radical."[49]

The strictness of this historical progress comes, of course, not from what anthropologist James Faubion has called the "themitical" (homeostatic and regulatory) modality of ethical life,[50] a point I will return to, but rather, to the contrary, from a sociohistorical and pragmatic disruption of ethical life; more specifically, Durkheim identifies the progressive development of severe interdictions against a person ending her or his own life in "Christian societies" as due to their new conception of the human personality. That is to say Durkheim offers a sketch of the general transformation in the worth of the human person from a "social value" belonging "wholly to the state" to "a kind of dignity which places him above himself as well as above society. . . . Man has become a god for men."[51] He puts the point succinctly when he writes that what had been uniquely a civil matter has become a religious one.

Durkheim challenges his own thesis: "but if *this* is why suicide has been classed among illicit actions, should we not henceforth consider the condemnation to be without basis? It seems that scientific criticism cannot concede the least value to these mystical conceptions."[52] To retain the authority of his science of the social, Durkheim then encompasses the valorization of the human person, beyond the value any single individual could give to it, by way of the "collective sentiment" that is expressed in such valorization. Stated differently, the individual can have worth only because and insofar as that worth is indexed to practices that refer to collective (i.e., social) life. Moral worth by definition for Durkheim is extrapersonal, and the moral form of that worth, which attracts, pushes, and pulls our actions, enjoys "real moral supremacy." His master stroke follows: "If it is demonstrable that *exaltation of human personality* is one of the aims pursued, and which *should be* pursued, by modern societies, *all moral regulation* deriving from this principle is justified by that fact itself, whatever the manner of its usual justification."[53] More persuasively still, in his judgment it is a "law of history" that societies progress from valorizing society over the individual to valorizing the individual as the object and objective whose worth is indexed to social life. Historically, he concludes, "the moment approaches when the only remaining bond among the members of a single human group will be that they are all men."[54] Societies constrain and dominate persons while societies are constrained by the ideal of humanity and the human person. Hence, societies are no longer able to dispose with persons or to articulate the ideal of the person as they see fit.

Durkheim was unable to imagine the turn that the twentieth century took. To his credit, he was blind to the gratuitous capacity of political regimes to bend the idea of the person and political justifications for the use of persons to their own ends. He was thus also blind to the fact that groups of persons wish to forge other forms of life, instantiate other norms, and seek to reorganize power relations among people. Durkheim could not see, indeed did not need to see, the capacity of persons to produce heterogeneous and obstinate forms of autonomy, with ambivalent relations to regulation: given the variegated and variously mediated forms of autonomy observable in Switzerland, one could say *le bonheur suisse* passed him by.

We can return to Durkheim's own test, however, to gauge his judgment of the historical development of moral forms of suicide: if exaltation of the person is and should be pursued by society, then society is justified in regulating morality according to this principle. For Durkheim the question is then finished: society no longer has the right to intervene on the person as it wishes; therefore, if society no longer has this right to do with persons as it wishes, then neither does any particular individual. He concludes that "under these conditions suicide must be classed among immoral acts; for in its main principle it denies this religion of humanity."[55]

PROBLEMATIZING HUMANITY AFTER 1975: NORMS, COUNTERNORMS, AND POWER

Following Durkheim's own logic, we are in a position now to observe the pushback against excessive moral regulation, itself derived from a principle of humanity, or dignity, and the valorization of the idea of the person. The post–Second World War moral and political landscape witnessed the invention and formation of venues for the discursive production of statements about protection of the intrinsic worth of human beings. The 1970s and 1980s then witnessed an inflection of this discursive formation through the reuse of the figure of human dignity within a configuration of power relations around medical authority, medical practice, and judgments about care at the end of life.

There has been a historical development in which suicide as the denial of humanity is put in question—that, in fact, societies have produced forms for the management of illness, both physical and psychiatric, that are heteronomous at minimum and morally despotic at a maximum. Such ethical disruption has political stakes for the management of requests for assistance with suicide. In its most extreme (and logical) form the rendering symmetric of Durkheim's schema poses the challenge of the legitimacy of suicide requests beyond and aside from any basis in a biological *cause* that would on its own act as justification (e.g., the justification of assisted suicide with reference to a "prognosis").

From the mid-1970s onward, in Europe and the United States, a distinct *topos* emerged: "death with dignity." What, then, are we to make of serious institutional developments since the 1980s and particularly the emergence of institutional forms for legitimating suicide under certain conditions along with juridical immunity (for the most part) of those who assist with suicide? We are in a position to respond to the test that Durkheim suggests. To undo a prohibition, the burden of proof is that some profound change in the basic conditions of collective life has occurred.

The year 1975 was crucial for the development of the theme of "death with dignity": a murder accusation of the head of medicine at the public hospital of Zurich launched a public and political debate in Switzerland, which coincided with (arguably launched) reflections at the level of the European Union: a year after the murder accusation and exoneration of the doctor for facilitating passive euthanasia, the European Council subsequently published resolution 613, "Rights of the Sick and Dying." This resolution declares that recourse to techniques for the prolongation of life does not always correspond to the veritable interests of suffering people. We see after this date a growing preoccupation with questions of what the interests of patients consist in and who can represent these interests. A debate had thus emerged on the relation of vital and social norms and the manner in which ethical judgments are made in their articulation.

In a radio broadcast from 1975 Canguilhem and Henri Péquignot, also a medical doctor and thinker, discussed the then-emerging question of the so-called right to die in this context. Canguilhem says the following:

> It seems to me that the question of the "right to die" could be taken up first of all outside of all reference to the current state of medical knowledge. . . . And well, I think that there is a right to die as there is any other right. Rights are the awareness, at a given moment, of the fact that, without having wanted it and without having sought it out, we are engaged in a situation that we can take up. . . . So then, the right to die is only the expression of this fact that the only thing I am able to do for life, for my life, at a given moment, is to choose the manner in which I will leave it.[56]

This is, of course, consistent with his approach to the vital normativity of living beings. What distinguishes a "right to die," however, particularly in the case of Switzerland, is precisely the manner and the means of ending one's life, which poses an awkward question of the institutional relations—and power relations—between the practice of medicine and this modality of voluntary death.

An assisted suicide is supposed to reduce the violence of voluntarily ending one's life. It is precisely in accessing the means to end one's life in a less violent manner (barbiturate overdose requiring a medical prescription) that heterogeneous norms come into contact and sometimes conflict in the judgment about whether to facilitate such access. The problem of such access and the pragmatic question of how to end life requires a refinement of Canguilhem's coherent but limited suggestion that the question of assistance with dying can be dealt with in the first place outside of medicine, since in the second place, medical authority and power frequently frames the means and manner of making the judgment to leave life. It is interesting that between 1982 and 1999 access to nonviolent means for accompanied suicides occurred largely with the hidden support of a small number of doctors. As of the late 1990s, the associations that facilitate such suicides vowed to operate in a visible manner, highlighting points of tension between medical practices and the facilitation of assisted suicides.

Where does that leave us with respect to Durkheim and a fourth virtue? Pragmatically, if we hypothesize the existence of the fourth virtue of obstinacy—amid a plurality of norms—and if the norms and normativity of clinical practice are part of that configuration, how, then, do we view the relation of medical practice, oriented to cure, the experience of illness for the sick person, and the biological and institutional parameters that sustain any possible relation between a doctor and the suffering person, particularly in a situation in which a person who is ill seeks medical help to end his or her life?

On the one hand, Canguilhem was right to say that there is no moral medical calculus that says *if* disease x, with prognosis y, after failed therapy z, *then* assisted suicide, or "the right to die." Furthermore, the fourth virtue indicates that it is precisely not a social institution instantiated in a single authority that will judge for the person whether or not they can leave their experience of illness. Yet it is not true for Canguilhem to suggest that a practice of a right to die is able to take place outside any reference to medical knowledge and judgment or outside of the power relations constituted by this major field and institution of modern medicine: obstinacy is configured in relation to a range of norms, virtues, practices, and the judgments of others, including doctors willing, or else not willing, to write a lethal prescription or facilitate the practice.

As we saw in parts 1 and 2, power relations and countereffectuations between associations and medical institutions are indicative of breakdowns for which there are no clear solutions. What remains is an active work for the associations to continue to listen to the experiences and wishes of patients and to give a form to these wishes, under the reigning power relations as they pertain to care proposed within institutionalized medical settings.

Canguilhem himself offers resources for a gesture of symmetry, so as to think about the relation of norms, counternorms, and power in the relation of clinical practice, illness, and ethical judgment. Canguilhem, in fact, provides a resource that can be used with respect to his own suggestion that the ethical judgment of ending life can be taken up in the first place distinct from the epistemic and ethical contours of medicine. In a text titled "The Idea of Nature in Medical Theory and Practice," Canguilhem observes the historical change in doctors' relation to "nature," and he specifies the emergence in the nineteenth century of virtues associated with the legitimacy of not treating "nature" as that which contains within itself the secrets of both cure and healing. He cites what could be taken for a nineteenth-century medical maxim: "ignorance would consist in not asking of nature what is not its own."[57]

Virtue, for a physician after the nineteenth century, is specified through a double negation of vice (understood as excessive or deficient practice): not to ask nature what it is but to ask of it what it is not, so as to know better how to intervene on it with what is not its own. We are squarely within the bounds of the legitimacy of modern virtues of curiosity, care, and intervention. Canguilhem offers us a glimpse of the development of virtues in medical practice, after the 1800s, a historical moment in which curiosity and impatience are rendered in positive ethical terms. The mid-eighteenth-century doctor Théophile de Bordeu is quoted diminishing the ethical virtue of the "expectant"— "wait and see," "let nature take its course"—method: "Those who employ it have always made up only a small number of the doctors, especially among people who are naturally *sharp, impatient,* and *apprehensive.*"[58]

It is a small step, then, to symmetrize (and thus countereffect) these virtues of heroic modern doctors to a contemporary ethos of those who suffer; indeed, it is in this ethical terrain that doctors, those suffering, and families, as well as legal and political actors, must meet: sharpness (in the discernment over how one wishes to die), impatience (to end an experience of suffering), and apprehension (for what a prognosis may bring) are not virtues unique to a profession that seeks to cure but also to an existence that asks "what are we to do?" when neither cure nor healing is possible.

Observation | The Neutral

Part 3 of this book has been dedicated to the exploration of knowledge domains that take "ethos" as an object of inquiry. The first way of taking up the practice of assisted suicide in terms of ethos was through a study of the conceptual repertoire and theoretical orientation available within psychoanalytic reflection. The psychoanalytic reading of ethos, as it pertains to questions of voluntary death, concerned the subject as "psyche" and "character," considered in terms of their constitution by way of psychological dynamics, and the forms, or structures, through which and within which those dynamics move. The attention of this knowledge practice to ethos as character primarily concerned the loss of objects, in partial connection with the loss to self, or the changes to an image of self, that can be associated with illness itself, narcissistic regression, and a tension, if not a dialectic (for certain analytic orientations), of repetition and a possible search for mastery of that loss.

The second way of taking up ethos and suicide was by way of a sociological reading of the social cause and form—isomorphic in that the kind of causation at stake is "formal"—of the kind of suicide that pertained to a counternormative virtue that I heuristically named as "obstinacy." Whereas Durkheim's sociological model was, broadly speaking, statistical, my conceptual determination was heuristic: a conceptual construction whose significance is situated in relation to its position within Durkheim's overarching model, which allowed me then, in heuristic fashion again, to use the model to better diagnose a particular aspect of the practice, as based on my experience, to wit, the "virtue" at stake in the practice, considered by way of its sociological form.

In addition to the question of the psychoanalytic truth of the desire to leave life, and the sociological determination of a virtue specific to pushing back against excessive moral regulation, I will now explore a third domain of knowledge through which this practice and the ethos through which it is put into practice can be grasped—namely, anthropology. Relative to an anthropological account of the particularity of the ethos that characterizes an assisted suicide (for the record, I do not think there is only one), its object, or rather as I will explain "the parameters" of taking ethos as an object of analysis, will need to be determined, as well as the manner of putting that object to the test. That manner is neither theoretical nor idea-typical, and its object is neither that of the psychodynamics of psychic investment and loss, and the structural configuration of drive, nor that of a social cause or form or the idea-typic identification of the social counternormative virtue that can heuristically characterize the practice.

To put it overly schematically: if, psychoanalytically speaking, assisted suicide can be characterized as "narcissistic," both in terms of regression and in terms of idealization, producing a desire for mastery whose lack appears in the repetition of an experience of loss, and if, sociologically, it can be characterized as "obstinate," how can we characterize the practice in terms of "anthropology"?

Moreover, I would like to ask, given that I am writing from the position of having been trained as an anthropologist, and given that I consider that this inquiry falls within a genre of, or rather, the search for a contemporary genre for anthropological inquiry, how can an anthropological characterization of the practice be situated in relation to the psychoanalytic and sociological readings?

Broadly, I will consider an anthropological orientation to the ethos of assisted suicide by way of what has come to be called an "anthropology of ethics," taking up specifically the centrality of the work of Michel Foucault (1926–84) for this domain of inquiry.[1] It is worth remembering that the Greek term *êthos*—ἦθος—refers principally to "manners," "customs," "disposition," "character," and "bearing."[2] The conceptual range of the term is thus part of its attraction and constitutes several traps to be avoided, principally, the wish to find formulas that can hold all senses of the term together, as has been frequently the case in prior anthropological usage in which ethos could grasp simultaneously, and within a common frame, personal disposition, individual bearing, and national, ethnic, or cultural character.

The question of whether there is something essentially "Swiss" about assisted suicide in terms of its ethos, in a "cultural" sense, is not a question I pose. I demur from a prior anthropological use of the term, such as that of Gregory Bateson in *Naven*, where he takes ethos up in the sense of "the characteristic spirit, prevalent tone or sentiment of a people or community; the 'genius' of an institution or system,"[3] or in *Balinese Character*, where he and Margaret Mead suggest it is "a culturally standardized system of organization of the instincts and emotions of behavior."[4] What is specific about the situation in Switzerland pertaining to the practice of assisted suicide, however, are the parameters of the "parazone" that I laid out in the first part of this book: the exclusion of the practice from professional activity; the sustained lack of clarity about rules; the vague sense of mistrust between the associations and institutional medical professionals; the tension between "technical" propositions and "aesthetics" of judgment in the acceptance or refusal of assistance; and the danger of reproach for those who undertake such assistance or, more seriously, juridical action against them.

Although the "doing" of an assisted suicide cannot reasonably be grasped as an "embodiment" of that cultural context, as Bateson and Mead did for example in their photographic analysis in *Balinese Character*, it is possible to ask how an ethos of a practice is able to be put into action within this particular setting. I take it as a more or less self-evident point that there is something about the setting, the parameters of the practice within the setting, including the fact that it pertains to suicide in an extramedical venue, and does not concern euthanasia in hospital, that there is something about this way of ending life that resonates with, or is interconnected with, the desires, wishes, and expectations of the person who makes the request. To put the point negatively, I can briefly mention the situation of a person in France, who after having made an initial investigation into assisted suicide in Switzerland, following a diagnosis of amyotrophic lateral sclerosis, decided that the form, the setting, the lack of "framing" (*le manque d'un cadre*) in Switzerland did not sit well with how he envisaged the end of his life. He subsequently endeavored to be accepted for euthanasia in a Belgian hospital. The ethos of the practice, to make a basic point, is not determined uniquely by either the social ecology or the psychological dynamics. This point, however, is insufficient for grasping, positively, ethos as an object of anthropological understanding.

Given a set of supports, tools, technologies, precepts, discourses, constraints, proscriptions, and so on, which are found in settings both outside and within Switzerland, the anthropological question of ethos that I seek to pose is, How might we grasp the way that people wishing to be assisted in their voluntary death recognize, and in which senses, the "ethos" of their "action" pertaining to the realization of an assisted suicide, as an object of concern?

AN ANTHROPOLOGY OF ETHICS

Michel Foucault's impact on the anthropological study of "ethos," understood as morally or ethically marked manners of being, is hard to overstate. The publication of volumes 2 and 3 of *History of Sexuality* was a major intervention in the way that historians and anthropologists could study how an "experience" was constituted at a given historical moment—in Foucault's case, an experience "that caused individuals to recognize themselves as moral or ethical subjects of a "sexuality." Experience, Foucault wrote, is understood as "the correlation between different fields of knowledge, types of normativity, and forms of subjectivity in a particular culture."[5]

Whereas he thought that he had developed, through previous inquiries, sufficient tools to analyze power relations through which normative comportment is regulated, as well as tools to analyze knowledge discourses without reducing them to ideologies, he realized that he lacked the tools to study "the modes according to which individuals are given to recognize themselves as sexual subjects" (4). The blockage point, he explains, was that "at the time the notion of desire, or of the desiring subject, constituted if not a theory, then at least a generally accepted theoretical theme" (4). To understand the "experience" of sexuality from the eighteenth century onward, Foucault considered he first had to clear the path by way of asking how individuals were "led to focus their attention on themselves, to decipher, recognize, and acknowledge themselves as subjects of desire, bringing into play between themselves and themselves a certain relationship that allows them to discover, in desire, the truth of their being" (5). What is important here, then, is that I consider Foucault's approach to ethical work of the subject on itself as an adjacent manner of taking up both the psychological and the sociological dynamics previously discussed. Regardless of what can be said about the truth of desire from within a psychoanalytic apparatus, with its postulate of the unconscious character of its dynamics and structure, what matters in relation to Foucault's orientation is how the problematization of a desiring subject becomes a matter of conscious reflection, work, and practice.

Foucault's question thus became a disconcertingly nuanced one: How does an individual come to recognize himself as a subject (of which the "subject of desire" is but one formula and formulation) and, by "forming" himself as a subject, engage in specific practices and discourses that in one way or another will discern or determine the truth or falsity of that self-formation? In other words, by what means does a person answer the question, Am I the person who I sought to become or take myself to be? The question of "whether I am the person I take myself to be" was central to what Foucault points out as being the ancient problematization of and preoccupation with "arts of existence" (technē tou biou). This question reaches its apotheosis in the practice of assisted suicide when the individual must answer the question, Are you sure you want to die? And then the question, Do you know what will happen if you ingest the solution or turn the tap on the perfusion? It is important to restate, though, that this question is the climax of unfolding work that a subject performs on itself, in relation to others. Foucault's reflection on ethics can assist me in asking how that work is constituted and how it is performed.

Foucault's methodological considerations turn first of all on what the object is of an inquiry that seeks to study the forms of a "morality" understood as the games of truth at stake in techniques of self. "By 'morality,'" he states, "one means a set of values and rules of action that are recommended to individuals through the intermediary of various prescriptive agencies such as the family (in one of its roles), educational institutions, churches, and so forth" (25). Such a morality can be more or less systematic. Foucault suggests, however, that even when "diffuse," the prescriptive ensemble—which includes "loopholes," "compromises," "injunctions," or "elements" that "counterbalance" or "cancel each other out on certain points"—can be termed a moral code.

Foucault quickly points out, though, that the code is not determinate; thus, "morality" refers—in addition to the code—to the "the manner in which they [individuals] obey or resist an interdiction or a prescription" (25). Between code and conduct there is what he would elsewhere call "governmentality" (action on action)—namely, the manner in which conduct is conducted relative to normative concerns about how conduct should be conducted: "the manner in which one ought to form oneself as an ethical subject acting in reference to the prescriptive elements that make up the code" (26).

If the sociological reading of obstinacy showed the existence of a social form that takes its content from a counternormative position, and the psychoanalytic framing considered the truth of (unconscious) desire, in a large part, to escape the subject's grasp, it is now necessary, anthropologically, to ask whether it is possible to conceptualize the specificity of the ethical work that takes place in this practice, in relation to both the truth of that desire and the counternormativity of the conduct of conduct, and to specify, by asking this question, what the object of such ethical work is, given that it is neither necessarily that of the psychological individual nor the sociological datum.

PARAMETERS

Foucault lays out four "parameters" for the study of how individuals conduct themselves in relation to a given discursive moral ensemble and preoccupation with such an ensemble. The first is through what he calls the determination of ethical substance: "Take, for example, a code of sexual prescriptions enjoining the two marital partners to practice a strict and symmetrical conjugal fidelity, always with a view to procreation; there will be many ways, even within such a rigid frame, to practice that austerity, many ways to 'be faithful'" (26). These many ways depend on "the way in which the individual has to constitute this or that part of himself as the prime material of his moral conduct": the ethical substance may concern "observance of interdictions," but it could also concern "mastery of desire" (not the same thing, clearly); it could also concern the "intensity, continuity, and reciprocity of feelings that are experienced vis-à-vis the partner" (26).

Such inquiry is also parameterized by what Foucault called "the mode of subjectivation": how an individual recognizes aspects of the moral ensemble and considers himself "obliged" to put that aspect into practice. Some examples of such modes: compliance with a precept may stem from acknowledgment of oneself as member of a group that accepts the precept or declares adherence to it, a more or less "conventional" mode; another modality could be "tradition," and a third could be the making of oneself an exemplar relative to a standard and form (beauty, perfection, dignity).

The third parameter is what he calls "ethical work," or *áskēsis*—exercise, practice, training; more generally the "mode of life"—that a subject performs on itself, "not only in order to bring one's conduct into compliance with a given rule, but to attempt to transform oneself into the ethical subject of one's behavior" (27). This mode includes the learning of precepts; checking of conduct; "a sudden, all-embracing, and definitive renunciation"; "relentless combat"; decipherment as painstaking, continuous, and detailed as possible, of the movements of desire.

Finally, there is the telos: "A moral action tends toward its own accomplishment; but it also aims beyond the latter, to the establishing of a moral conduct that commits an individual, not only to other actions always in conformity with values and rules, but to a certain mode of being, a mode of being characteristic of the ethical subject" (27). Different final aims can include mastery of the self, detachment from the world, tranquility of the soul, immortality of the soul, and salvation.

Foucault was willing to go so far as to make a general claim: "there is no specific moral action that does not refer to a unified moral conduct; no moral conduct that does not call for the forming of oneself as an ethical subject; and no forming of the ethical subject without 'modes of subjectivation' and an 'ascetics' or 'practices of the self' that support them. Moral action is indissociable from these forms of self-activity, and they do not differ any less from one morality to another than do the systems of values, rules, and interdictions" (29). What are the consequences that Foucault draws out for analysis?

One significant consequence is a better specification of the object and objective of analysis. To study the extent to which action is consistent with prescribed rules and values is to take "moral behaviors" as the object of analysis; to analyze the "different systems of rules and values that are operative in a given society" with their enforcement (or not) and their variability in form (or not) is to take "codes" as the object of analysis; finally he suggests that "a history of the way in which individuals are urged to constitute themselves as subjects of moral conduct would be concerned with the models proposed for setting up and developing relationships with the self, for self-reflection, self-knowledge, self-examination, for the decipherment of the self by oneself, for the transformations that one seeks to accomplish with oneself as object" (29). Behaviors and codes and models, then, are three objects that can be either interconnected or studied in their partial connection and disconnection, since "codes of behavior and forms of subjectivation . . . may develop in relative independence from one another" (29). As he points out, some moralities focus more on the side of "code" or codification, in which "subjectivation occurs basically in quasi-juridical form." In other moralities

> the dynamic element is to be sought in the forms of subjectivation and the practices of the self. In this case, the system of codes and rules of behavior may be rather rudimentary. Their exact observance may be relatively unimportant, at least compared with what is required of the individual in the relationship he has with himself, in his different actions, thoughts, and feelings as he endeavors to form

himself as an ethical subject. Here the emphasis is on the forms of relations with the self, on the methods and techniques by which he works them out, on the exercises by which he makes of himself an object to be known, and on the practices that enable him to transform his own mode of being. (30)

The originality, and influence, of Foucault's conception of inquiry into ethics is that the ethical domain links the practice of the government of self and others to the reflexive practice through which a subject takes itself as an object of concern, to be judged within a veridictional manner. The parameters he specified are useful to the degree that, on the one hand, they avoid simply taking a practice and showing how it conflicts with norms, conventions, laws, or else multiplying the "domains" from which a particular moral practice can be viewed (e.g., "religious," "legal," "scientific" points of view on sexuality). On the other hand, more positively stated, the parameters, because they stemmed from a particular inquiry, always had as their objective the analysis of a singular form of moral experience through which other inquirers can ask themselves whether the same parameters are diagnostically useful.

ASIDE FROM ROUTINE

James Faubion, in his *An Anthropology of Ethics*, endeavored to revise and expand Foucault's parameters for inquiry into the ethical domain. I will not review the schematics of his conceptual architecture but rather will indicate one point on which I consider his revisionist work to be fruitful for the anthropological account of ethos that I intend to pursue now—namely, an account of what Faubion calls "ethical complexity." This will include a discussion of his insistence on a systems-theoretic approach, inspired by the work of German sociologist Niklas Luhmann, that necessitates identifying the stabilized, routinized, and reproductive aspect of ethical work that Faubion considers essential to an account, his account, of ethics.

The core distinction that Faubion works with is between the ethical domain as a totality and what is themitical within that totality. The term *themitical* derives from the Greek *themis*—θέμις—meaning "that which is laid down or established by law, decrees of the gods," or "ordinances."[6] In Faubion's use the neologism refers, essentially, to the homeostatic aspect of system adaptation within the ethical domain as a totality. The distinction between the ethical and the "themitical" is thus subsequent to a more primary systems-theoretic distinction between "system" and "environment": the "originary moment" of ethics, for Faubion, is not system autopoiesis or reproduction but system adaptation to environment, an adaptation that begins with a dynamic change but must then engage in, or endeavor to pursue, a homeostatic quality of auto-poiesis. It is the latter aspect that Faubion terms the themitical within the ethical. Sociologically, one might be inclined to read "obstinacy" as precisely the aspect of the themitical within the ethical, except for precisely one caveat: Obstinacy, as a virtue, derives its normative sense and significance precisely from its position as a counterconduct. Thus, even though it is a normative orientation, and consists in a virtue, in no way could it be said to partake of "ordinances" or be elevated to the level of a moral code for righteous action.

What is noteworthy, nevertheless, about this proposition is that Faubion argues that the legitimacy of the ethical domain, thought of systems theo-retically, and relative to Weber's triumvirate of types of legitimate authority (*Herrschaftstyp*), stems from the charismatic and not from either tradition or rational-legal authority, which are both "marked by routine."[7] Charisma, in general, in Faubion's rendering, is precisely the suspension of themitical nor-mativity. Weber's trio of *Gedankenbilden* (heuristic constructs for thinking) is useful in our situation: to put it in a matter-of-fact way, the associations for assisted suicide in Switzerland rely on a form of authority based in rational grounds, that of the right to prescribe medications, yet the specific use they make of this rational authority, and this right to prescribe, breaks with the routinized form, as indicated in exemplary fashion in the trial of Peter Bau-mann; indeed, the ultimately personal judgment of those who accept a request for help are, as Faubion puts it at a schematic level, revealing "the inadequacy of the established social and cultural order."[8] For charismatic authority (lead-ership) to be able to constitute an ethics—that is, for the "follower" to not only be subjected to charismatic authority—the latter must recognize in turn the "chrism of the other."[9] This recognition can disrupt its routinization.

Faubion claims, by virtue of the fact that the ethical domain and the ethi-cally marked positions within the domain tend to carry on, or endure, that there is then a "routinization" of semantic qualifications of what he calls "ethical value," subsequent to the "charismatic" moment through which sub-jects are subjectivated to norms and values that are public, shared, and have this tendency to become in one way or another routinized, if not stable. To state it baldly: Faubion sees no need (etymologically) to distinguish between morality and ethics and no need (conceptually) to distinguish among ethical practice, norms, and values.

By contrast, what I would like to underscore is that in the cases we have been considering, reflection on ethos and ethics within this practice is not equivalent to the moral and political discourse that people, including those people I have followed, have about the practice. This is to say that often they do have precisely such a discourse, one that would seek to routinize, or render themitical, their engagement in moral and political terms yet is entirely separable from the ethics of the practice of the movement toward a voluntary death.

STATING VALUES

In what follows, I seek first of all to indicate how some version of a "moral code" or a claim to justification by way of "values" is made and then to consider the possibility that the ethical subject of this practice is located elsewhere than relative to the supposed moral values that frequently constitute the discourse of the practice.

Some instances: During my inquiry into Peter's illness and request, I came across a letter written by Peter to the director of the Swiss association that was to assist him. The letter is of interest insofar as it outlines in a simple and modest way his explicit ethical and political stance, germane, it seems to me, for contextualizing his rapport with the form of his death, and of the political and ethical pertinence of the term *freedom*, constituted in terms of a counter-movement against tyranny, albeit framed in terms of a political conception of "individuals" as the unit of political life:

> In a free society individuals are encouraged to follow their own beliefs, providing they do not adversely affect others. Those religious zealots who oppose assisted suicides are free to reject such activities for themselves. However, they are not entitled to make such decisions for other people. Many UK citizens are not Christians and have varying religious convictions, many at odds with Christianity. I suspect the UK government as well as the Swiss authorities tend to appease those with such Christian views, in the mistaken view that they are appealing to the majority. At least in Switzerland it appears that such specific issues are put to a democratic vote. It is interesting to note how enlightened are your countrymen in this and other matters. One can already recognise the enlightenment exercised by your country in the seventeenth century on providing sanctuary to exiled regicides, such as Edmund Ludlow, one of my forebears, now buried in the English churchyard in Vevey. It is well recognised that Switzerland was unique in its support of democracy and freedom of the individual. It viewed the oppressive practices of King Charles I and his coterie of royalist supporters with distaste and when action was taken to end this dictatorial and undemocratic practices [sic] resulting in the

English Civil War Switzerland responded in seeking to safeguard those persons being pursued following the restoration of the monarchy and reintroduction of many of the former oppressive practices. Switzerland has good reason to be proud of its impressive record in these matters.

Edmund Ludlow (1617–92) exemplifies, then, the recognition of "negative" liberty, an answer to the question of the areas of life within which subjects are left to do as they like. Moreover, following Isaiah Berlin's distinction,[10] it can be noted that Ludlow also had an answer to the "positive" question of freedom, "by whom am I governed?" He was a parliamentarian who fought for Oliver Cromwell during the English Revolution but who also fell afoul of Cromwell and refused to give assurance not to act against the government. Ludlow's memoires stage the following exchange between the Lord Protector and Ludlow, after having announced his refusal to assure the government that he would play along: "What can you desire more than you have?" Cromwell asked him. "That the nation might be governed by its own consent," Ludlow claims to have replied.[11] A principle of self-determination, self-government connected to the government of others, links these two conceptions of liberty.

A second instance I take from the letter that Florian wrote to the then president of the French Republic, Francois Hollande. Florian uses a French republican and enlightenment political idiom rather than the idiom of English liberalism to distinguish individual freedoms from collective freedoms:

> Monsieur Le Président de la République Française, Allow me first of all to assure you of my sympathy; I have, ever since I was old enough to vote, had a left-wing sensibility. The values of justice, equality of rights between human beings, the fight against all forms of discrimination and racism have always been part of who I am. We have the good fortune to live in this beautiful country, France, country of the Enlightenment, country of the Rights of the Man and the Citizen, country of the hardest struggle for the equity that each and every one can make claim to. I am a 33-year-old man and as of 5th May 2011 my life has literally fallen into hell. An incurable progressive neurological disease called Spina Bifida appeared at that time. For me, a life is worth living only when it makes sense: what is the meaning of all this? . . . What person (from the "simple" Citizen to the Deputy and to the Senator) would have the presumption to tell me to continue to undergo all this suffering, all these treatments, all these hospitalizations, all these surgeries? Why are we so behind compared to our neighboring European neighbors (Switzerland, Belgium, etc.) who have already legalized [assistance with dying]? . . . If I decide to resort to Voluntary Assisted Dying, it would be a matter of individual freedom, it would not change the course of my neighbor's life because we have to differenti-

ate individual liberties (like this one, like Marriage Equality, etc.) and Collective Freedoms (such as the 35 hour working week, Pensions, Labor Laws, etc.). Why do the self-righteous have the last word on my own death? I do not want to exile myself to die: I love my country, I do not want to force my relatives to accompany me abroad in order to follow me to die, I also want to save them from having to go through this. Stranger to myself, I want it to stop and by not legislating, you add suffering to suffering, you accentuate our/my [*notre*] desire to go to die abroad and you pooh-pooh a human and sociological reality.

If we were to qualify these two statements, I think broadly speaking we can qualify them as advocating a principle of autonomy. This principle has been configured with the linking of two elements: the declamation that autonomy with regard to how one dies is a feature of human dignity and that there is, or should be, a right to die "with dignity." Hence the frequent use of the phrase "the right to die with dignity," which is used in heterogeneous settings. What is crucial to recall, however, is that in Switzerland it is not a matter of exercising a right; rather, the person who requests assistance is exercising a margin of freedom with the aid of others. It is precisely the "routinization" of this aid, of this ethic, that has not been put into place.

The case of Clément is instructive: of all those people I had met and followed, he was not only the person who had been a member of different associations for the longest time—he had become a member of the French *Association pour le droit de mourir dans la dignité* (ADMD) more than a decade before he ended his life—but also, he was by far the most actively involved. I stated earlier, more or less in passing, that he had founded and facilitated groups for mutual assistance, first in Bordeaux and then in Cherbourg. These groups were conceived on the model of a well-known Dutch physician, Boudewijn Chabot, a key figure in the Dutch "Right to Die" movement. Practically, Clément drew on Chabot's experience and reflection to create small support and self-help groups, each group limited to ten people over the age of sixty-five, who, in addition to meeting once a month to discuss end-of-life issues, constituted themselves as a practical network to distribute the materials necessary for an assistance with suicide among all the members so that, when necessary, the group could come together to help the person to end his or her life.

In 2005 Clément conceived of a model for support groups that he called *"groupe de réflexion et d'entraide"* (mutual support and discussion groups). The Dutch group, which had served as the model for Clément, had published on techniques that could be used for assisted suicide in contexts where it was difficult or illegal to access pentobarbital. The groups had several inclusion criteria: to be at least sixty-five years old, to be in principle in accord with the practice of euthanasia and assisted suicide, and for the groups to have no more than ten participants. There were then some fundamentals of practice: for the group to meet at least once a month in a convivial manner, to focus on creating the conditions for well-being within the group, and to organize information sessions and debates as part of the regular activity. With respect to the more specific issue of ensuring practical means for a person to be able to end his or her life, the groups had the following protocol: after a collective decision about the means to be used, which should be a lethal combination of medications that are more easily accessible than pentobarbital, each member procures a tenth of the necessary dose. In the event that a member of the group makes the judgment to end his or her life, the group meets and brings together the dispersed doses. The person who requests the use of the lethal dose must have informed his or her family, and both the other members and the family can accompany them. Several groups were created in the southwest of France and several in Normandy.

The reader will recall that the only member of Clément's groups to have ended her life was a medical doctor who did it without informing the group, through her own access to lethal drugs. This fact, that doctors frequently give themselves the means that others are not able to access, is one of the core points that the associations make about the reason for their existence: that there is a double standard. The work of these groups and their apparent nonfunctioning with respect to the practical aspect of assistance with dying—the fact even that Clément himself, founder of the groups, did not use the group technique but rather was accompanied by his son and myself, without his two daughters—indicates a clear gap between a moral discourse and discursive practice for reflection on the theme of self-determination at the end of life and the matter of how such self-determination actually unfolds in practice. This is not to say that such a moral discourse is in itself irrelevant but rather that if my aim now is to grasp the ethos of the practice, anthropologically, then I consider that to focus on the moral discourse, and the routinization of ethical value, would take the inquirer further away from rather than closer to grasping the ethos of the practice.

The work of these associations, especially those in settings in which assistance with suicide is illegal, and those in Switzerland that accept requests from foreigners, consider their work "political" or, to use Faubion's term, "themitical," to the degree that what is sought to be routinized is a specific "mode of subjectivation," respect for the self-determination of the individual regarding the end of life. The gap between the "mode of subjectivation" that is discursively valorized, the self-determination of the individual, and the mode that is put into practice indicates that the ethically marked subject position is occupied not only by the individual but often by a set or configuration of subjects. The first consequence is the obvious one that therefore the domain of the ethical is adjacent to a given semiotic engagement with specific values on the part of an individual. Less obvious, or more difficult to grasp, is how the "ethical moment" at stake in this inquiry, and perhaps more broadly than this inquiry, is the moment in which a subject that is considering searching for a form through which to leave the experience of suffering invites another to participate in and observe and facilitate that search. This invitation, this "moment," is, it seems to me, fundamentally ethical but probably has little to do with either values or norms in any routinized sense.

COMPOSITE SUBJECT OF ETHICS: SUBSTANCE

There is in Faubion's *An Anthropology of Ethics* a key point, however, that aids me in grasping the specificity of this "ethical moment." A systems-theoretic approach enables him to be open about the elements that occupy any particular ethically marked subject position, an orientation that he characterizes as grasping "ethical complexity."[12] Ethical complexity is characterized by way of two not mutually exclusive forms: a subject can occupy at the same time two or more ethically marked positions within the ethical domain. The work of Caroline Humphrey has partly focused on how individual subjects that are "assembled" through diverse practices in contingent historical situations are for the most part "not non-humans, or parts of human, or combinations of humans and something else, but individual intentional human beings."[13] Nevertheless, her conceptual concern has been to capture descriptively the "internal complexity" of such subjects.

The occupants of an ethically marked position may, however, show another form of complexity, which is perhaps better qualified as "composite" rather than complex. Unlike the internal complexity of which Humphrey has written, Faubion has experimented with a narrative form to give to a composite ethical figure constituted through the relation of inquirer (himself) and informant, in this case, the protagonist Branch Davidian from his 2001 *Shadows and Lights of Waco*, Amo Roden.[14] The composite ethical subject was named "Araucaria." Although not a subject in a standard sense, Faubion is explicit about the work, fundamentally ethical work, undertaken by the pair, and between the pair, in order to occupy this subject position. I take from Faubion the point about ethical complexity, or compositeness, finding it generative for understanding the character of the ethically marked positions that I both observed and participated in. I decouple the point about such complexity, however, from any insistence that a wish or endeavor to extend ethical "chrism," as he calls it, in the guise of a commitment, or engagement, is tantamount to its routinization.

In Faubion's case, or rather Araucaria's, routinization was consequent to a "contract," a letter sent by Faubion to Roden in the hope that he could be clear with her about his intentions, about the scope and limits of his capacity: "Structurally and themitically, Araucaria owed much to the constitution or contract that I put forward to Ms. Roden early in our relationship."[15] He wrote to her: "I cannot be your Matthew. At best, I can be your 'translator,' someone who tries to render your situation in terms that might do it proper justice and that even outsiders might understand. I would ask . . . to be given the benefit of the doubt. I'm merely a scholar. Whatever else I may or may not be, I'm quite sure that I'm not evil."[16] The endeavor to contractualize the ethical engagement was, as Faubion points out, "bound to be ambiguous and incomplete," but it was critical to his conception and narration of the subject position they occupied: in his own rendering the *"mise-en-scènario"* in which expectations were announced came before the mutual assignation of rules, which in turn preceded the *mise-en-scène* of highly variable sorts.

The theatrical *Gestus* of fieldwork—the configurations of gesture, discourse, and attitude—could be read nevertheless in relation to the contract, or the opening claim to be Ms. Roden's translator, and for Faubion to be quite sure that he is not evil. Whether the latter claim is stated in relation to the specific activity of seeking to "translate" her, or if it is a more overarching claim about his personhood, is not stated. But the point is a serious one: the aim of translation was an internal good; Faubion calls Araucaria's telos autotelic. Its substance is their "voice"—the achievement of a weakly dialectical motion from the ethical encounter to its normative routinization, as voice, in practice and in text.

For my part, given the type of encounters in which I sought to engage, I could not offer anything resembling a contract: I, as inquirer, had no telos beyond the vague interpretive anthropological desire to "understand" how a person decides to end their own life. At the time, and indeed looking back on some of the encounters, I cannot be so sure that I didn't make mistakes, particularly in relation to what I went through with Christine, Sylviane, Clément, and Florian, of my shifting endeavor to not be too close and to not be too far. I wouldn't use the term *evil*, either, but I certainly did and do wonder whether my comportment may have been deficient, ethically. The hope of vindication cannot be realized by claims of self-justification.

The substance of the composite ethical figures that I think I managed to participate in, at least in the situations with Clément and Florian, was thus not one of a shared "voice." The kind of "compositeness" of the ethical subjects at stake in the inquiry was something of a fudge between Humphrey's focus on complex interiority and Faubion's systems-theoretically informed nonindividualizing ethical figure.

In each of the four situations, what was at stake, in part, was the capacity for an anthropologist to occupy a position so as to observe the request and realization of an assisted suicide, by another person. The inquiry itself turned on the acceptance of a person to be observed in her or his request. The acceptance of being observed by an anthropologist, I think, is an addition of an order of observation, to a situation that is necessarily already one of observation.

Assisted suicide is by definition a situation in which a subject's relation to her or his life is being observed and grasped. What form of observation and grasping? Individuals will variably accept or refuse medical observation, and in any event, those who seek assistance with suicide replace such an apparatus with another kind of observational assemblage, another form and mode of (self-)observation that will give them a way out. The addition of "apparatuses" of observation can both add orders of observation and change the character of that observation. That being said, I see no reason to qualify those people who have solicited apparatuses of observation, whether in the form of documentary films or anthropologists, or both, as wanting to "stage" (*mettre en scène*) their death, in contradistinction to those who are accompanied only by family or friends. The basic commonality is of being observed, often held, during the act of ending life. The situation of observation has de facto its *mise-en-scène*.

Subjects are observed by those who are present. They are often also observed by a video camera capable of telling its truth about what happened, capable of carrying the person's image and voice so as to prove that they did what they wanted to do—unless, that is, some other apparatus is able to put that intention in question, as we saw with Andreas U. The request and realization is fundamentally an ethical act not only because it concerns suicide, or dying, or a decision with irreversible consequences, but also because the subject constitutes itself as an object of self-observation by way of the regard, the attention, and the position of others. The ethical substance of these composite relational subjects is that of the dynamics of self-observation, a dynamic that is reciprocal to the degree that these dynamics can be more or less in accord or discordant, as the situations with Clément and Florian indicate.

When it comes to thinking about the ethical problematization of the form given to assisted suicide in Switzerland, unlike in contexts where there is precisely a legal and institutional framework, the ethical work of those who participate in it is ultimately recalcitrant to "themitical" routinization—both for the subject qua individual, who requests assistance with death, and for the composite ethical subject of the relation between myself as inquirer and the person or persons willing (or not) to open a position for me. Moreover, and this is the more important point, the ethical moment is produced within the demand to be observed, held, watched over, within a configuration of positions.

These positions include, minimally, the one who requests assistance with suicide, the association and the medical professionals who agree to such a request (or not), and a family member or friend who can accompany them. In my case, necessarily, there is an added element of observation and participation, the position of the one who wants to observe that observation, to accompany the accompaniment. I will argue for the claim that the addition of this second-order observer position is an intensification of a process that is in any event present, or under way. That is to say, I do not think that assisted suicide without an additional layer of observation is of a different ethical nature than assisted suicide with such an additional layer of observation. Rather, I think that the identification of observation as ethical substance renders describable a form of ethical work that takes place between the person who requests assistance and the person who accepts to accompany them.

FROM HOLDING TO LEANING-ON: MODE OF SUBJECTIVATION AND ÁSKĒSIS

From a psychoanalytic perspective the choice of an assisted suicide can be conceptualized as a narcissistic object choice, destined to repeat images of mastery and loss; from a sociological perspective it can be understood as a refusal of dominant norms: what neither of these points of view adequately accounts for, however, is the position of the other, the other person, that is necessary for the practice, within or in relation to that subject position.

By considering the mode of subjectivation, and the form in which this subjectivation is exercised, it is possible to grasp this configuration. I insist here on considering the mode of subjectivation and its "exercise" together, precisely in order not to consider the mode of subjectivation as "deontological" in distinction to the exercise of practice. Self-observation as the object of ethical concern is part of a setting, an environment constituted of and with others. If "autonomy" names the mode of subjectivation in terms of discursive value, practically, the ethical moment of the call for accompaniment, of observation, puts that self-control, that mastery, into a configuration: self-observation and self-mastery are recognized as an object of attention by way of the gesture of support of others in the situation.

We can distinguish the kind of mode of subjectivation between observer and observed, which includes the relation between two persons and the relation each has to themselves, from a concept and practice of gesture well known from the psychoanalytic literature: holding. As opposed to holding, I propose to consider the relation of participant-observers to self-observation as one of leaning-on (*étayage*). The French term *étayage*, as translation of Freud's *Anlehnung* (leaning-on), has a specific and complicated position within the psychoanalytic literature. It usually refers to the objectless sexual drive "leaning-on" drives of a biological nature; on self-preservative drives, such as thirst and hunger; or on gestures such as self-soothing, as in thumb-sucking.[17] For my purposes, I seek to use the term in such a way as to transgress and transverse the psychological, sociological, and anthropological registers, focusing on how the place of the other, physically and affectively, is a form of support for the desire and ethics of the subject in question.

In his book *Le moment du soin: A quoi tenons-nous?* the philosopher Frédéric Worms has made a case for how to observe situations of dying. He specifies these situations as those in which death is certain (in the near future, one should add) yet are the kind of situation in which practices of care remain necessary and possible. Palliative situations, Worms suggests, can be thus taken up as privileged sites in which to investigate whether and how "tests of care" produce (what he terms) "the signification of death or of dying" (*la signification de la mort ou du mourir*).

Worms's orientation is generative: his specification of "palliative situations" as a kind of situation in which tests of care produce "signification" seems germane and promising for grasping medical practice and assistance with suicide, as tests of care in palliative situations. What does it mean, he asks, for practices of care to remain necessary and possible even when cure or ameliorative intervention can no longer be pursued, either because there is no treatment possible or because the person no longer wishes to pursue treatment?

There is a moment in the practice of care, Worms writes, that reconfigures a situation from one whose orientation was aimed toward cure into an orientation of accompaniment. Worms thus attempts to characterize two different kinds of arrangements and their interaction: a medical arrangement and an arrangement he calls *soins parentaux*: parental care.

For Worms there is, today, a problematic configuration at the heart of institutions whose goal is to care for people. The problem of the configuration centers on a series of tensions that can be seen in the interrelation of these two models of care:

(1) a relational model of care instantiated in gestures of holding. Such parental care is not a "natural" relation of care fixed through biological or structural kin relations but rather are relations that are arranged and given viscosity (capacity to resist deformation) through gestures of care;

(2) a medical model of care in which medical-therapeutic gestures are normally justified by questions of efficacy oriented to their capacity to ameliorate if not cure the specific malady or ailment.

Worms draws on the work of the pediatrician and psychoanalyst D. W. Winnicott to suggest that Winnicott's concept of holding is useful for understanding the constitutive character of "primary" gestures of care in the formation of subjectivities. Rather than a psychological concept per se, holding, in Winnicott's work, is simultaneously an ethical and ontological anthropological concept: holding refers to a gesture that is constitutive of the elements held in relations, the relations, and the milieus in which the relations and elements can be constituted. Holding indexes (1) that which is held, (2) that which holds, (3) relations between holder and held, and (4) the "holding environment."

Holding, in the domain of parent-child relations, has as its ultimate aim the safeguarding of the continuity of the child's experience, an experience threatened by disintegration since we are dealing in the case of infants with a form of *anthrōpos*, human being, that has yet to develop the capacity to integrate and keep together different parts of subjectivity. We can surmise, although he doesn't explain this, that Worms thinks Winnicott's concept of holding is important, helping to explain the use of the phrase "parental care" to describe a primary mode of care in palliative situations, because dying is fundamentally an experience of disintegration or the anticipation of such disintegration that calls for, or can call for, both kinds of gesture: "parental holding" and "medical handling." Palliative situations thus test capacities and effects of gestures, in which there is an ethical and ontological question of how to endeavor to compose subjects and their relations for the time that remains in life.

Acknowledging that medical care is itself also tied to this first mode and model of care, a practice that he specifies as prior and fundamental given its presence in the formation of primary attachments and object relations, Worms nevertheless distinguishes medical care as a distinct mode and model: medical care is always also care of a precise need (with an instrumental technique) or a determined pathology (based on medical knowledge), even if these needs and pathologies are (or should be) taken up in terms of the person's relation to him- or herself and his or her milieu.

Although Worms draws the political significance of the problem of care in broad sociological strokes (how to manage and organize social relations and access in societies of care?), the manner in which he develops his thought about the problem of care itself is more anthropological and operates on the plane of interactions with close attention to gestures.

His central claim is trenchant, and the claim will function as a pivot and testing ground for my own effort at anthropological observation of gestures in situations of the ending of life: that practices of care in palliative situations aim not only to confront the absence of curative treatment but also to work on the absence or limits to parental care based on holding relations. Parental care is in turn constitutive of the subjects who are party to those relations of care. That is to say, gestures of care are as much constitutive of subjects and their interrelations as they are precise technical interventions into illness.

Here, then, lies the test of care: the intimate connection, as Worms puts it, between attachments as the very conditions of our lives and concrete practices of care creates affordances in situations of marked absence or indeterminations of how to care. Such intimate connection affords "if not their compensation or their substitution, at the least and in principle their support and their consolidation" during moments of testing.[18] The test is constituted by the problem and the task of how to articulate the intimate connection of two modes of care in situations of their excess, deficiency, or absence.

Worms illustrates such a test of care—the compensation, possible substitution, and articulation of medical and parental modes of care—by focusing on a culminating scene from Ingmar Bergman's film *Cries and Whispers* (1972), which portrays a final gesture of care. *Cries and Whispers* is a story of two sisters, Karin and Maria, both married, who return to attend the bedside of a third sister, Agnes, who is dying. The dying sister is aided in her agony by a faithful servant, Anna. The sisters refuse to care for her, refuse to attend to her medically, and moreover, they refuse to accompany her as sisters; they refuse the touch and the gesture of close kin. Within the domestic scene and the configuration of familial ties, it is the relation with Anna that substitutes for the relation and gesture of care that is lacking. The scene that Worms focuses on presents Anna taking the dying Agnes in her arms, in the deathbed, shrouded in a white sheet, breast naked as she holds the dying body of her mistress. Worms asks as to how she is positioned: "Is she servant, nurse, or also mother, sister, lover? With what deep affect are these bodies charged on the threshold of death and of love? How is the fact that Anna herself had lost her daughter mixed up with this situation?" All these questions, Worms suggests, "are swept away by the simplicity and the plain fact of the image and of the bodies." He continues: "The film underlines with an unequalled intensity the effect of the absence of parental care, and that of a substitution. The film drives us to formulate some remarks on the reinforcement of such care, or its possible institution, which returns us, as though through another limit, that which is expected on the side of medical care itself."[19] Here I take Worms to mean that the image is powerful because it shows the capacity for a third party to occupy a place in which to provide a fundamental or primary gesture of care in a situation of illness.

The image thus functions in Worms's account iconographically: the model "likeness" affording or calling for a mode and form of participation. As Worms wrote, the icon presents a form of care that returns us to that which is expected of medical care. For me, as an anthropologist observing Worms's observation, the image operates heuristically for inquiring into the presence of such a primary gesture in medicalized situations of the ending of life. Worms underlines that the care shown by Anna is not medical: the aim is not to treat a determinate harm with a determinate technique; neither, however, is the aim of the care psychological nor (uniquely) emotional. On the contrary, the practice of care is concrete, as Winnicott writes of holding. But in being concrete, this care is no less subjectivational and even constitutive of subjectivity. That is why the absence of this care in the sisters touches them not only as sisters; it reveals, on the contrary, the rupture of their whole subjectivity, as lovers and spouses, as women and individuals in general. The narrative line of the film shows in part how the sisters become deficient human beings through their incapacity to care concretely as sisters.

Worms's orientation to "tests of care," however, should be supplemented in two respects: the first is that I think it is necessary initially to make a distinction between what he called "the signification *of* death or dying," produced in tests of care, and significations produced *in* dying, understood as the ending of life. The latter must include indeterminations and breakdowns in signification, attempts, as well as incapacities, to produce significations through these practices, gestures, and tests in the practice of accompaniment.

By making this distinction, I am indicating that I think, on the one hand, the task for anthropological inquiry into situations of care is certainly to attempt to ask how indeterminations and determinations around signification are made visible and sayable through practices, specifically through attention to gesture during dying. With this orientation I agree with Worms that manners of dying are privileged sites to inquire into problems and practices of care. On the other hand, unlike Worms, I am cautious as to whether it is possible to grasp "the signification of dying"—an orientation that implies both that dying (and death) has such a meaning and that it can be grasped, both of which points need, I think, to be shown rather than assumed. Furthermore, it is prudent to operate on the basis of an openness to the plurality of significations and practices that "tests" in the ending of life can produce. I take it as a methodological caution to distinguish between the signification "of death" and significations in the practices in the ending of life.

Additionally, it is essential to interconnect inquiry into indeterminations on the plane of signification with a second kind of breakdown—namely, ones of discordancy: that is to say, breakdowns in practice that pose for participants and observers questions as to how the normative frames of working and living through breakdowns in situations could be remediated and given different form. Such breakdown is connected to, although not reducible to, indetermination on the plane of "signification." By contrast, to characterize the mode of subjectivation at stake as one of "leaning" as opposed to "holding" is to grasp the mode through which a moral value such as "autonomy" is actually shored-up in practice.

TELOS

And to what end such leaning-on?

As participant, I refused a pure instrumentalization of the exercise of "leaning-on" and its subjectivational outcome in the relation of inquirer to the one requesting assistance with suicide: as in the case of Sylviane and Florian. That is not to say, however, that I was not aware of my instrumental participation. The point is that together with the other person, there had to be some possibility of introducing a gap between any given discursive engagement and the possible understanding to which it could lead. This does not mean that I took as the aim the transformation of the subject (the one who requests) by way of an other (me, as inquirer) in relation to their request. That would be more appropriate within the context of a psychotherapeutic or analytic setting.

Rather, within the position we could occupy together, the aim was to forge the possibility of a narrative mood that could inhabit the register of what Barthes has called "the Neutral." As the sequence of situations unfolded, and let it be recalled that they were narrated chronologically, I went from a position of external observation (Peter), to failed internal observation (Fabienne), to a request for excessive participation (Sylviane), to a (in my judgment) mean form of second-order participation (Clément), to a request for excessive participation transformed into external observation (Florian). The extent to which the telos of the composite subject was successful in the relation between myself and Clément, and unsuccessful in the relation with Florian, was the extent to which a mood of the Neutral was able to be forged both within the subject position and in its textual rendering.

Why the Neutral? The form of control expressed in assisted suicide, on the one hand, like Worms's reading of "holding," endeavors to determine the signification *of* dying in advance, proleptically—a death with dignity, a good death, a choice; on the other hand, the grasping of what happened is restive to complete determination, requiring a listener to the story of the death, or a family member's experience and recollection of their grief, to give it a specific form (not to say to complete it, once and for all). The form of the practice, and the signification for self and others, it could be said, is not a correlate of a technique (*technē*) but rather becomes a site of narrative testing (*épreuve*).

Roland Barthes aids the anthropologist who is in search of an ethos and manner through which to grasp and test the simultaneous imposition of meaning and its disruption, by way of his accounts of "desire for the Neutral": an ethical category (i.e., pertaining to excess and deficiency in practice and the formation of judgments of practice) that assists the observer to grasp at once the meaning imposed and that which accompanies, and perhaps even undermines, the "paraded" or imposed meaning.

In thinking about the ending of life and its gestures, it would be understandable if the incompleteness of signifying apparatuses were taken up with a narrative mood of tragedy and the limited efforts to intervene, the limits to the *technē* and technologies of such efforts to manage the ending of life, were taken up with irony. Such a combination of moods of irony and tragedy, referring to the finite condition of human beings and the limited arts of healing that are available, is something I have often observed during fieldwork with home palliative care teams, especially when the person who is dying is treated as an object of intervention and not as a subject, principally because the person is often in a liminal state of consciousness between presence and absence.

By contrast, with respect to those undertaking assisted suicide, since they are very much active participants in the arrangement and conduct of dying, the moods that suffuse the practice are closer to those of comedy or pathos. Narratively, these moods are ways of forging a "point of view" or an orientation toward the scene of action that establishes a relation between the reader relative to the writer, as well as that which is told, in both the time of the telling and the situation described in the time of the told. The temporal hiatus of participation can be given form through different narrative moods, moods I have explored previously in my collaborative work with Paul Rabinow.[20] Tragedy primes the incapacity of those narrated for self-affectation in their historico-temporal situation, which, when effective, provides a simultaneous identification and splitting of the narrator and (hopefully) the reader with the time of the told. A comedic mood, by contrast, offers the possibility of a temporary resolution primarily through the capacity of those narrated for self-affectation and thus for temporary reconciliations relative to the breakdowns and indeterminations that make up lives—to wit, what I endeavored to describe previously as the posture of *otium* or leisure taken by Clément, and the affect of serenity that he, that we, in part assembled.

The mood of pathos is an important companion to the comedic, with respect to what we read in Clément's case, since as a mood it turns on break-down and repair, leading to more breakdown and repair. There is no delusion that he is simply "going to sleep," despite his efforts to insist to us that that was "simply" what was happening. It certainly takes the historical situation and capacity for self-affectation of those narrated into account as a dominant vector providing major determinations of situations and action. Nevertheless, as a mood it acknowledges and seeks to give a form to what has broken down, marked in the account of Clément by the tender gesture of his son holding his feet, which can be reconnected to an older repertoire of gestures of lamenta-tion in iconography.

Through discussion it became apparent that indetermination about the signifying character of gesture in assisted suicide could be taken up relative to the ethical stakes, and ethical indetermination, of the meaning of salvation, particularly the pre-Christian conception of *sōzein*, the present infinitive active of the verb "to save" or "with a sense of motion to a place, to bring one safely to." Such a term has deep layers of determination and indetermination when taken up in the present, relative to concerns for the signifying elements of gesture, and their semiotics, in the wake of ten centuries of Christian iconog-raphy of gestures of compassion and lamentation. The signification of such a gesture of dying, for his son, could only be "completed," could only be "under-stood," by taking into account his father's escape from the Nazis, as a young boy in Paris, while his parents were captured and sent to die in the camps.

The wager is that such a narrative orientation is able to grasp the relation between the *technē* in play, the manner of living (*bios*) specific to those who undertake assisted suicide, and the narrative tests for all those involved, the anthropologist included. Crucially, however, this does not rest at a level of simply reproducing the narratives of those who participate, subsequently to forge, for example, a proximate tragic sympathy, or aloof protective irony, with respect to their accounts.

Rather, for me, the mode of engagement that is most appropriate is to acknowledge that the semiotic "commitments" of those who participate (i.e., a first-order narrative engagement) such as the claim to "dignity" are, on the one hand, part of the situation but, on the other hand, cannot be said to be determining, thus opening a space of semiotic and ethical "neutrality," which is precisely not an axiological neutrality.

What is perplexing about the practice of assisted suicide is precisely the admixture of signifying elements, and of affects, ramifying one another, neutralizing one another, which leave room for indetermination and temporal narrative transformation—revisiting the past and allowing for projections into the future.

> "The desire for the Neutral is desire for:
>
> —first: suspension (*épochè*) of orders, laws, summons, arrogances, terrorisms, puttings on notice, the will-to-possess.
>
> —then, by way of deepening, refusal of pure discourse of opposition. Suspension of narcissism: no longer to be afraid of images (*imago*); to dissolve one's own image . . .
>
> The desire for the Neutral continually stages a paradox: as an object, the Neutral means suspension of violence; as a desire, it means violence."[21]

Whatever the cause of such desire, to participate and observe, to know, in this manner, its significance does not reside in its "signification"—few can honestly say today that death has meaning—but rather in how it is incorporated into a form for living, as well as for leaving.

NOTES

INTRODUCTION

1. Genesis 25:8. Robert Alter renders the Hebrew as "sated with years." See Robert Alter, *The Five Books of Moses: A Translation with Commentary* (New York: Norton, 2008). My sincere thanks to Roy Fisher for pointing out the Alter translation.

2. Max Weber, "Wissenschaft als Beruf," in *Gesammelte Aufsätze zur Wissenschaftslehre* (Tübingen: J. C. B. Mohr, 1922), 536–37: "Abraham oder irgendein Bauer der alten Zeit starb 'alt und lebensgesättigt,' weil er im organischen Kreislauf des Lebens stand, weil sein Leben auch seinem Sinn nach ihm am Abend seiner Tage gebracht hatte, was es bieten konnte, weil für ihn keine Rätsel, die er zu lösen wünschte, übrig blieben und er deshalb 'genug' daran haben konnte. Ein Kulturmensch aber, hinein gestellt in die fortwährende Anreicherung der Zivilisation mit Gedanken, Wissen, Problemen, der kann 'lebensmüde' werden, aber nicht: lebensgesättigt." Quoted in Max Weber, "Science as a Vocation," in *The Vocation Lectures*, trans. Rodney Livingstone, ed. David Owen and Tracy B. Strong (Indianapolis, IN: Hackett, 2004), 1–31.

3. Stephen J. Collier, Andrew Lakoff, and Paul Rabinow, "Biosecurity: Towards an Anthropology of the Contemporary," *Anthropology Today* 20, no. 5 (2004): 3–7; Paul Rabinow et al., *Designs for an Anthropology of the Contemporary* (Durham, NC: Duke University Press, 2008); Paul Rabinow, *Marking Time: On the Anthropology of the Contemporary* (Princeton, NJ: Princeton University Press, 2009); Paul Rabinow and Anthony Stavrianakis, *Designs on the Contemporary: Anthropological Tests* (Chicago: University of Chicago Press, 2014).

4. See Robert Savage, "Translator's Afterword," in Hans Blumenberg, *Paradigms for a Metaphorology* (Ithaca, NY: Cornell University Press, 2010), 140–41. See also Hans Blumenberg, *Die Ontologische Distanz: Eine Untersuchung über die Krisis der*

Phänomenologie Husserls (unveröffentlichte Habilitationsschrift, Univ. Kiel; Unpublished Habilitation Thesis, University of Kiel, 1950).

5. Savage, "Translator's Afterword," 141.

6. Savage, 141.

7. Rabinow, *Marking Time*, 2.

8. See Paul Rabinow and Anthony Stavrianakis, "Movement Space: Putting Anthropological Theory, Concepts, and Cases to the Test," *HAU: Journal of Ethnographic Theory* 6, no. 1 (2016): 403–31, 425.

9. Jean-Claude Passeron and Jacques Revel, *Penser par cas* (Paris: Éditions de l'École des Hautes Études en Sciences Sociales, 2005); John Forrester, *Thinking in Cases* (New York: John Wiley and Sons, 2016).

10. Max Gluckman, "Ethnographic Data in British Social Anthropology," *Sociological Review* 9, no. 1 (1961): 5–17, 10.

11. See Edmund Leites, *Conscience and Casuistry in Early Modern Europe* (Cambridge: Cambridge University Press, 2002); James F. Keenan and Thomas A. Shannon, *The Context of Casuistry* (Washington, DC: Georgetown University Press, 1995); and Albert R. Jonsen and Stephen Edelston Toulmin, *The Abuse of Casuistry: A History of Moral Reasoning* (Berkeley: University of California Press, 1988).

12. Rabinow and Stavrianakis, "Movement Space," 425.

13. His most recent reflection on the concept of the contemporary can be found in Paul Rabinow, *The Accompaniment: Assembling the Contemporary* (Chicago: University of Chicago Press, 2011); and Paul Rabinow, *Unconsolable Contemporary: Observing Gerhard Richter* (Durham, NC: Duke University Press, 2017).

14. On the question of anthropological inquiry after modernism see Paul Rabinow and Anthony Stavrianakis, *Inquiry after Modernism* (Oakland, CA: ARC, Wilsted and Taylor, 2019).

15. Max Weber, "Die 'Objektivität' sozialwissenschaftlicher und sozialpolitischer Erkenntnis," in *Gesammelte Aufsätze zur Wissenschaftslehre*, hrsg. von Johannes Winckelmann, 6 erneut durchgesehene Auflage (Tübingen: J. C. B. Mohr [Paul Siebeck], 1985 [1. Auflage 1922], 166: "Nicht die 'sachlichen' Zusammenhänge der 'Dinge,' sondern die gedanklichen Zusammenhänge der Probleme liegen den Arbeitsgebieten der Wissenschaften zugrunde: wo mit neuer Methode einem neuen Problem nachgegangen wird und dadurch Wahrheiten entdeckt werden, welche neue bedeutsame Gesichtspunkte eröffnen, da entsteht eine neue 'Wissenschaft'" (my translation and emphasis).

16. Weber, "Science as a Vocation,"17.

17. I take the terms *characteristic* and *didactic* from organizing headings of the two parts to Immanuel Kant's *Anthropology from a Pragmatic Point of View* (Cambridge: Cambridge University Press, 2006).

18. Responsibility for one's position as a subject is an observed state of affairs, not a goal. I take the point from Jacques Lacan's text "Science and Truth," in *Écrits*, trans. Bruce Fink (New York: Norton, 2006), 729.

PARAZONE

1. Kurt Goldstein, *The Organism* (New York: Zone, 1995). In Georges Canguilhem's words, "As Goldstein puts it, the norms of pathological life are those that oblige the organism to henceforth live in a 'shrunken' milieu, which differs qualitatively, structurally, from its former milieu of life; the organism is obliged by its incapacity to confront the demands of new milieus (in the form of reactions or undertakings dictated by new situations) to live exclusively in this shrunken milieu." George Canguilhem, "The Normal and the Pathological," in *Knowledge of Life* (1965; New York: Fordham University Press, 2008), 132.

2. John Dewey, *Art as Experience* (1934; New York: Perigee, 2005), 15.

3. Sianne Ngai, *Ugly Feelings* (Cambridge, MA: Harvard University Press, 2005), 27.

4. See Tom Burke, *Dewey's New Logic: A Reply to Russell* (Chicago: University of Chicago Press, 1994), 179; and Paul Rabinow and Anthony Stavrianakis, *Designs on the Contemporary: Anthropological Tests* (Chicago: University of Chicago Press, 2014).

5. Ngai, *Ugly Feelings*, 14.

6. I prefer to translate Max Weber's term *Idealtypus* as "idea-type" rather than the conventional "ideal type." As formulated by Weber—one among a number of different formulations, the idea-type "has the significance of a purely ideal *limiting* concept with which the real situation or action is *compared* and surveyed for the explication of certain of its significant components. Such concepts are constructs in terms of which we formulate relationships by the application of the category of objective possibility. By means of this category, the adequacy of our imagination, oriented and disciplined by reality, is *judged*." Max Weber, "'Objectivity' in Social Science and Social Policy," in *Max Weber on the Methodology of the Social Sciences*, trans. and ed. Edward A. Shils and Henry A. Finch (Glencoe, IL: Free Press, 1949), 93.

7. Nicole Steck, Christoph Junker, and Marcel Zwahlen, "Increase in Assisted Suicide in Switzerland: Did the Socioeconomic Predictors Change? Results from the Swiss National Cohort," *BMJ Open* 8, no. 4 (April 2018): https://doi.org/10.1136/bmjopen-2017-020992.

8. Patrice Pinell, "The Genesis of the Medical Field: France, 1795–1870," *Revue française de sociologie* 52, no. 5 (2011): 117–51.

9. "Celui qui, poussé par un mobile égoïste, aura incité une personne au suicide, ou lui aura prêté assistance en vue du suicide, sera, si le suicide a été consommé ou tenté, puni d'une peine privative de liberté de cinq ans au plus ou d'une peine pécuniaire" (Code pénal suisse, 1937, art. 115).

10. S. Y. H. Kim, R. G. De Vries, J. R. Peteet, "Euthanasia and Assisted Suicide of Patients with Psychiatric Disorders in the Netherlands 2011 to 2014," *JAMA Psychiatry* 73, no. 4 (2016): 362–68.

11. Weber, *On the Methodology*, 144.

12. Sharon Kaufman, *And a Time to Die: How American Hospitals Shape the End of Life* (New York: Scribner, 2005).

13. Frances Norwood, *The Maintenance of Life: Preventing Social Death through Euthanasia Talk and End-of-Life Care—Lessons from The Netherlands* (Durham, NC: Carolina Academic Press, 2009).

14. Swiss National Advisory Commission on Biomedical Ethics, "Assisted Suicide," Opinion no.9/2005, www.nek-cne.admin.ch/inhalte/Themen/Stellungnahmen/en /suizidbeihilfe_en.pdf.

15. E. Hafter, "Zum Tatbestand: Anstiftung und Beihilfe zum Selbstmord," *Monatsschrift für Kriminalpsychologie und Strafrechtsreform*, tome 8 (1912), 398–99: "Es widerstrebt einem feineren menschlichen Empfinden, den Freund zu strafen, der dem von der Welt durch ein Verbrechen ehrlos gewordenen, in seiner Existenz vernichteten Freund das Mittel zum Selbstmord verschafft, gleichgültig ob im einzelnen Fall Anstiftung oder Beihilfe vorliegt. Es widerstrebt der Gerechtigkeit, den Gehilfen zu strafen, der einen unrettbar Kranken, zum Tod Entschlossenen in seinem Entschluss, sich selbst den Tod zu geben, bestärkt und ihm die Mittel dazu in die Hand gibt" (my translation).

16. See N. D. A. Kemp, *Merciful Release: The History of the British Euthanasia Movement* (Manchester: Manchester University Press, 2002).

17. "La mission des médecins prenant en charge des patients en fin de vie consiste à soulager et accompagner le patient. Il n'est pas de leur devoir de proposer une assistance au suicide, bien au contraire, ils ont le devoir de soulager les souffrances qui pourraient être à l'origine d'un désir de suicide. Toutefois, les directives reconnaissent qu'un patient en fin de vie ne supportant plus sa situation peut exprimer son désir de mourir et persister dans ce désir. Dans une telle situation, la décision morale personnelle du médecin d'apporter une aide au suicide doit être respectée." "Prise en charge des patientes et patients en fin de vie: Directives médico-éthiques de l'Académie Suisse des Sciences Médicales (ASSM)," *InfoKara* 21, no. 4 (2006): 169–73 (my translation).

18. Georg Bosshard, "Assisted Dying—in Search of Appropriate Assistants," *King's Law Journal* 23 (2012): 141–48; G. Bosshard, "Beihilfe zum Suizid—medizinische, rechtliche und ethische Aspekte," *Schweizerische Rundschau für Medizin—PRAXIS* 101 (2012): 183–89; G. Bosshard, B. Broeckaert, D. Clark, L. J. Materstvedt, B. Gordijn, and C. Müller-Busch, "A Role for Doctors in Assisted Dying? An Analysis of Legal Regulations and Medical Professional Positions in Six European Countries," *Journal of Medical Ethics* 34 (2008): 28–32; G. Bosshard et al., "Assisted Suicide Bordering on Active Euthanasia," *International Journal of Legal Medicine* 117, no. 2 (2003): 106–8; Georg Bosshard, Esther Ulrich, and Walter Bar, "748 Cases of Suicide Assisted by a Swiss Right-to-Die Organization," *Swiss Medical Weekly* 133, no. 21–22 (2003): 310–17.

19. Eliane Pfister and Nikola Biller-Andorno, "Physician-Assisted Suicide: Views of Swiss Health Care Professionals," *Journal of Bioethical Inquiry* 7, no. 3 (2010): 283–85; Susanne Brauer, Christian Bolliger, and Jean-Daniel Strub, "Haltung der Ärzteschaft zur Suizidhilfe" (2014): www.samw.ch{{gt}}dam{{gt}}studie_samw_suizidhilfe_schlussbericht_2014.pdf.

20. Susanne Fischer, Carola Huber, Lorenz Imhof, Romy Mahrer, Matthias Furter, Stephen J. Ziegler, and Georg Bosshard, "Suicide Assisted by Two Swiss Right-to-Die Organisations," *Journal of Medical Ethics* 84 (2008): 810–14.

21. See J. Pereira, P. Laurent, B. Cantin, D. Petremand, and T. Currat, "The Response of a Swiss University Hospital's Palliative Care Consult Team to Assisted Suicide within the Institution," *Palliative Medicine* 22, no. 5 (2008): 659–67.

22. Workshop, "Les réalités du suicide assisté," EESP, Lausanne, 14 March 2018.

23. Infrarouge, "La mort en libre accès pour les seniors ?" Radio Télévision Suisse, 6 June 2014, https://playtv.fr/programme-tv/978316/infrarouge.

JUDGMENT ON TRIAL

1. A methodological note: it will be a case of analyzing the chronology of events, arguments, normative orientations, and evidence mobilized, made public, and criticized throughout the trial. I began by interviewing Peter Baumann's lawyer, who provided me with his defense plea, as well as an analysis of the expert report of the psychiatrist for defense. Using SwissLex (Swiss Legal Database), I have consulted the judgment of the Appellate Court of Basel-Stadt (court of appeal, 2008) and the judgment of the Federal Supreme Court of Switzerland (2009) but not the judgment of the Basel Criminal Court (2007), which was not included in this database. I could only rely on the summary in the judgment of the Court of Appeal, concerning the position of the court of first instance. In addition, the second limit of the investigation, the forensic psychiatrist who testified for the prosecution, did not respond to my requests for interview. I had to reconstruct his argument from the judgments, the defense plea, and the writings published by Baumann himself before his death in 2011. I also used the television interview given by Baumann in 2002. Finally, I studied all the press articles published in the *Basler Zeitung* and the *Neue Züricher Zeitung*, which provided me with elements such as statements from the prosecution, from Baumann himself, and reports on how those political actors approached the trial.

2. Art. 161A. De la personnalité en général / II. Exercice des droits civils / 2. Ses conditions / d. Discernement: "Toute personne qui n'est pas privée de la faculté d'agir raisonnablement en raison de son jeune âge, de déficience mentale, de troubles psychiques, d'ivresse ou d'autres causes semblables est capable de discernement au sens de la présente loi."

3. See Guenter Lewy, *Assisted Death in Europe and America: Four Regimes and Their Lessons* (Oxford: Oxford University Press, 2010), 87–89.

4. See A. Frei, S. Tanja-Anita, F. Asmus, K. Kurt, D. Volker, and H.-R. Ulrike, "Assisted Suicide as Conducted by a 'Right-to-Die'-Society in Switzerland: A Descriptive Analysis of 43 Consecutive Cases," *Swiss Medical Weekly*, 30 June 2001, 375–80.

5. Frei et al., 380.

6. Peter Baumann, *Suizid und Suizidhilfe: Eine neue Sicht* (Norderstedt: Books on Demand, 2007), 33–40.

7. Baumann, 35–36.

8. It is curious that the interview segment is conducted by a standing Brennwald, whilst the interviewee, Baumann, sits in a grotesquely large, raised seat.

9. I am indebted to Timon Mürer for his help with the translation from Swiss German.

10. Defense Plea, Basel Criminal Court, 2 July 2007.

11. Defense Plea.

12. Defense Plea.

13. Swiss Penal Code, Art. 112: "Where the offender acts in a particularly unscrupulous manner, in which the motive, the objective or the method of commission is particularly depraved, the penalty is a custodial sentence for life or a custodial sentence of not less than ten years."

14. Claudia Kocher, "Das war eine Bastelei: Stümperhaft," *Basler Zeitung,* 7 July 2007, 11.

15. Baumann, *Suizid und Suizidhilfe,* 55.

16. Baumann, 50.

17. Accusation as described in Baumann's lawyer's plea.

18. Basel Court of Appeal, 2008, 4.

19. Basel Court of Appeal, 5: All das reicht aber nicht aus, um die Urteilsfähigkeit des Suizidenten ex ante nachzuweisen.

20. "Der Nachweis der Urteilsunfähigkeit des Suizidenten ist mit dem Gutachten Dittmann und den Umständen des Suizids in einem Masse erbracht, das keinen Zweifel offen lässt."

21. "Angesichts seiner beruflichen Qualifikation als Psychiater kann das Verhalten des Angeklagten nur dahingehend verstanden werden, dass er von der Abklärung der Urteilsfähigkeit im genannten Sinne offenbar nicht viel hält und, wie er sich selber ausdrückt, einen Suizidwunsch auch von mit sicherer Diagnose psychisch Kranken (Zwangskranken) immer dann erfüllen möchte, wenn er ihm persönlich menschlich einfühlbar und verständlich ist. Indem er sich aber derart um eine sachgerechte Abklärung der Urteilsfähigkeit und die Objektivierung seiner Einschätzung der Lage foutiert hat, hat er eventualvorsätzlich gehandelt und ist entsprechend der Appellation der Staatsanwaltschaft der vorsätzlichen Tötung in mittelbarer Täterschaft nach Art. 111StGB schuldig zu sprechen."

22. "Gnade für Suizidhelfer Grosser Rat erlässt Peter Baumann die Strafe," *Basler Zeitung,* 7 April 2010, 19.

PETER

1. *Terry Pratchett: Choosing to Die,* dir. Charlie Russell (UK: KEO Films, 2011).

2. See Margaret K. Dore, "Physician-Assisted Suicide: A Recipe for Elder Abuse and the Illusion of Personal Choice," *Vermont Bar Journal* 27, no. 1 (2011): 1–4; Gerald A. Larue, Derek Humphry, Robert Risley, Joseph Fletcher, Helga Kuhse, and Peter Admiraal, "The Case for Active Voluntary Euthanasia," *Free Inquiry* 9, no. 1 (1987): 3–21; and Timothy E. Quill and Margaret P. Battin, *Physician-Assisted Dying: The Case for Palliative Care and Patient Choice* (Baltimore: Johns Hopkins University Press, 2004).

3. Personal communication between the author and Dignitas, 24 Oct. 2016. In 2015 the association had 7,291 members and had assisted 222 people with their voluntary assisted death.

4. Personal communication between the author and Dignitas, 24 Oct. 2016.

5. The reader will be aware by now that I have intentionally left out certain details about Peter, such as his age and his background, albeit offering one pertinent contextualization of his socioeconomic position (high). The statistical fact that, among Swiss citizens who died through assisted suicide from 2003 to 2008, the majority of persons who did so were of a high socioeconomic position is, of course, important but beyond the scope of the narrative insofar as it does not touch on the core stakes of the inquiry—namely, the determinations and indeterminations in ethical signification of such a form of death. Despite the fact that Peter is referred to by his full name in the film, by referring to him only as Peter here, I wish to underscore the manner in which I take up his situation as an individuation of a manner of living and dying. I do not want to treat Peter as a sociological instance or a medical case or as an example standing in for a general phenomenon. Peter's age, for example, is not, from his point of view or the point of view of any of the other persons concerned, a pertinent category in his decision or their decision to help him. What is important is that he had motor neurone disease (MND) and did not want to die with the effects of advanced MND. The sociological reading of this practice will be confronted in part 3.

6. See Axel Honneth, *The Struggle for Recognition: The Moral Grammar of Social Conflicts* (Cambridge: John Wiley and Sons, 1995).

7. See Tom Burke, *Dewey's New Logic: A Reply to Russell* (Chicago: University of Chicago Press, 1994), 179.

8. Administrative Court of the Canton of Zurich, "On the Question of a Building Permit Requirement for Dignitas to Carry Out Assisted Suicides in Residential Areas. Question of the Proportionality of the Prohibition." "Frage der Baubewilligungspflicht für von Dignitas durchgeführte Freitodbegleitungen in Wohnzone. Frage der Verhältnismässigkeit des Nutzungsverbots." Verwaltungsgericht des Kantons Zurich, Geschäftsnummer: VB.2007.00473, Endentscheid vom 21.11.2007.

9. See Anthony Stavrianakis, "Thinking the Obvious: Determination and Indetermination in a Voluntary Death," *Terrain: Anthropologie & sciences humaines*, 20 Jan. 2017, http://journals.openedition.org/terrain/16103.

10. I take the pair of terms *diastolic* and *systolic* from Georges Didi-Huberman's article "Pathos et Praxis: Eisenstein contre Barthes," *1895: Mille huit cent quatre-vingt-quinze*, no. 67 (2012): http://1895.revues.org/4522. Didi-Huberman identifies the specificity and originality of Russian filmmaker Sergei Eisenstein's intervention into the movement of images by his use of a double, vital, rhythm, read principally through his 1925 film *Battleship Potemkin*. The terms take on both literal and symbolic dimensions. At a surface level we are led to observe, from its etymological root, the diastolic movement of separation or expansion outward; and reciprocally, with systolic movement, we are led to observe contraction, or closing in. Accompanying the observation of these literal movements are the iconographic resonances that can be identified.

11. See Gregory Bateson and Margaret Mead, *Balinese Character: A Photographic Analysis* (New York: New York Academy of Sciences, 1942), 68.

12. Paul Rabinow and Anthony Stavrianakis, *Inquiry after Modernism* (Oakland, CA: ARC, Wilsted and Taylor, 2019), 37–39.

FABIENNE AND SYLVIANE

1. The phrase is from Roland Barthes, "L'effet de réel," *Communications* 11, no. 1 (1968): 84–89.

2. Radio Télévision Suisse, "Voilà comment je veux mourir," 13 Oct. 2016.

DESIRE | NARCISSISM

1. Sigmund Freud, "Contributions to a Discussion on Suicide," in *The Standard Edition of the Complete Psychological Works of Sigmund Freud*, vol. 11, *Five Lectures on Psycho-Analysis, Leonardo da Vinci and Other Works* (London: Hogarth, 1957), 231–32 (trans. mod.).

2. Sigmund Freud, *The Ego and the Id*, in *The Standard Edition of the Complete Psychological Works of Sigmund Freud*, vol. 19, *The Ego and the Id and Other Works* (London: Hogarth, 1961), 1–66, 13.

3. Max Schur, *Freud: Living and Dying* (London: Hogarth and the Institute of Psycho-Analysis, 1972), 527; see also Michael Beldoch, "The Death of the Hero: An Essay on Max Schur's *Freud: Living and Dying*," *Bulletin of the Menninger Clinic* 38, no. 6 (Nov. 1974): 516–26.

4. Schur, *Freud: Living and Dying*, 528.

5. Schur, 529.

6. Roy B. Lacoursiere argues that another physician, Josephine Stross, was in fact the doctor who watched over Freud at the end of life and administered the injections; see Roy B. Lacoursiere, "Freud's Death: Historical Truth and Biographical Fictions," *American Imago* 65, no. 1 (2008): 107–28.

7. Schur, *Freud: Living and Dying*, 528.

8. Schur, 528.

9. Lacoursiere, "Freud's Death," 127.

10. Peter Gay, *Freud: A Life for Our Time* (New York: Norton, 1998), 650.

11. I did not set out to do "psychoanalytic anthropology" but in pursuing my inquiry found myself confronted with psychoanalytic concerns; see Robert A. Paul, "Psychoanalytic Anthropology," *Annual Review of Anthropology* 18, no. 1 (1989): 177–202.

12. Geneviève Morel, "Spectres et idéaux les images qui aspirent," in *Clinique du suicide*, ed. Geneviève Morel (Toulouse: Erès, Kindle Edition, 2012): "Freud suppose un narcissisme primaire de l'individu, par lequel le corps est investi par la libido ou énergie sexuelle. De ce corps-réservoir de libido sont émis secondairement des investissements sur les objets et il s'ensuit un va-et-vient apparemment réversible : dans l'amour, l'objet attire presque toute la libido : dans la maladie ou le rêve, elle retourne dans le moi."

13. Freud, *The Ego and the Id*, 24.

14. See Jean-François Gouin and Isabelle Martin Kamieniak, "Argument: Caractère," in "Caractère," special issue, *La revue française de psychanalyse* 78, no. 4 (Oct. 2014): 953–56.

15. Sigmund Freud, "Mourning and Melancholia," in *The Standard Edition of the Complete Psychological Works of Sigmund Freud*, vol. 14, *On the History of the Psycho-Analytic Movement, Papers on Metapsychology and Other Works* (London: Hogarth, 1957), 244.

16. Freud, 248.

17. Freud, 248.

18. Freud, 251–52 (emphasis added).

19. Freud, 251.

20. Karl A. Menninger, "Psychanalytic Aspects of Suicide," *International Journal of Psychoanalysis* 14 (1933): 376–90.

21. Quoted in Wiener Psychoanalytische Vereinigung, *On Suicide: With Particular Reference to Suicide among Young Students*, ed. Paul Friedman (New York: International Universities Press, 1967), 87.

22. Jacques Lacan, *The Seminar of Jacques Lacan, Book XI: The Four Fundamental Concepts of Psychoanalysis*, ed. Jacques-Alain Miller, trans. Alan Sheridan (New York: Norton, 1998), 203.

23. Lacan, 126.

24. Jacques Lacan, "The Mirror Stage as Formative of the *I* Function as Revealed in Psychoanalytic Experience," in *Écrits: The First Complete Edition in English* (New York: Norton, 2006), 75–81.

25. Morel, "Spectres et idéaux," Loc. 427. "Le moi se constitue par identification à l'image du corps dans le miroir; sa consistance est donc celle d'une image. Cette opération fonde le narcissisme du sujet, donne sa matrice au moi et délimite la place de l'idéal du moi qui restera un point de repère pour le sujet. Le moi-idéal est l'image désignée comme désirable, au moment du stade du miroir, par l'adulte situé à la place de l'idéal du moi. A l'avenir, le sujet tentera de faire coïncider son image - c'est-à-dire son moi – avec son moi idéal, en se réglant sur son idéal du moi."

26. Freud, "Mourning and Melancholia," 255.

27. For an erudite discussion of Freud's theoretical development of the death drive, in relation to other scientific development in the early twentieth century concerned with human self-regulation, see Stefanos Geroulanos and Todd Meyers, *The Human Body in the Age of Catastrophe: Brittleness, Integration, Science, and the Great War* (Chicago: University of Chicago Press, 2018). See also Ulrike May's painstaking and insightful account of the development of drive theory: Ulrike May, *Freud at Work: On the History of Psychoanalytic Theory and Practice, with an Analysis of Freud's Patient Record Books* (New York: Routledge, 2018).

28. Jean Laplanche and Jean-Bertrand Pontalis, *Vocabulaire de la psychanalyse* (Paris: Presses universitaires de France, 2007)

Le besoin vise un objet spécifique et s'en satisfait. La demande est formulée et s'adresse à autrui ; si elle porte encore sur un objet, celui-ci est pour elle inessentiel, la demande articulée étant en son fond demande d'amour. Le désir naît de l'écart entre le besoin et la demande ; il est irréductible au besoin, car il n'est pas dans son principe relation à un objet réel, indépendant du sujet, mais au fantasme ; il est irréductible à la demande, en tant qu'il cherche à s'imposer sans tenir compte du langage et de l'inconscient de l'autre, et exige d'être reconnu absolument par lui.

29. Jean Laplanche and Jean-Bertrand Pontalis, *The Language of Psycho-Analysis* (London: Karnac, 1988), 314.

30. Jean Laplanche and J. B. Pontalis, *Fantasme originaire: Fantasmes des origines, origines du fantasme* (Paris: Hachette, 1998).

31. I am not saying that in actuality it is so simple, but during the inquiry I ran out of means of finding out more about how it is problematic. My repeated questions and descriptions of how medical judgments are made did not go beyond what could be called the "network" of elements, a network that is describable by following the associations made by the different actors of the elements that are necessary to hold the associations together.

32. Michael Pollak, *L'expérience concentrationnaire: Essai sur le maintien de l'identité sociale* (Paris: Métailié, 1990); see also N. Dodier, *Leçons politiques de l'épidémie de sida* (Paris: Éditions de l'EHESS, 2003).

33. See Nicole Steck, Christoph Junker, Maud Maessen, Thomas Reisch, Marcel Zwahlen, Matthias Egger, and Swiss National Cohort, "Suicide Assisted by Right-to-Die Associations: A Population Based Cohort Study," *International Journal of Epidemiology* 43, no. 2 (2014): 614–22.

34. Paul Ricoeur, "The Metaphorical Process as Cognition, Imagination, and Feeling," *Critical Inquiry* 5, no. 1 (1978): 143–59, 147.

CONDUCT | OBSTINACY

1. A Swiss chocolate invented in 1942. During the Second World War chocolate was in limited supply, so the company made a chocolate bar characterized by the large quantity of nuts in it.

2. Roma Chatterji, "The Experience of Death in a Dutch Nursing Home," in *Living and Dying in the Contemporary World: A Compendium*, ed. Veena Das and Clara Han (Berkeley: University of California Press, 2016), 696–71.

3. See Robert Desjarlais, "A Good Death, Recorded," in *Living and Dying in the Contemporary World: A Compendium*, ed. Veena Das and Clara Han (Berkeley: University of California Press, 2016), 648; James Laidlaw, "A Life Worth Leaving: Fasting to Death as Telos of a Jain Religious Life," *Economy and Society* 34, no. 2 (2005): 178–99, 193.

4. For a classic Durkheimian argument see Thomas Widger, "Suicide and the Morality of Kinship in Sri Lanka," *Contributions to Indian Sociology* 46, no. 1–2 (2012): 83–116.

5. Ludek Broz and Daniel Münster, "The Anthropology of Suicide: Ethnography and the Tension of Agency," in *Suicide and Agency: Anthropological Perspectives on Self-Destruction, Personhood, and Power*, ed. Ludek Broz and Daniel Münster (Farnham, UK: Ashgate, 2015), 3–26, 6.

6. Luc Boltanski, *Mysteries and Conspiracies: Detective Stories, Spy Novels and the Making of Modern Societies* (London: Polity, 2014).

7. Jean-Etienne Dominique Esquirol, *Des maladies mentales* (Paris: J. B. Baillière, 1838).

8. Gabriel Tarde, *Études de psychologie sociale* (Paris: Giard and Brière, 1898).

9. Emile Durkheim, *Le suicide: Étude de sociologie* (Paris: Felix Alcan, 1897), 7 (unless otherwise indicated, all translations are my own).

10. Durkheim, 263. It was thanks to Bruno Karsenti that I began this work of engagement with Durkheim's *Le suicide*, rethinking what I thought I knew about the text and engaging with it, as he argues for, as a treatise on ethics. I equally thank Gildas Salmon for his philosophic counsel and patient reading of this text.

11. Francesco Callegaro, "The Idea of Society and Its Relation to the Individual: Recovering the Novelty of Durkheim's Sociology. Part I: The Ideal of the Person," *Journal of Classical Sociology* 12 (2012): 455.

12. See Bruno Karsenti, "Sociology Face to Face with Pragmatism: Action, Concept, and Person," *Journal of Classical Sociology* 12, no. 3–4 (2012): 398–427; Anne W. Rawls, *Epistemology and Practice: Durkheim's "The Elementary Forms of Religious Life"* (Cambridge: Cambridge University Press, 2004).

13. James Laidlaw, "For an Anthropology of Ethics and Freedom," *Journal of the Royal Anthropology Institute* 8 (2002): 311–22, 312.

14. James Laidlaw, *The Subject of Virtue: An Anthropology of Ethics and Freedom* (Cambridge: Cambridge University Press, 2014).

15. Patrice Pinell, "The Genesis of the Medical Field: France, 1795–1870," *Revue française de sociologie* 52, no. 5 (2012): 117–51.

16. Immanuel Kant, *Kant: Anthropology from a Pragmatic Point of View* (Cambridge: Cambridge University Press, 2006), 3.

17. Durkheim, *Le suicide*, 5.

18. See Francesco Callegaro, *La science politique des modernes: Durkheim, la sociologie et le projet d'autonomie* (Paris: Economica, 2015).

19. Durkheim, *Le suicide*, 314.

20. Durkheim, 336.

21. Durkheim, 420.

22. Durkheim, 321.

23. Virtue (*aretē*), for Aristotle, is a question of the excellence of a practice, which admits of excesses, deficiencies, and "the middle" or mean in the conduct of different kinds of *technē* and, moreover, *technē tou biou* (the art of ordering life, producing, in its critical dimension, a worthwhile manner of living). Work on the human good, or reflection on ethics, is preparatory for concerns about how people can live together. But as Aristotle explains, even this seems incomplete, as possession of virtue is not enough; one actually has to exercise virtues.

24. Durkheim, *Le suicide*, 311.

25. Sharon R. Kaufman, *Ordinary Medicine: Extraordinary Treatments, Longer Lives, and Where to Draw the Line* (Durham, NC: Duke University Press, 2015), 127.

26. Gilles Deleuze, *Essays Critical and Clinical*, trans. Daniel W. Smith and Michael A. Greco (New York: Verso, 1998), 68–90.

27. Jane Desmarais, "Preferring Not To: The Paradox of Passive Resistance in Herman Melville's 'Bartleby,'" *Journal of the Short Story in English / Les cahiers de la nouvelle* 36 (2001): 25–39.

28. Nicole Steck, Christoph Junker, Maud Maessen, Thomas Reich, Marcel Zwahlen, Matthias Egger, "Suicide Assisted by Right-to-Die-Associations: A Population-Based Cohort Study," *International Journal of Epidemiology* 34, no. 2 (2014): 622.

29. See Jason Szabo, *Incurable and Intolerable: Slow Death in the Nineteenth Century* (New Brunswick, NJ: Rutgers University Press, 2009).

30. See Peter Noll, *In the Face of Death* (New York: Viking, 1989).

31. Harry M. Marks, "Chemonotes," *Social History of Medicine* 25, no. 2 (2012): 520–39, 524.

32. Durkheim, *Le suicide*, 360.

33. Durkheim, 383 (emphasis added).

34. Callegaro, "The Idea of Society," 455.

35. Callegaro, 453.

36. See Paul Rabinow, *French Modern: Norms and Forms of the Social Environment* (Chicago: University of Chicago Press, 1989).

37. Rabinow, 10.

38. Georges Canguilhem, *Le normal et le pathologique*, 2nd ed. (Paris: PUF, 1966), 182–83; quoted in Rabinow, *French Modern*, 10.

39. Rabinow, *French Modern*, 10.

40. Durkheim, *Le suicide*, 264.

41. Durkheim, 272.

42. Durkheim, 272.

43. Durkheim, 273.

44. Durkheim, 275.

45. Georges Canguilhem, *Œuvres complètes*, vol. 4, *Résistance, philosophie, biologique et histoire des sciences, 1940–1965* (Paris: Vrin 2015), 648.

46. Henri Bergson, *Les deux sources de la moralité et de la religion* (1932; Paris: PUF, 2012).

47. Durkheim, *Le suicide*, 396, 371.

48. Durkheim, 376.

49. Durkheim, 377.

50. James D. Faubion, *An Anthropology of Ethics* (Cambridge: Cambridge University Press, 2011), 104–15.

51. Durkheim, *Le suicide*, 378.

52. Durkheim, 379.

53. Durkheim, 381 (emphasis added).

54. Durkheim, 382.

55. Durkheim, 383.

56. Céline Lefève, "Le droit à la mort peut-il être reconnu par la médecine? A propos du dialogue radiophonique 'le droit à la mort' entre Georges Canguilhem et Henri Péquignot (1975)," *Les cahiers du Centre Canguilhem*, no. 4, 13–52 (Paris: PUF, 2010), 31.

57. Georges Canguilhem *Écrits sur la médecine* (Paris: Seuil, 2002), 29.

58. Quoted in Canguilhem, 33.

OBSERVATION | THE NEUTRAL

1. In returning to the anthropology of ethics, and to Foucault's work on ethics, I have had occasion to revisit prior determinations that Paul Rabinow and I had made about inquiry into "ethos," specifically in *Designs on the Contemporary: Anthropological Tests* (Chicago: University of Chicago Press, 2014). Readers should also consult Michel Foucault, *Ethics: Subjectivity and Truth* (New York: New Press, 1997); James D. Faubion, "Toward an Anthropology of Ethics: Foucault and the Pedagogies of Autopoiesis," *Representations* 74, no. 1 (2001): 83–104; James D. Faubion, "The Subject That Is Not One: On the Ethics of Mysticism," *Anthropological Theory* 13, no. 4 (2013): 287–307; James Laidlaw, "For an Anthropology of Ethics and Freedom," *Journal of the Royal Anthropological Institute* 8, no. 2 (2002): 311–32; James Laidlaw, "The Undefined Work of Freedom: Foucault's Genealogy and the Anthropology of Ethics," in *Foucault Now: Current Perspectives in Foucault Studies*, ed. James D. Faubion (Cambridge: Polity, 2014), 23–37; James Faubion, *The Ethics of Kinship: Ethnographic Inquiries* (Oxford: Roman and Littlefield, 2001); James Faubion, *An Anthropology of Ethics* (Cambridge: Cambridge University Press, 2011); Monica Heintz, ed., *The Anthropology of Moralities* (Oxford: Berghahn, 2009); Webb Keane, *Ethical Life: Its Natural and Social Histories* (Princeton, NJ: Princeton University Press, 2015); James Laidlaw, *The Subject of Virtue: An Anthropology of Ethics and Freedom* (Cambridge: Cambridge University Press, 2013); Michael Lambek, Veena Das, Didier Fassin, and Webb Keane, eds., *Four Lectures on Ethics: Anthropological Perspectives* (Chicago: HAU, 2015); and Joel Robbins, "Beyond the Suffering Subject: Toward an Anthropology of the Good," *Journal of the Royal Anthropological Institute* 19, no. 3 (2013): 447–62.

2. H. G. Liddell and R. Scott, *A Greek-English Lexicon: With a Revised Supplement* (Oxford: Oxford University Press, 1982), s.v. ἦθος.

3. Gregory Bateson, *Naven: A Survey of the Problems Suggested by a Composite Picture of the Culture of a New Guinea Tribe Drawn from Three Points of View* (Stanford, CA: Stanford University Press, 1958).

4. Gregory Bateson and Margaret Mead, *Balinese Character: A Photographic Analysis* (New York: New York Academy of Sciences, 1942).

5. Michel Foucault, *The Use of Pleasure*, vol. 2 of *The History of Sexuality*, trans. Robert Hurley (New York: Vintage, 1990), 4 (subsequent references to this text will be cited parenthetically by page number in the text).

6. Liddell and Scott, *A Greek-English Lexicon*, s.v. θέμις.

7. Faubion, *An Anthropology of Ethics*, 81; Max Weber "The Types of Legitimate Domination," in *Economy and Society: An Outline of Interpretive Sociology* (Berkeley: University of California Press, 1978), 941–55; Max Weber, "Die drei reinen Typen der legitimen Herrschaft," *Preussische Jahrbücher* 187, no. 1–2 (1922): 1–12.

8. Faubion, *An Anthropology of Ethics*, 83.

9. Faubion, 86.

10. Isaiah Berlin, *Four Essays on Liberty* (Oxford: Oxford University Press, 1969).

11. Edmund Ludlow, *The Memoirs of Edmund Ludlow, Esq. . . .: With a Collection of Original Papers, Serving to Confirm and Illustrate Many Important Passages Contained in the Memoirs* (London: A. Millar, 1751), 2:11.

12. Faubion, *An Anthropology of Ethics*, 14.

13. Cited in James Laidlaw, Barbara Bodenhorn, and Martin Holbraad, "Introduction: Freedom, Creativity, and Decision in Recovering the Human Subject," *Recovering the Human Subject: Freedom, Creativity, and Decision* (Cambridge: Cambridge University Press, 2018), 8.

14. James D. Faubion, *The Shadows and Lights of Waco: Millennialism Today* (Princeton, NJ: Princeton University Press, 2018).

15. Faubion, *An Anthropology of Ethics*, 244.

16. Faubion, *Shadows and Lights of Waco*, 157–58.

17. See Jean Laplanche, *Life and Death in Psychoanalysis* (Baltimore: Johns Hopkins University Press, 1976), 30.

18. Frédéric Worms, *Le moment du soin: À quoi tenons-nous?* (Paris: Presses universitaires de France, 2010), 59.

19. Worms, 60.

20. See Paul Rabinow and Anthony Stavrianakis, *Designs on the Contemporary: Anthropological Tests* (Chicago: University of Chicago Press, 2014).

21. Roland Barthes, *The Neutral: Lecture Course at the Collège de France (1977–1978)*, ed. Thomas Clerc and Eric Marty (New York: Columbia University Press, 2005), 12.

BIBLIOGRAPHY

Administrative Court of the Canton of Zurich. "On the Question of a Building Permit Requirement for Dignitas to Carry Out Assisted Suicides in Residential Areas: Question of the Proportionality of the Prohibition." "Frage der Baubewilligungspflicht für von Dignitas durchgeführte Freitodbegleitungen in Wohnzone: Frage der Verhältnismässigkeit des Nutzungsverbots." Verwaltungsgericht des Kantons Zurich. Geschäftsnummer: VB.2007.00473. Endentscheid vom 21.11.2007.

Alter, Robert. *The Five Books of Moses: A Translation with Commentary*. New York: Norton, 2008.

ASSM. "Prise en charge des patientes et patients en fin de vie: Directives médico-éthiques de l'Académie Suisse des Sciences Médicales (ASSM)." *InfoKara* 21, no. 4 (2006): 169–73.

Barthes, Roland. "L'effet de réel." *Communications* 11, no. 1 (1968): 84–89. https://doi.org/10.3406/comm.1968.1158.

Barthes, Roland, Thomas Clerc, and Eric Marty. *The Neutral: Lecture Course at the Collège de France (1977–1978)*. New York: Columbia University Press, 2005.

Basel Court of Appeal. "Urteil des Appellationsgerichts des Kantons Basel-Stadt vom 1. Oktober 2008 (BS): Verleitung und Beihilfe zum Selbstmord und fahrlässige Tötung."

Bateson, Gregory. *Naven: A Survey of the Problems Suggested by a Composite Picture of the Culture of a New Guinea Tribe Drawn from Three Points of View*. Stanford, CA: Stanford University Press, 1936.

Bateson, Gregory, and Margaret Mead. *Balinese Character: A Photographic Analysis*. New York: New York Academy of Sciences, 1942.

Baumann, Peter. *Suizid und Suizidhilfe: Eine neue Sicht*. Norderstedt: Books on Demand, 2007.

Beldoch, Michael. "The Death of the Hero: An Essay on Max Schur's *Freud: Living and Dying*." *Bulletin of the Menninger Clinic* 38, no. 6 (1974): 516–26.

Bergson, Henri. *Les deux sources de la moralité et de la religion.* 1932. Paris: PUF, 2012.

Berlin, Isaiah. *Four Essays on Liberty.* Oxford: Oxford University Press, 1969.

Blumenberg, Hans. "Die Ontologische Distanz: Eine Untersuchung über die Krisis der Phänomenologie Husserls." Unpublished habilitation thesis, University of Kiel, 1950.

———. *Paradigms for a Metaphorology.* Ithaca, NY: Cornell University Press, 2011.

Boltanski, Luc. *Mysteries and Conspiracies: Detective Stories, Spy Novels and the Making of Modern Societies.* London: John Wiley and Sons, 2014.

Bosshard, Georg. "Assisted Dying—in Search of Appropriate Assistants." *King's Law Journal* 23 (2012): 141–48.

———. "Beihilfe zum Suizid—medizinische, rechtliche und ethische Aspekte." *Schweizerische Rundschau für Medizin—PRAXIS* 101 (2012): 183–89.

Bosshard, Georg, B. Broeckaert, D. Clark, L.J. Materstvedt, B. Gordijn, and C. Müller-Busch. "A Role for Doctors in Assisted Dying? An Analysis of Legal Regulations and Medical Professional Positions in Six European Countries." *Journal of Medical Ethics* 34 (2008): 28–32.

Bosshard, Georg, D. Jermini, D. Eisenhart, and W. Bär. "Assisted Suicide Bordering on Active Euthanasia." *International Journal of Legal Medicine* 117, no. 2 (2003): 106–8.

Bosshard, Georg, E. Ulrich, and W. and Bär. "748 Cases of Suicide Assisted by a Swiss Right-to-Die Organisation." *Swiss Medical Weekly,* May 31, 2003, 310–17.

Brauer, Susanne, Christian Bolliger, and Jean-Daniel Strub. "Haltung der Ärzteschaft zur Suizidhilfe" (2014): www.samw.ch{{gt}}dam{{gt}}studie_samw_suizidhilfe_schlussbericht_2014.pdf.

Broz, Ludek, and Daniel Münster. *Suicide and Agency: Anthropological Perspectives on Self-Destruction, Personhood, and Power.* Franham, UK: Ashgate, 2015.

Burke, Tom. *Dewey's New Logic: A Reply to Russell.* Chicago: University of Chicago Press, 1998.

Callegaro, Francesco. "The Idea of Society and Its Relation to the Individual: Recovering the Novelty of Durkheim's Sociology. Part I: The Ideal of the Person." *Journal of Classical Sociology* 12 (2012): 449–78.

———. *La science politique des modernes: Durkheim, la sociologie et le projet d'autonomie.* Paris: Economica, 2015.

Canguilhem, Georges. *Écrits sur la médecine.* Paris: Seuil, 2002.

———. *Knowledge of Life.* New York: Fordham University Press, 2009.

———. *Le normal et le pathologique.* 2nd ed. Paris: PUF, 1966.

———. *Œuvres complètes.* Vol. 4, *Résistance, philosophie, biologique et histoire des sciences, 1940–1965.* Paris: Vrin 2015.

Collier, Stephen J., Andrew Lakoff, and Paul Rabinow. "Biosecurity: Towards an Anthropology of the Contemporary." *Anthropology Today* 20, no. 5 (Oct. 2004): 3–7. https://doi.org/10.1111/j.0268–540X.2004.00292.x.

Das, Veena, and Clara Han, eds. *Living and Dying in the Contemporary World: A Compendium.* Berkeley: University of California Press, 2015.

Desmarais, Jane. "Preferring Not To: The Paradox of Passive Resistance in Herman Melville's 'Bartleby.'" *Journal of the Short Story in English/Les cahiers de la nouvelle*, no. 36 (March 2001): 25–39.

Dewey, John. *Art as Experience*. 1932. New York: Penguin, 2005.

Didi-Huberman, Georges. "Pathos et Praxis: Eisenstein contre Barthes." *1895: Mille huit cent quatre-vingt-quinze: Revue de l'association française de recherche sur l'histoire du cinéma*, no. 67 (June 2012): 8–23. https://doi.org/10.4000/1895.4522.

Dodier, Nicolas. *Leçons politiques de l'épidémie de sida: Cas de figure*. Paris: Éditions de l'École des hautes études en sciences sociales, 2015. http://books.openedition.org /editionsehess/1760.

Dore, Margaret K. "Physician-Assisted Suicide: A Recipe for Elder Abuse and the Illusion of Personal Choice." *Vermont Bar Journal* 27, no. 1 (2011): 1–4.

Faubion, James D. *An Anthropology of Ethics*. Cambridge: Cambridge University Press, 2011.

———. *The Ethics of Kinship: Ethnographic Inquiries*. Oxford: Roman and Littlefield, 2001.

———. *The Shadows and Lights of Waco: Millennialism Today*. Princeton, NJ: Princeton University Press, 2018.

———. "The Subject That Is Not One: On the Ethics of Mysticism." *Anthropological Theory* 13, no. 4 (2013): 287–307.

———. "Toward an Anthropology of Ethics: Foucault and the Pedagogies of Autopoiesis." *Representations* 74, no. 1 (2001): 83–104.

Fischer, S., C. A. Huber, L. Imhof, R. Mahrer Imhof, M. Furter, S. J. Ziegler, and G. Bosshard. "Suicide Assisted by Two Swiss Right-to-Die Organisations." *Journal of Medical Ethics* 84 (2008): 810–14.

Forrester, John. *Thinking in Cases*. New York: John Wiley and Sons, 2016.

Foucault, Michel. *Ethics: Subjectivity and Truth*. New York: New Press, 1997.

———. *The Use of Pleasure*. Vol. 2 of *The History of Sexuality*. Translated by Robert Hurley. New York: Vintage, 1990.

Frei, Andreas, Tanja-Anita Schenker, Asmus Finzen, Kurt Kräuchi, Volker Dittmann, and Ulrike Hoffmann-Richter. "Assisted Suicide as Conducted by a 'Right-to-Die'-Society in Switzerland: A Descriptive Analysis of 43 Consecutive Cases." *Swiss Medical Weekly*, 30 June 2001, 375–80.

Freud, Sigmund. "Contributions to a Discussion on Suicide" (1910). In *The Standard Edition of the Complete Psychological Works of Sigmund Freud*. Vol. 11, *Five Lectures on Psycho-Analysis, Leonardo da Vinci and Other Works*. London: Hogarth, 1957.

———. "The Ego and the Id" (1923). In *The Standard Edition of the Complete Psychological Works of Sigmund Freud*. Vol. 19, *The Ego and the Id and Other Works*. London: Hogarth, 1961.

———. "Mourning and Melancholia." In *The Standard Edition of the Complete Psychological Works of Sigmund Freud*. Vol. 14, *On the History of the Psycho-Analytic Movement, Papers on Metapsychology and Other Works*. London: Hogarth, 1957.

Gay, Peter. *Freud: A Life for Our Time*. New York: Norton, 1998.

Geroulanos, Stefanos, and Todd Meyers. *The Human Body in the Age of Catastrophe: Brittleness, Integration, Science, and the Great War*. Chicago: University of Chicago Press, 2018.

Gluckman, Max. "Ethnographic Data in British Social Anthropology." *Sociological Review* 9, no. 1 (March 1961): 5–17. https://doi.org/10.1111/j.1467–954X.1961.tb01082.x.

"Gnade für Suizidhelfer Grosser Rat erlässt Peter Baumann die Strafe." *Basler Zeitung*, 7 April 2010, 19.

Goldstein, Kurt. *The Organism: A Holistic Approach to Biology Derived from Pathological Data in Man*. New York: Zone, 1995.

Gouin, Jean-François, and Isabelle Martin Kamieniak. "Argument: Caractère." In "Caractère." Special issue, *La revue française de psychanalyse* 78, no. 4 (Oct. 2014): 953–56.

Hafter, Ernst. "Zum Tatbestand: Anstiftung und Beihilfe zum Selbstmord." *Monatsschrift für Kriminalpsychologie und Strafrechtsreform* 8 (1912): 397–98.

Heintz, Monica, ed. *The Anthropology of Moralities*. Oxford: Berghahn, 2009.

Honneth, Axel. *The Struggle for Recognition: The Moral Grammar of Social Conflicts*. Cambridge: John Wiley and Sons, 1995.

Infrarouge. "La mort en libre accès pour les seniors?" Radio Télévision Suisse, 6 June 2014, https://playtv.fr/programme-tv/978316/infrarouge.

Jonsen, Albert R., and Stephen Edelston Toulmin. *The Abuse of Casuistry: A History of Moral Reasoning*. Berkeley: University of California Press, 1988.

Kant, Immanuel. *Kant: Anthropology from a Pragmatic Point of View*. Cambridge: Cambridge University Press, 2006.

Karsenti, Bruno. "Sociology Face to Face with Pragmatism: Action, Concept, and Person." *Journal of Classical Sociology* 12, no. 3–4 (2012): 398–427.

Kaufman, Sharon. *And a Time to Die: How American Hospitals Shape the End of Life*. New York: Scribner, 2005.

———. *Ordinary Medicine: Extraordinary Treatments, Longer Lives, and Where to Draw the Line*. Durham, NC: Duke University Press, 2015.

Keane, Webb. *Ethical Life: Its Natural and Social Histories*. Princeton, NJ: Princeton University Press, 2015.

Keenan, James F., and Thomas A. Shannon. *The Context of Casuistry*. Washington, DC: Georgetown University Press, 1995.

Kemp, N.D.A. *Merciful Release: The History of the British Euthanasia Movement*. Manchester: Manchester University Press, 2002.

Kim, Scott Y. H., Raymond G. De Vries, and John R. Peteet. "Euthanasia and Assisted Suicide of Patients with Psychiatric Disorders in the Netherlands 2011 to 2014." *JAMA Psychiatry* 73, no. 4 (April 2016): 362–68. https://doi.org/10.1001/jamapsychiatry.2015.2887.

Kocher, Claudia. "Das war eine Bastelei: Stümperhaft." *Basler Zeitung*, 7 July 2007, 11.

Lacan, Jacques. *Écrits: The First Complete Edition in English*. Translated by Bruce Fink. New York: Norton, 2006.

————. *The Seminar of Jacques Lacan, Book XI: The Four Fundamental Concepts of Psychoanalysis*. Edited by Jacques-Alain Miller. Translated by Alan Sheridan. New York: Norton, 1998.

Lacoursiere, Roy B. "Freud's Death: Historical Truth and Biographical Fictions." *American Imago* 65, no. 1 (2008): 107–28.

Laidlaw, James. "For an Anthropology of Ethics and Freedom." *Journal of the Royal Anthropological Institute* 8, no. 2 (2002): 311–32.

————. *The Subject of Virtue: An Anthropology of Ethics and Freedom*. Cambridge: Cambridge University Press, 2014.

————. "The Undefined Work of Freedom: Foucault's Genealogy and the Anthropology of Ethics." In *Foucault Now: Current Perspectives in Foucault Studies*, ed. James D. Faubion (Cambridge: Polity, 2014), 23–37.

Laidlaw, James, Barbara Bodenhorn, and Martin Holbraad. *Recovering the Human Subject*. Cambridge: Cambridge University Press, 2018.

Lambek, Michael, Veena Das, Didier Fassin, and Webb Keane, eds., *Four Lectures on Ethics: Anthropological Perspectives*. Chicago: HAU, 2015.

Laplanche, Jean, and J. B. Pontalis. *Fantasme originaire: Fantasmes des origines, origines du fantasme*. Paris: Hachette, 1998.

Laplanche, Jean, and Jean-Bertrand Pontalis. *The Language of Psycho-Analysis*. London: Karnac, 1988.

————. *Vocabulaire de la psychanalyse*. Paris: Presses universitaires de France, 2007.

Larue, Gerald A., Derek Humphry, Robert Risley, Joseph Fletcher, Helga Kuhse, and Peter Admiraal. "The Case for Active Voluntary Euthanasia," *Free Inquiry* 9, no. 1 (1987): 3–21.

Lefève, Céline. "Le droit à la mort peut-il être reconnu par la médecine? A propos du dialogue radiophonique 'le droit à la mort' entre Georges Canguilhem et Henri Péquignot (1975)." *Les cahiers du Centre Canguilhem*, no. 4, 13–52 Paris: PUF, 2010.

Leites, Edmund. *Conscience and Casuistry in Early Modern Europe*. Cambridge: Cambridge University Press, 2002.

Lewy, Guenter. *Assisted Death in Europe and America: Four Regimes and Their Lessons*. Oxford: Oxford University Press, 2010. www.oxfordscholarship.com/view/10.1093/acprof:oso/9780199746415.001.0001/acprof-9780199746415.

Liddell, H. G., and R. Scott. *A Greek-English Lexicon: With a Revised Supplement*. Oxford: Oxford University Press, 1982.

Ludlow, Edmund. *Memoirs of Edmund Ludlow, Esq. . . .: With a Collection of Original Papers, Serving to Confirm and Illustrate Many Important Passages Contained in the Memoirs*. London: A. Millar, 1751.

Marks, Harry M. "Chemonotes." *Social History of Medicine* 25, no. 2 (May 2012): 520–39. https://doi.org/10.1093/shm/hkr171.

Morel, Genevieve, ed. *Clinique du suicide*. Toulouse: Eres, Kindle Edition, 2012.

Ngai, Sianne. *Ugly Feelings*. Cambridge, MA: Harvard University Press, 2009.

Noll, Peter. *In the Face of Death: 2*. New York: Viking, 1989.

Norwood, Frances. *The Maintenance of Life: Preventing Social Death through Euthanasia Talk and End-of-Life Care—Lessons from The Netherlands.*. Durham, NC: Carolina Academic Press, 2009.

Passeron, Jean-Claude, and Jacques Revel. *Penser par cas.* Paris: Éditions de l'École des hautes études en sciences sociales, 2005.

Paul, R. A. "Psychoanalytic Anthropology." *Annual Review of Anthropology* 18, no. 1 (1989): 177–202. https://doi.org/10.1146/annurev.an.18.100189.001141.

Pereira, J., P. Laurent, B. Cantin, D. Petremand, and T. Currat. "The Response of a Swiss University Hospital's Palliative Care Consult Team to Assisted Suicide within the Institution." *Palliative Medicine* 22, no. 5 (July 2008): 659–67. https://doi.org/10.1177/0269216308091248.

Pfister, Eliane, and Nikola Biller-Andorno. "Physician-Assisted Suicide: Views of Swiss Health Care Professionals." *Journal of Bioethical Inquiry* 7, no. 3 (2010): 283–85.

Pinell, Patrice. "The Genesis of the Medical Field: France, 1795–1870." *Revue française de sociologie* 52, no. 5 (2011): 117–51. https://doi.org/10.3917/rfs.525.0117.

Pollak, Michael. *L'expérience concentrationnaire: Essai sur le maintien de l'identité sociale.* Paris: Métailié, 1990.

Quill, Timothy E., and Margaret P. Battin. *Physician-Assisted Dying: The Case for Palliative Care and Patient Choice.* Baltimore: Johns Hopkins University Press, 2004.

Rabinow, Paul. *The Accompaniment: Assembling the Contemporary.* Chicago: University of Chicago Press, 2011.

———. *French Modern: Norms and Forms of the Social Environment.* Chicago: University of Chicago Press, 1995.

———. *Marking Time: On the Anthropology of the Contemporary.* Princeton, NJ: Princeton University Press, 2009.

———. *Unconsolable Contemporary: Observing Gerhard Richter.* Durham, NC: Duke University Press, 2017.

Rabinow, Paul, George E. Marcus, James D. Faubion, and Tobias Rees. *Designs for an Anthropology of the Contemporary.* Durham, NC: Duke University Press, 2008.

Rabinow, Paul, and Anthony Stavrianakis. *Demands of the Day: On the Logic of Anthropological Inquiry.* Chicago: University of Chicago Press, 2014.

———. *Designs on the Contemporary: Anthropological Tests.* Chicago: University of Chicago Press, 2014.

———. *Inquiry after Modernism.* Berkeley: ARC, Wilsted and Taylor, 2019.

———. "Movement Space: Putting Anthropological Theory, Concepts, and Cases to the Test." *HAU: Journal of Ethnographic Theory* 6, no. 1 (June 2016): 403–31. https://doi.org/10.14318/hau6.1.021.

Radio Télévision Suisse. "Voilà comment je veux mourir." 13 Oct. 2016.

Rawls, Anne Warfield. *Epistemology and Practice: Durkheim's "The Elementary Forms of Religious Life."* Cambridge: Cambridge University Press, 2005.

Robbins, Joel. "Beyond the Suffering Subject: Toward an Anthropology of the Good." *Journal of the Royal Anthropological Institute* 19, no. 3 (2013): 447–62.

Ricoeur, Paul. "The Metaphorical Process as Cognition, Imagination, and Feeling." *Critical Inquiry* 5, no. 1 (1978): 143–59.

Russell, Charlie. *Terry Pratchett: Choosing to Die.* London: KEO Films, 2011.

Schur, Max. *Freud: Living and Dying.* London: Hogarth and the Institute of Psycho-Analysis, 1972.

Stavrianakis, Anthony. "Thinking the Obvious: Determination and Indetermination in a Voluntary Death." *Terrain: Anthropologie & sciences humaines,* 20 Jan. 2017, http://journals.openedition.org/terrain/16103.

Steck, Nicole, Christoph Junker, Maud Maessen, Thomas Reich, Marcel Zwahlen, Matthias Egger. "Suicide Assisted by Right-to-Die-Associations: A Population-Based Cohort Study." *International Journal of Epidemiology* 34, no. 2 (2014): 614–22.

Steck, Nicole, Christoph Junker, and Marcel Zwahlen. "Increase in Assisted Suicide in Switzerland: Did the Socioeconomic Predictors Change? Results from the Swiss National Cohort." *BMJ Open* 8, no. 4 (April 2018): https://doi.org/10.1136/bmjopen-2017-020992.

Swiss National Advisory Commission on Biomedical Ethics. "Assisted Suicide." *Opinion,* no. 9 (2005): http://nek-cne.admin.ch/inhalte/Themen/Stellungnahmen/en/suizidbeihilfe_en.pdf.

Szabo, Jason. *Incurable and Intolerable: Chronic Disease and Slow Death in Nineteenth-Century France.* New Brunswick, NJ: Rutgers University Press, 2009.

Weber, Max. *Gesammelte Aufsätze zur Wissenschaftslehre.* Tübingen: Mohr Siebeck, 1985.

———. "Die drei reinen Typen der legitimen Herrschaft." *Preussische Jahrbücher* 187, no. 1–2 (1922): 1–12.

———. "The Types of Legitimate Domination." In *Economy and Society: An Outline of Interpretive Sociology.* Edited by Guenther Roth and Claus Wittich, 941–55. Berkeley: University of California Press, 1978.

Weber, Max, David S. Owen, and Tracy B. Strong. *The Vocation Lectures.* Indianapolis, IN: Hackett, 2004.

Weber, Max, Edward Shils, and Henry A. Finch. *The Methodology of the Social Sciences.* New York: Free Press, 1949.

Widger, Thomas. "Suicide and the Morality of Kinship in Sri Lanka." *Contributions to Indian Sociology* 46, no. 1–2 (2012): 83–116.

Wiener Psychoanalytische Vereinigung. *On Suicide: With Particular Reference to Suicide among Young Students.* Edited by Paul Friedman. New York: International Universities Press, 1967.

Worms, Frédéric. *Le moment du soin: À quoi tenons-nous?* Paris: Presses universitaires de France, 2010.

INDEX

Founded in 1893,
UNIVERSITY OF CALIFORNIA PRESS
publishes bold, progressive books and journals
on topics in the arts, humanities, social sciences,
and natural sciences—with a focus on social
justice issues—that inspire thought and action
among readers worldwide.

The UC PRESS FOUNDATION
raises funds to uphold the press's vital role
as an independent, nonprofit publisher, and
receives philanthropic support from a wide
range of individuals and institutions—and from
committed readers like you. To learn more, visit
ucpress.edu/supportus.